Sailing the Bay

Sailing the Bay

KIMBALL LIVINGSTON

The WHITE BRIDGE GROUP

This book is dedicated to the men and women of the United States Coast Guard.

Because, it's not a thank-you job.

Sailing The Bay

Kimball Livingston

Published by
The White Bridge Group
201 El Camino del Mar
San Francisco, CA 94121-1114

Second Edition
First published 1981

Library of Congress Catalog Card Number 98-60545

ISBN 0-9663808-0-0

Book and cover design by Bill Prochnow
Cover photo by Don Hilbun
Frontispiece photo by John Riise, *Latitude 38*
Author photo by Frank Hubach: aboard *Nalu IV* in the South China Sea
Printed on recycled paper [20%pcw]

CONTENTS

ACKNOWLEDGEMENTS

Just about anybody who ever sailed a boat on San Francisco Bay and hung around to talk about it made some contribution to this book. I am especially grateful to Paul Cayard for keeping the place on the map. Thanks also to those who contributed their expertise — Jeff Madrigali speaking on the Olympic Circle, Shimon-Craig van Collie on windsurfing, Steve Taft on the Alcatraz Cone, Diana Jessie on where to cruise and many more. Without them, I might never have reached the bottom line, and it wouldn't be the same book if I did.

Take away the photographs, and again, it's not the same book. There is a special passion to picture taking, this urge to capture the beauty, the action, and sometimes the serenity that drive that other passion, the urge to sail. Alphabetically, here are my heroes: Diane Beeston, Don Hilbun, Dr. John E. Hutton, Jr., *Latitude 38* writer-shooters John Riise and Rob Moore, Keith Nordahl, and Patrick Short. (When Diane Beeston sent me her *negatives*, I puckered up like a guy balancing a Lalique vase on his head, and I went straight for the safe deposit box.)

SAIL originally published "The Devil's Own Grin," which stood up to yet another editing and refused to go away. I am also grateful to The San Francisco *Chronicle* for allowing me to re-print a few chestnuts from my days in the newspaper trade.

Frank Hoburg, Bar Pilot #37 and tide book printer extraordinaire, provided essential data and an up-to-date outlook. Ralph Ta-shun Cheng at the U.S. Geological Survey got me into this tide stuff; he led the team that launched the tide and wind pages on the net. Dave Brayshaw, software guru, not only donated the "live" current chart in Chapter 3, he also created the Local Knowledge program that brings the tide books to life — on a higher plane of consciousness.

Renee Wilmeth contributed a read-and-respond.

Dave Cahn took me sailing while the devil was grinning.

Jim Cascino kept the fires of determination burning.

Bill Prochnow not only designed the book, he stood watch and shared the helm.

Bruce Krefting and Joe Shoulak smiled and cranked out illustrations.

Tamara and David Kennedy at Arm Chair Sailor kept saying, "So, Kimball, when are you going to do the new book?"

John Ravizza took me on my first sailboat race.

L.L. and The Jet put up with my bad habits.

Lay the blame on them.

FOREWORD

FOR ME, NO PLACE COMPARES TO SAN FRANCISCO BAY. Call it windy, call it scenic, but the real attraction will never come down to words. It's such a combination of sights, sounds, chills, and salt smells that, in the end, it's simply a feeling you carry with you. And no feeling will stick as deeply as what you remember from age 17, doing what you did every day.

For me and my friends, sailing was it. We didn't have a ball or a playground. Instead, we had Lasers and the Bay. Sure, we went to school, but we arranged that around the sailing. I will never forget the tingly feeling in my feet standing in a hot, fresh water shower after five hours of a cold salt water shower — practicing gybes in 25 knots of true wind, on an ebb tide, by the red nun buoy west of the South Tower.

There were many days like that, when we tested ourselves and tempted Mother Nature.

Before I was 20 years old, I had the good fortune to crew for two of the kings of the Bay, Dennis Surtees and Tom Blackaller. Don Trask mentored a whole generation that went off to represent San Francisco Bay around the world. Together, they got me off to a great start in a great game that I will never completely master. And now that I have played the game, from the Laser Slalom to the Southern Ocean and the America's Cup, I know one thing. If we ever get the America's Cup to our little patch of water, we'll show the world how good sailing can be.

For as long as I've read about sailing in San Francisco, I can remember articles by Kimball Livingston. Like all good writers, Kimball has done what he writes about. He has sailed to Point Reyes in 30 knots with water running down his neck, muttering to himself, "My wife isn't all that bad. I should have stayed home." But, instead of saying home, Kimball went out, and he came back ready to tell about the hard times and the easy times both.

Sailing The Bay has something for everyone. From the analysis of tides and currents — both scientific and practical — to tips on favored anchorages, *Sailing The Bay* covers the Bay. And, it is tied together with stories that you don't have to read with a straight face.

If you're experienced in boats, you can count on some good grins, just reading this book. If you're less experienced, expect the same, and expect to find yourself growing a bit more seasoned, page by page. Sooner or later you'll be out there on an August afternoon with the seabreeze trying to blow your ears off, and you'll feel right at home.

Enjoy the book. Enjoy your sailing.

— PAUL CAYARD

THE DEVIL'S OWN GRIN

A STRONG CURRENT AND OPPOSING WIND MAKE THE CLASSIC ROUGH-WATER MIX. The waves square off, the troughs thin out, and the tops go to slapping salt in your face. Working to weather becomes a science of minimizing the jolts, and the jolts in a racing dinghy come hard and fast. So it was, on a windy day, in the windy month of March. The prudent and the already-broken gathered on the beach to watch. Their wetsuits were dripping, their bodies were bruised, and every one of them had a clear idea what their diehard friends were up against: a westerly blowing thirty knots and gusting; the tide fighting it at four knots; the waves vertical, close together, topped with long whitecaps. It was a normal day on San Francisco Bay. In the background, as bare as during the Gold Rush, rose the northern escarpment of an ocean pass. The miners of the 1840s, and the merchants who greeted them, called it the Golden Gate. The ebb rushed out, and the wind rushed in …

San Francisco Bay is the windiest patch of water on the Blue Planet where people actually like to sail.

And, it's always been a windy spot.

In the dim past, as the ice caps grew and the oceans shrank, the Golden Gate was left behind, a river canyon draining a mountain valley. Even then the wind fairly ripped through the canyon. Any prehistoric beast that came to drink at the river got a snootful of natural air conditioning. They were grazers, most of them, camel, bison and ground sloth species long since extinct. But it's a good bet that John Andron and Bob McNeil were not thinking about the ice ages at all on our windy day in the windy month of March. Nothing came easy as they closed on the weather mark. Their fingers felt like icicles, and they had enough to do just hanging on.

Viewed from the beach, Andron and McNeil simply disappeared among the whitecaps. The rig was a bobbing white triangle rounding the mark. Then, they took off in a hail of spray. You could see white water, and sails sticking out, and a flash something of yellow changing backgrounds, fast.

They had the lead, and they could see the win.

They were ready to go for it.

The crowd roared when they set the chute.

In San Francisco, we've inherited a Wild West take on life. It's been squeezed pretty hard, but it's not squeezed out. Along Victorian Row, the purr of Mercedes blends with the rumble of chopped Harleys. On San Francisco Bay, sailboat racing is a bronc-buster's game.

But, learning to love this stuff can warp you.

Andron and McNeill nearly made it to the leeward mark.

The crowd roared for the capsize.

How bright their frail deeds might have danced in a green bay. [PHOTO BY DON HILBUN]

EVEN AT THE HEIGHT OF HAPSBURG POWER, Vienna was said to retain a provincial air, with the scent of lush forests on the four winds. In San Francisco, it's the salt on the westerly that keeps the senses alert. Wind is what we have, and wind is what we're known for. However (and fortunately), the story of the bay is not only a story of wind and more wind. Winters are mild here, in the absence of storms. Even the signature summer seabreeze cycles up and down, so we have our golden mornings. From time to time we have our golden afternoons as well, when the seabreeze is as gentle as a kitten. Those days don't leave us with many gripping tales - you might see an enthralling sunset, but when was the last time you witnessed a *heartpounding* sunset? And yet, we mustn't fail to honor the golden days of San Francisco Bay. We cherish them. We gripe about them too for the way they come too seldom and when they do, that's the day we're stuck in the office with the hard drives crashing and the telephones screaming.

> *"Take calculated risks. That is quite different from being rash."* — PATTON

Many people live in California solely for personal safety, knowing that one day an earthquake of epic proportions will tip the rest of the country into the Atlantic with a single, massive groan. And wherever they live, there are people who must sail. What proliferates on San Francisco Bay as elsewhere is the simple sailing nut. How simple? is not a polite question. But a regular feeding of fifteen- to twenty-five-knot winds is sure to pay out somewhere.

Look at the schoolkids. They don't bundle up if they can help it. You say it's morning and it's sixty degrees and foggy, and the seabreeze blew all night at twenty-two knots and now it's building? That's shirt-sleeve weather on the playgrounds of San Francisco. Then, jumping ahead a few years, we discover the same people grown up and on their own, snorting salt water and bruising their buns on the way to a relaxing, sunbaked lunch at Angel Island.

On the bay, in theory, you can pick your weather — the Marin side for sun, and the Angel Island lee that extends all the way to the Richmond Riviera. Sunseekers might also choose the South Bay or Alameda or points upriver. Our sailing can be as soothing as a day off Virgin Gorda. The joker in the deck — depending on where you start, and where you're going later — is that your sunbaked lunch just might be bracketed by passages through a runaway Hobbesian Maytag cycle: nasty, brutish, and not necessarily short. So the local breed is a rugged lot. But let's not be smug about it. The Aussies and Kiwis yield nothing on this score, and if you ever visit the Solent, tucked between the British "mainland" and the Isle of Wight, you're likely to discover scores of stiff-upper-lipped vacationers yachting along in the summer squalls, entire rosy-cheeked families buttoned up against the cold and the rain and each as happy as a clam. Which returns us to the basics: The second dunking is never as cold as the first, and the sailing nut sails no matter what.

SO LET'S GET BACK TO THE SCARE STORIES. How windy can it get? A look at events on record turns up plenty of breezy races on San Francisco Bay. There was that one race in a Star Worlds where the casualty count ran, "Sank four, recovered two." But the all-time bell ringer goes way back to 1972. With heavy air expected at the Kiel Olympics (it was light that year), the U.S. Olympic Trials were held on San Francisco Bay to put some hair on contenders' chests. Turned it gray, is more like it.

Homer could have scripted the Berkeley Circle scene: The short, white, wall-sided chop of gale over shallow water, and strong men torn upon the rack of the gobbly sea. Tom Blackaller was in his prime then, and he compared the white-water reaches to, "going into a fire hose that's shooting twenty knots." The water, that is. The wind on the final Trials day gusted to fifty, and Blackaller, a two-time world champion in the Star, on this day "just drove it under." Later, being a bay sailor through and through, he hastened to explain that the series wasn't really all that rough because, "Until the last day, we never saw any winds over twenty-five knots."

Now, fifty-knot gusts are a bad bear, and a rare bear, even in these parts. But thirty knots and gusting (not so rare) will blow salt in your face faster than tears can wash it away. On a day like that, a race course is littered with crack, crash, and burn victims. Only the strong survive, and so it was for the 505s that we left punching their way through the chop, one stubbed toe at a time. On that windy day in the windy month of March, even the crashboat drivers were crying for mercy as a few hardy sailors entered the final leg. At the head of the pack, Harriet Minkwitz trapezed to the finish, skimming the foam off the wavetops — some of them — and swallowing the rest. Minkwitz figures this kind of sailing is just fine, "as long as you're with somebody you know can swim, really well." She has the devil's own grin.

Sic semper furiosus. When San Francisco Bay's natural ventilation system is pumping full throttle, this is better sport than throwing Christians to the lions, or vice versa. Take the strange case of Corry and Jimmy, who after all was said and done did not swear off sailing (except briefly), as they too worked the final leg. And then it came time to tack. And in the tack they felt a bump, the kind of bump that provokes the question: Oh heavens, Aunt Martha, what have we hit now?

But the boys trimmed right on out on the new tack, and they let their reflexes bring the boat back to speed, gathering stability enough for a look around the boat only to find themselves richer by one shark, just like that. It was a modest shark, of a species of no great reputation, but a shark nonetheless — nearly four feet worth of sand shark wedged right by the centerboard trunk. Jimmy sat with his feet in the straps, steering with the tiller extension. He began to ease the sails. His voice was not normal, He was saying, "Out! Out! Get him out!" Boats were sailing right past them. "Get him out!"

Corry was meanwhile hanging outside the boat on the trapeze wire and eyeballing the shark. The shark's tail was twitching one Sunday punch at a time. One shark eye was staring right back at him, and Corry looks over and says, "You get him out." A credit to the crew's union, that boy.

In the background, as bare as during the Gold Rush, rose the northern escarpment of an ocean pass.

"Dammit, Corry, it's your boat!"

The air was crystal clear.

"Are you kidding? That's a shark!"

The ebb rushed out, and the wind rushed in …

One stubbed toe at a time [PHOTO BY DON HILBUN]

THE BIG PICTURE

Four hundred square miles on the surface.

Two trillion gallons in the volume.

That's San Francisco Bay.

THE WATERS ARE NEVER STILL: The moon draws the tides. Sea waters press in as the rivers press out. Strong currents oppose, bypass, or marry. The winds of the Pacific drive in at an unpacific rate.

This is where sea and continent meet, where sea weather and land weather meet. This is the front line. San Francisco Bay is a fine place to sail a boat, and a demanding one.

If we look back a century and more, we can imagine a San Francisco in which all the inhabitants were in tune with the ways of sail. Many had sailed to California, or they took weekend trips under sail to outlying towns. A good yacht race — or better yet, a Master Mariners race for working craft — would cut business in the saloons (briefly) and raise a fat pool among the wagering folk on Telegraph Hill. Today the city and its environs have a large population of people who are strangers to sail, yet the waters around us shape our thoughts. You can see it in the morning in the commuters from Marin, bussing south on Golden Gate Transit. You can see it as they set aside their morning papers for whatever time it takes to span the Golden Gate. They sit there, feet crossed at the ankles, staring mutely out to sea. "There is magic in it," Melville wrote. "Let the most absent-minded of men be plunged in his deepest reveries — stand that man on his legs, set his feet a-going, and he will infallibly lead you to water …"

With forethought, it is possible to sail the bay the easy way, in the warm hours from the warm anchorages. For some people, however, the call of the wild is the only call, and for them the wind slot is right there, working hard most of the year. Anyone already expert in the ways of boats will find that the bay adds a few elements of its own: not the strongest currents in the world, but challenging; not the strongest winds in the world, but challenging, too. For those brand new to boats and still stumped between porthole and starboard, the bay will demand a high level of learning. The average surface temperature at the Golden Gate is 56 degrees, not a forgiving environment, and the flow is powerful. From mean lower low water and a surface area of 400 square miles, the bay expands to 460 square miles at mean higher high water — all in about six hours. Each ordinary flood tide or ebb tide pushes water through the Golden Gate at a rate of some 5,000,000 cubic feet per second. How much water is that? The Mississippi River in its highest flood stage in fifty years topped out at a flow of 1,962,000 cubic feet per second.

No one really knows whether it was Sir Francis Drake's Golden Hinde in 1579 or Juan Manuel de Ayala's San Carlos in 1775 that first sailed through the Golden Gate. Most historians place Drake's landfall to the north, at the bight we call Drake's Bay. We do know that many Spanish ships sailed the coast without discovering the narrow strait and

"Don't ever tell me the odds." Han Solo [PHOTO BY DR. JOHN E. HUTTON, JR.]

13

the deep, natural harbor beyond it. When a Spanish seaman finally came, he came with orders to search for a broad bay that Captain Gaspar de Portola's land expedition had stumbled upon by accident. Portola had suffered the embarrassment of mule-training right past Monterey, but he had made a major find. In his report to the authorities, Portola speculated that the waters he found were connected to Point Reyes, where Spanish ships customarily stopped for supplies and refurbishing. Ayala would learn otherwise, but only after making a hard trip of it through the Golden Gate. The countercurrent, ebbing against the westerly, set up a forbidding, whitecapped welcome to strange waters. Night had fallen and a chill had set in by the time the San Carlos cleared the narrows at last and turned north to the closest lee shore. Anchor watch was a happy duty by comparison. Morning found the San Carlos swinging to a hook opposite a clump of willows, a sauzalito. Later the ship set out to explore the bay, stopping in what we now call Ayala Cove and giving a name to the Isla de Nuestra Señora de los Angeles (Angel Island). Many a Sunday cruise has followed Ayala's path, but Ayala was engaged in serious work. The San Carlos nosed into much of the bay, sampling the South Bay and sailing east as far as the river beyond Carquinez Strait. That was far enough to convince the captain that he was exploring, not an arm of Tomales Bay, but a grand refuge from the Pacific Ocean, a harbor of great strategic significance.

In the two hundred years since Ayala came, man has made the bay a safer place with buoys, lighthouses and foghorns. Man has also made the bay more complicated. The influence has been sudden, unlike the hand of nature, though nature has been more thorough.

Ours is the fourth edition of San Francisco Bay. Three previous editions dried out in the ice ages. More ice at the poles meant less water in the oceans, and San Francisco Bay was left high and dry to become a (no doubt lovely) river valley. When the last ice age ended some 15,000 years ago, the inch-by-inch rising of the waters brought us this San Francisco Bay; the one Ayala found; the one we sail.

How long ago the first human tribes settled here we do not know. The ancestors of the Miwok and Costanoan and Ohlone tribes passed the generations hunting and gathering. Theirs were among the simplest of the continent's native cultures when the European explorers came. Their ancestors' homesites — if they existed ten thousand years ago — would have been built near the stream beds, long since flooded and scoured clean by the tides. We do not know whether it was whimsy, or artful guesswork, or memories handed down through the generations that lay behind the native tales recorded in 1818 by Mariano Payeras. Those tales told of oak groves where the port of San Francisco now stands, and a river that passed at the foot of the hills.

The royal Spanish flag flew here for only 46 years after the San Carlos survey. In that time the Spanish repaired ships, traded illegally with Russian fur hunters and built a mission to instill guilt in the heathen. They also built a few houses and perfunctory forts, but they left the natural order untouched. The Miwok paddling his high-ended tule raft still recognized his home, if not his relationship to sin and deliverance. The brief day of Mexican rule saw even less change. But Manifest Destiny was rolling west.

Fremont raised the flag of the Bear in 1848, the year of the Mexican War and, later, of the gold find at Sutter's mill on the American River. Within a decade, a city had sprung up on the hills above the bay, a city with rich banks on the downtown corners and vices on a heroic scale. Saloons and churches boomed. There were tall ships in the harbor and sailing scows hauling produce from upriver farms. The Farallon Islands were soon pillaged of eggs, and bird populations collapsed. Today, a century and a half after the Bear Flag Republic's quick metamorphosis into the State of California, 37 percent of the bay has disappeared to shoaling, diking and landfill. In the early Gold Rush years, hydraulic mining in the Sierra stirred up great clouds of mud that rode the streams tumbling down from the mountains. Much of this mud dropped and stayed in Suisun and San Pablo Bays, raising the bottom foot by foot, before geologic time could wink an eye.

It is this much-altered body of water that today is watched over by the Eleventh Coast Guard District. It is home to pleasure boats by the thousands, from kayaks to grand yachts. It is the shining jewel of a great city, the meeting place not only of ocean and continent, but also of wilderness and urbanization. The Pacific is wilderness, and the bay carries its wild salt scent to the empty wards of Alcatraz, to the deer and raccoon of Angel Island, to the bicycle messengers of Montgomery Street.

However urban the shoreline, however trafficked the shipping lanes, just a few meters of water between shoreline and transom will clear the city dweller of city cares. There is no way, overland, to get away so far so fast as sailing, motoring, rowing, drifting, dreaming on San Francisco Bay.

GETTING STARTED

When the boat bug bites, it bites deep. The obvious reaction for anyone in the chips is to rush out and buy a boat. But that might be moving too fast. Sausalito once hosted a bright yellow sloop, about twenty-six feet long. It was the new owner's first boat, and he couldn't talk about anything else. The fellow spent day after day aboard, scrubbing, fingering the gear, or talking to his neighbors in the harbor. Sometimes he relaxed in the parking lot in his green school bus. On the side of the bus was a painting of Smokey the Bear and large letters reading, "Only You Can Prevent Forest Fires." As the owner explained, "It saves problems. When I go by, people smile and wave, and the cops never look twice." At night he would fire up the bus for home, there to read about boats and sailing. The next day would find him back, puttering, watching the fog roll over Wolfback Ridge, and talking. Always talking.

He had never, ever, sailed. He had even purchased the boat without so much as taking it away from the dock. And there was something in his manner, as if he had passed up the test sail because he was a bit, well, intimidated. A committee of neighbors was therefore formed to get the new skipper on the road. After dark ages of delay, a date was set, and the morning came mild and clear. The Army Corps of Engineers debris-picker *Coyote* passed, outbound,

The West wasn't built by cowboys. [PHOTO BY DON HILBUN]

in the channel while the little sloop's auxiliary was warmed up and lines were cast off. For two of the three people aboard, it was just another day out, an opportunity to touch yet another boat and to share their sailing fervor with a new recruit.

In the lee of Sausalito's Banana Belt, they hoisted the mainsail and a working jib. They ghosted slowly in a breath of an easterly, an eddy from the westerly seabreeze building and flowing over the hills from the west. It should have been idyllic. The first sign of something haywire came when one crewman bent down to shut off the motor and the owner shouted out a high, plaintive, "No!" Two brows furrowed in wonderment. Then, reassurances were made and accepted, and the iron wind was put to sleep at last. The moment was given over to the peaceful lapping of water past the hull. The yellow sloop sailed slowly, daintily under the windows of the restaurants, where early brunchers looked on with approval. Through it all, the boat's new owner sat wide-eyed. Intense. Tense.

The yellow sloop soon passed out of the wind eddy and into a calm. The sails went slack, then filled with the seabreeze, and the boat slipped forward again. Off the bow, far across the bay, the steel towers of commerce were backlighted and blue in the morning. Much closer, the crew could see the first whisper of a building breeze. There were no big blasts. Two-penny puffs rippled across the water, enough to caress the sails and bring the boat to fifteen degrees of heel.

"Start the motor!" the owner screamed.

"What?" said the crew? "What?"

"Start the motor! Take the sails down! I want to go in. Now!"

Silence.

"You want to what?"

The next day a For Sale sign hung on the mast. Grass soon grew around the waterline, and Smokey the Bear disappeared from the parking lot. That's one guy who could have saved a heap of time and trouble, and money, for a sawbuck's worth of sailing lessons.

For those who have never been there, the world of boats is magical and confusing and so thick with information that it might seem downright contradictory. More often, it is merely a bit perverse. Newcomers have the joy of learning, to wit: a northerly wind blows *from* the north; a northerly current sets *toward* the north. Your right hand may point east, west, north, or south, but the starboard (right hand) side of a boat is always and only starboard. Boats are a wonderful world to inhabit, and most of the stories have no ending. When the boat bug bites, it chews in and itches forever. You don't just want a boat, you need a boat. And yet, it is difficult for neophytes to know just what they need in a boat until they have used a few. What's easy is to find folks willing to regale you with nautical expertise, whether they know what they're talking about or not.

Around Northern California, there are many boat dealerships staffed by professionals who know and love and live the sport. They're in the game for the long run, and when they sell a boat, they're hoping the buyer will be satisfied enough to come back to them in two years, or ten years, or whenever it's time to buy the next one. They try to do right by the boat and the buyer. Experienced sailors will know these salespeople already, or they'll recognize them immediately. A newcomer could just as easily encounter someone hired off this ad culled from the San Francisco classifieds:

"Largest and oldest yacht dealer in Bay
Area seeks two professional salespeople …
Sales exp required, boat exp not."

THERE ARE MANY WAYS TO LEARN TO SAIL. The hardest, and the least recommendable, is to buy the boat first. That raises the risk of choosing the wrong boat. Or, even if you get the right boat, you could still spend a lot of your time on the water feeling nervous instead of content. Unlearned sailors are dangerous to themselves and others. They suffer public embarrassments, and all too often they don't have much fun. So, if you didn't grow up in a yacht club junior program, and your ancestors didn't found the Cruising Club of America, how do you get into this deal? Simple. Go to school, or crew. The choice is a matter of outlook and circumstance. You don't have to be a yuppie to go the sailing school route, and you don't have to be a twenty-something to hang around the docks and shag rides on racing boats (but there's a correlation).

Sailing schools operate in all corners of the bay, and it's in their interest to set the hook. They'll get you onto the water in a hurry. The good ones, meaning most of them, will teach you more, and sooner, than you would get on your own. When you're ready to move to the next level, they'll have instruction ready. Again, it's in their interest. Some schools have a young-and-racy feel. Others focus on cruising skills. Ask first, and take a good look around, to make sure you're choosing a school that fits. Later, when you've done some sailing and experienced more than one kind of boat and observed the prejudices of your fellow sailors — schoonermen vs. sportboat drivers vs. wood vs. aluminum vs. fiberglass vs. junk rigs for easy sail handling vs. catamaran hulls for thrills — you will be far more qualified to put your money down.

Clubs, schools and civic organizations also offer beginning and advanced instruction. Universities turn out first-rate sailors. Many new-boat owners, would-be owners, families, and friends profit from classes given by the U.S. Coast Guard Auxiliary and the U.S. Power Squadron for only a small materials fee. Terminology, rules of the road, knot-tying and safety tips are only a few of the topics. The Coast Guard Auxiliary is administered by the Coast Guard, but its members are nonmilitary. Besides offering free classes, Auxiliary members in Northern California participate in the Courtesy Motorboat Examinations program and often aid at marine events. The Power Squadron, with some eighty thousand members nationwide, was formed in 1914 when there was a special need for education in the ways of motorboats. In the 1990s, the Power Squadron also teaches sailing and has many sailing members.

The other way to go sailing, for those short on the means to buy a boat, is to join a racing crew. However intimidating and inaccessible that may sound, it doesn't have to be.

Forget (for starters) the glamour boats at the high end. There are many skippers of good boats who will gladly take on a new sailor who offers loyalty, a good attitude, loyalty, commitment to learning, loyalty, steady improvement in skills, and loyalty, not necessarily in that order. Once the basic skills are mastered, any healthy enthusiast can find a

> *"The University of Hawaii? I went there because the sailing team travels a lot. I figured I'd study on the plane."*
> — MORGAN LARSON

boat to crew on. It may take time. It may take hanging around the docks and suffering a few rejections. It may even take sailing with some real turkeys. But it is possible in a few years' time to become good enough at this to sail your pants off year-round, or to find yourself cringing at the sound of another Friday night call because you've already told three skippers, "Sorry, I'm committed."

Whether your instruction comes from friends or from pros, one fact is basic. Good boat handling is accomplished with quiet ease. Hollering is not a good sign.

Crewing races works as well for women as for men. Some jobs on a seventy footer draw upon brute strength — more than almost anybody has — but the valuable commodities on the average boat are stamina and skill, or, in the beginner, a determination to learn. The novelty of women in sailing wore off a long time ago, so it shouldn't be difficult to find another opening. There are all-woman crews, too. They have been known to serve as a right-of-passage for women who go on to live the sailing life on their own terms. Trial and error is an essential step in learning skill and confidence. Trial and error, however, can be greatly complicated by the presence of the opposite sex, especially a spouse. For many family women, the all-woman crew can be the best thing that ever happened, even if it's just for a season.

When it comes to crewing, here's one qualifier worth knowing at the outset: Most crew openings for beginners are on keelboats over twenty feet. If you later develop an urge to steer and call the shots, you will need much more background to do it well, and the best way to learn complete racing skills is to get out of keelboats and into dinghies, or start with dinghies in the first place. The opportunities are there. For just one example, a person could look into the Cal Sailing Club (it's in Berkeley, but it's not part of UC) for dinghy training at sweat-equity rates. For anyone who has the spirit, and especially for the young, small craft are the way to go.

Another fact about crewing: The atmosphere on a racing boat is competitive by nature. Whenever strangers sail a race together, part of that competitive drive goes into establishing the pecking order. At its worst, it's ludicrous. At its best, it becomes an exercise in personality management. In the very best circumstances, when good sailors who are good friends sail together, it's a running joke.

For a beginner, fitting into the pecking order is a matter of learning who to listen to, then concentrating on the job at hand. The less glamorous jobs — tending the foreguy on a spinnaker run, for example — are just as necessary as trimming the spinnaker sheet. Both are team positions. But spinnaker trim requires more skill, and it's a starring role. Picture this: The trimmer is expected to be talking to the helmsman, watching the course, and giving orders when necessary. The foreguy is merely a downhaul helping to control the spinnaker pole. It is adjusted only when the position of the spinnaker pole is changed. The foreguy follows the pole. Tending the foreguy is mostly a following job, so there is a temptation to go dreamy in the beauty of the boats and the way the water picks up the colors of sails and which pocket did I put that candy bar in — until somebody starts yelling, "Foreguy! For Chrissake! Will you please ease the foreguy!" At which point you've let down the team. So here's another basic principle: A rookie who stays alert and aggressive and keeps a simple job under control is a rookie who is on the way to a better job.

RIGHT AND WRONG

There is no single answer to the question, what kind of boat should I buy? Yachts are not purchased rationally. A sixty-year-old, gaff-rigged schooner will not go to weather in the Golden Gate wind funnel with a modern, plastic sloop of the same length. It will not have as much room below, and it will eat up much more time and money in maintenance. But the wooden yacht has an aura, and maybe a soul, that cannot be created on those fiberglass production lines.

If a small boat suits you, a windsurfer or a centerboard dinghy, you're going to face fewer storage problems than those who go sailing on bigger boats — boats with lids — that stay in the water or are dry-sailed close to the water all the time. With a small boat, you learn the basics in a basic machine, and that can't be wrong. John Rousmaniere, author of the *Annapolis Book of Seamanship*, once attended a safety seminar on the bay, and he recalled a day when he was approached by a man who was all set to go ocean cruising. The man asked him, "Do you think I ought to buy a Magellan GPS, a Trimble GPS, or a Garmin GPS?" The way Rousmaniere told the story, he knew something about the man's background and abilities, so his answer was, "I think you ought to take that money and go out and buy yourself a Laser, and learn how to sail."

In these pages, no matter what size boat you have, you may safely call it a yacht, because it is. "Yacht" is a very good word, but it seems to bother Americans something fierce. The governing body of the sport in America — U.S. Sailing — adopted its current moniker in 1991 to escape the supposedly stuffy connotations of the old name, the U.S. Yacht Racing Union, and that same drive to consumerize the sport is global. The London-headquartered International Yacht Racing Union has metamorphosed into ISAF, www.isaf.com, the International Sailing Federation. Say the word "yacht" and you evoke images of gold faucets and uniformed stewards. But a yacht by definition is any relatively small boat used for pleasure. J.P. Morgan's yacht was smaller (barely) than the average battleship, and more power to him. There are three-foot models that sail on Spreckels Lake in Golden Gate Park that are achingly beautiful too, as beautiful as any J-boat that Vanderbilt ever launched to race for the America's Cup. X-class models carve wind with a fine edge, and they leave a clean wake. Heaven knows, those are yachts. It's not a word that requires any apology, not when you consider the price of Harley Davidsons or Winnebagos.

Yachts have different personalities to suit the different personalities that select them. Among windsurfers (sailboards, if you must), the differences are often too subtle for anyone but an aficionado to recognize. To that person, however, the differences are night and day: it turns fast, or it doesn't want to turn at all; it's a floater (all the time), or it's a sinker (if it slows down). These things *matter*.

Dinghy sailors have their own choices. Lasers are popular, with 160,000 sold around the world. They're a great trainer for anyone, but they're a youngster's boat if you're talking serious competition. On the bay, we have a longtime rivalry (and camaraderie) between the Inter-

The junior program is a birthing place of legends. [PHOTO BY DIANE BEESTON]

national 14 and the 505 — both being quick, athletic boats with trapezes. Then the 49er was added to the Olympic list, and we had a whole new standard for wet and wild. Ignoring that scene entirely, another group has brought about a resurgence in the Snipe class, largely because it can be sailed without an athlete for a crew. And the list goes on.

Choosing a keelboat depends upon your level of athletic skill or aspiration. Some people belong in a hotrod boat that keeps them busy. Other people belong in a boat that takes care of itself. This will probably be a heavier but not necessarily "heavy" boat, with a fuller underbody that imparts a feeling of stability and security; a boat that will sail itself in a straight line without a lot of fiddling; a nonathlete's boat. The full displacement boat will provide a comfortable platform for watching the hotdogs get thrashed. It will also provide a comfortable platform for watching them blast right by. There are no right or wrong types of boats, only right or wrong reasons for buying them.

Cruisers, however, should not make the mistake of assuming that the slowest, stodgiest boat is the safest. First of all, a sailing boat has to sail. If you're going places, you want a boat that's going places too, and if you're planning to make long passages, you have to assume that sooner or later your boat will be called upon to claw its way upwind, against breaking seas, with rocks at your back and the motor dead. There are examples of popular (and otherwise successful) boats that won't make it. A cruising sailor doesn't need a poky boat to feel comfortable any more than a Sunday horseman needs a plow horse to enjoy a relaxing ride. That's true whether the goal is Petaluma Creek or the Seychelles. Somewhere between the plow horse and a racing thoroughbred lies the happy medium.

WHEN WATER CASTS ITS SPELL, one of the high-risk bewitchments is the urge to build a boat and sail around the world. There have been some famous and inspiring successes in this group. There have been many more cases of partly-fin-ished hulls showing up in the classifieds at "please, please buy me" prices. First it was plywood trimarans. Then it was cement monohulls.

In the real world, the cost of the hull material represents only a fraction of the finished boat, and any saving on hull material represents a fraction of that fraction, so the notion of the cheap but ultimate boat just might be elusive.

Some people become heroes in building and sailing wonderful boats. For a few people, you could even say that it's necessary to build a boat to feel satisfied with their lives. On the other hand, it's amazing how many people have spent two, three, or even five years in a back-yard working on a boat that was not right in the first place, does not look good, and will not sell for much. Even more amazing is how many people will build or buy a boat to cross oceans without first learning how to sail.

Stories surface from time to time about someone who went to sea knowing nothing but learned underway, saw the world, and loved it. The failures receive less advertising. On the West Coast, they tend to rally in San Diego and never leave. San Diego is the last continental American port before the jump to Never Never Land, and the waters around San Diego's Shelter Island shelter many a broken dream — dreams broken upon the discovery that the Pacific Ocean is not set up for sunbathing and sybaritic joy. Yes, there are days when the sun, sea and sky glow with a single smile. Yes, there are days when the dolphin come to call, yakking and blowing and riding the foam of the bow wave. The Pacific in its smiling mood is close to paradise. But the sea, first of all, is wilderness. The sea has power and beauty, but no mind. Some take to that; some do not. According to the individual, wilderness is either liberating or appalling. If blue water voyaging is the object, there is no middle attitude.

Two themes run through the conversation of successful voyagers when they come home. First they say, "Go now; it's changing fast." Then they echo this observation of the late Pete Sutter, a career sail-maker who got in some good cruising in his final years. "You wouldn't believe how many people there are out there who don't even know

TIP OF THE DAY: San Francisco piers have odd numbers if they're north of the Bay Bridge, even numbers if they're south of it.

how to trim their sails," Sutter said. "They can't get anywhere fast, so they motor all the time, and you see them in these little, out of the way harbors spending two miserable days rowing back and forth in the dinghy, filling jerry cans with diesel fuel and dumping it into the tank."

So dream deep. Dream with your eyes open. Take short trips first. Learn to sail.

For all the lure of distant lands, most boats live their lives close to home and never venture far. Few totally unsuitable boats reach the new-boat market on San Francisco Bay. Some boats are too lightly rigged for our weather, but Northern California dealers, by and large, have learned to forestall embarrassments by doing their own rigging where necessary.

Most boats are built for the weekend sailor, with a little coastwise port hopping in mind but not ocean voyaging. Often, the difference is less in the quality of construction than in the tradeoffs. The long-distance boat has the capacity to carry lots of water and fuel that would be wasted on a weekend boat. The long distance voyager will show a serious concern for storage and perhaps even provide a workbench where the weekender goes for sprawl space and entertaining convenience. Every boat is a compromise. Even if the deep-down structure is meant for light use only, that's not an evil in itself — but it's important to know. We needn't criticize the famous yacht designer who described very honestly, in a national magazine article, how he developed one model for a weekenders' market. He made the assumption, and said so openly, that the hulls would never encounter extreme conditions. What seemed odd was the manufacturer's full-color advertisement, in the same issue, touting that design as a yacht for the seven seas.

THE BEST KIND OF YACHTING

For some unfathomable reason, a natural antipathy has been alleged between "raghangers" and "stinkpotters," abhorrent terms both, and best forgotten. It is a blessing to love all boats great and small.

How could anyone use the word stinkpotter after sampling the view from a grand yacht, a classic Stephens or an elegant DeFever, high above the water, with a spread of Gorgonzola and one of those rare, Barnett Cabernets from Rattlesnake Hill?

But if I'm planing along on a Laser, I'm there for the thrills. With the wind high and the water near, it's hard to believe that anything else could match that moment — certainly not sailing on a big boat, some chunky old lead mine.

From the deck of a solid, powerful keel yacht, however, those little mosquitoes look mighty skittish and cold.

When some shrieking speedboat explodes the peace and quiet, I wrinkle my nose. But just put me in the driver's seat and watch me go. Those sailboats are *slow!*

And yet, how could that compare to a morning row in a 75-year-old Whitehall, in communion with the cormorants and seals?

Two things I know: The best kind of yachting is whatever I'm doing, right now. And you can figure the importance of a sailboat race by how many powerboats it takes to run it.

In the early days of Britain's Royal Yacht Squadron, the elevated gentlemen who commissioned the building of yachts made it a custom to bow to the improvement of naval architecture: ruling the waves and all that. The brigantine yachts they came up with engaged in training maneuvers with the Royal Navy. Would a tax dodge like that work today? Probably not. But Lord Belfast's *Waterwitch* bested the naval fleet so badly in the 1830s that public opinion forced the Admiralty to buy it.

The schooner yacht that won the 100 Guineas Cup from the Royal Yacht Squadron in 1851 — the America's Cup — was no wee chick. The *America* was 101 feet long. In 1893 the America's Cup was defended by *Vigilant*, 124 feet long, but grand yachting was cresting then. The International America's Cup Class yachts introduced in 1992, while the San Diego Yacht Club held the Cup, are 75 feet long, with space to tout the sponsors.

Taken altogether, the yachting boom of the second half of the 20th century was born of a combination of downsizing, deficit financing, and fiberglass production lines. It follows that sailing is not the exclusive sport it once was, when all boats were custom-built of wood, and every sailor knew every yacht on San Francisco Bay. Long distance racing and cruising are commonplace now, and local waters attract crowds. Along with the boom in the boating population came a boom in sailing associations and yacht clubs. No one needs a club, of course, to enjoy a boat. The waters are free. That is one of the enticements. But many people find that club memberships open good facets of the sailing life, and clubs, for the most part, are not exclusive.

The Bay Area features clubs to fit every budget and taste. Some lean toward families who like to cruise, some toward racing dinghies, and some toward racing big boats. Still others are populated by the owners of motorboats with a yen this way or that. The smaller the club, the more likely it is to specialize; the larger, the more likely it is to have members of all persuasions.

Yacht club membership is required to enter most competitive events. This contributes a form of accountability as well as a medium of exchange. Clubs with a sailboat-racing membership become constituents in turn of the San Francisco Bay Yacht Racing Association, Small Yacht Racing Association, Small Boat Racing Association, and so on. These organizations negotiate the season schedule, and the clubs then take turns sponsoring the races, fielding committees, and reporting results. There are budget-minded clubs that will get a newcomer started for not much more than the price of a pair of Topsiders.

SEASICK? ME?
© San Francisco Chronicle, by Kimball Livingston

THERE'S NO SICKNESS like seasickness. Nothing else is so catching, so unnerving, so thorough in its undoing. You can take your remedies — the drugs, the acupressure points, the thousand-yard stare at the horizon, or Mama's chicken soup. The truth was told long ago in a homely homily of the British navy: "The only cure for seasickness is to go sit down on the shady side of an old brick church in the country."

In theory, everyone gets seasick. In real life, some people seem immune. A while back I sailed a bit on a 40-footer owned by a guy named Lu Taylor. Now, there was a cast iron stomach, and here's my story.

It was a dark and stormy night …

I was called from a warm bunk. Half asleep. Lost in a dreamy trance of rhythm and sound: the boat pitching over waves, spray flying as we hammered our way upwind toward Point Reyes. The wind moaned in the rigging and howled down the aluminum hollow of the mast. It was not a night to make you think, "Oh boy, I get to go sailing."

I had been sleeping with my just-in-case boots on. Over them, still lying flat, I pulled on my foul weather pants.

I stayed flat because, in a prone position, I'm less prone to inner-ear distress. And with the boat crashing around, it was just plain easier. Then I stood up and quickly zippered and buttoned the necessaries. Quickly, because I can get queasy in a hurry, standing around in a closed cabin, and I could feel it coming on. I was still zippering as I stopped at the foot of the ladder to exchange pleasantries with Lu Taylor and found him calmly reading a book … Munching a salami and pickle sandwich … Sipping a green death ale … Smoking a cigar.

I've never climbed a ladder so fast in my life.

To quote one motion sickness expert, Dr. Kenneth Dardick of Storrs, Connecticut, "Tolerances vary greatly from one person to another." I already knew that.

Motion sickness becomes an issue west of the Golden Gate Bridge. People don't get sick inside the bay unless they're bonkers-susceptible or they spend too much time belowdecks. There, the eyes accept an apparently-stationary surrounding while the critical nerve fibers of the inner ear disagree, spewing out conflicting information and …

Seasickness is one version of motion sickness, a clammy, cold-sweat misery that runs the gamut from vaguely uncomfortable to incapacitating. There's a wealth of folklore: Eat a raw egg. Never touch sprouts. Just stay busy and you'll be fine. Maybe.

Medical researchers still debate the causes. A 1990 Air Force study identified low-frequency brain wave patterns in nausea sufferers that were similar to patterns produced by epileptics during convulsions. Ongoing research asks whether motion sickness is caused by a partial seizure in the brain or brain stem. Meanwhile, there's no sure fix. Susceptibility is higher in children, slightly higher in women, and tends to run in families. Short trips before a long one can help. So can a headrest to keep the head stable.

A listing of clubs, complete with rosters of officers and member yachts, can be found in the *Yachting Year Book*, a solid and useful guide published under the aegis of the Pacific Inter-Club Yacht Association. The PICYA has more than ninety member clubs, and the *Year Book* contains historical data, the rosters of many one-design classes, and information about the racing associations that make the sport tick. And, there's an upside for a potential boatbuyer: some of the one-designs that post themselves in the Year Book are active racing classes. There are examples of solid used-boat values. They're a long way from glamorous, mind you, but boats such as the Santana 22, Cal 20 or Columbia Challenger (to name just a few) can be purchased second-hand or seventh-hand in the low thousands, sailed for a few years, and resold with no more loss than the cost of sails, berthing, insurance, and sandwiches. Add more thousands, and there are larger boats that fit the same equation. There's no more cost-effective way to own your own yacht on San Francisco Bay.

The PICYA, organized in 1896, also sponsors Opening Day, an evolving, cheerful anomaly that sailors think of in terms of flag-festooned feluccas. To the Bar Pilots, faced with all that small-boat traffic, it's Black Sunday.

Fresh air is good. Strange smells are bad. Upwind is worse than downwind. Being able to watch the horizon is better than being cooped up inside, but, sometimes, a view of the horizon is enough to make you sick. First you're afraid you'll die. Then you're afraid you won't.

NASA says that 70 percent of the astronauts it shoots into space report some level of motion sickness. But unlike pilots in the lower atmosphere, astronauts are allowed to take drugs, and since all the effective drugs cause drowsiness, astronauts add chemicals such as Dexedrine to keep them alert. Many an ocean race was won on the same combination, until Dexedrine was added to the dangerous drug list. ("What, me tired? No way. I'll stand your watch. Here, let my grind on that. I'll ... Oh, sorry. Let's just eeease it back out. So, you wanna talk about something? Whatcha wanna talk about???")

How to cope? Antihistamines, including Dramamine, Bonine, and Benadril, are generally effective, but they cause the drowsies, and they have to be taken before symptoms set in.

A nauseous person won't be able to hold them down. Acupressure bands are supposed to work by exerting just enough pressure between the wrist's main tendons to interfere with the sensory messages that cause nausea; they have their believers, and they have their doubters. Scopolamine is a prescription drug, formerly available as Transderm Scop, a dime-sized "patch" worn on the skin to transmit a steady dose for three days. The manufacturer claimed a 75 percent reduction of motion-induced nausea in clinical trials, but the FDA pulled the patch from the market for alleged misuse by its public (dumb misuse, not for kicks). Maybe it will be back, but frankly, those patches have their problems. In rough weather, if you're pulling wet gear over your head, you might lose the patch unless you protect it. Dry mouth and drowsiness affect some people, and Scopolamine users are warned against operating heavy and dangerous machinery (for example, a boat on the ocean?). Not to be unfair, Scopolamine is an effective drug for the job, and it is still available by prescription, but not with the patch.

Ephedrine and Phenergan are a reasonably effective prescription, combined to beat the drowsies. And ginger — 500 milligrams per day — has a fan club. I've never tried it myself.

Legend has it that British admiral Lord Nelson was queasy every time he went to sea. Fishermen say the feeling is at its worst when the boat is stopped and rolling in the troughs. And even someone who is well adapted can blow it (sorry) if conditions are bad enough.

Some people sail, knowing they'll be sick. They love it that much. Once, two days into a Honolulu race, I radioed home a newspaper story about a crewman who had sailed enough Transpacs to know that, without a doubt, he was going to be dog-sick for the first three days. But still, he just had to race. I wrote how determination shone through his misery. I wrote how he suffered. And I got pretty graphic. I used the phrase, "blowing his grits." My *Chronicle* editors killed the story. They said, "It made us sick."

And they have the gall to call it, *The Sporting Green*.

In the early years, each club held its own opening day and chose its own date. The Encinal Yacht Club kicked off its 1894 season with a day of maneuvers off its South Beach clubhouse in Alameda, with a procession of twenty yachts attended by sailing canoes and Whitehalls. Woodruff C. Minor's history of Encinal Yacht Club, *On The Bay*, offers a vivid picture of Commodore Joseph A. Leonard's *Little Annie* in the lead of the 1894 parade, raising and lowering the signal flags while members observed from the clubhouse — each dressed for the occasion in the club uniform of blue trousers, blue shirt with white collar, and a white duck cap. The celebration continued with rowing races and a rousing game of water polo played with a large inflatable ball. The ball was batted about between boats and canoes. All in all, not a bad way to welcome summer. Opening Day is also a reminder of eastern traditions that took hold when the sport was young. In those earliest days of San Francisco yachting, boats were laid up for the winter, eastern style, and the games resumed in the spring. A number of harbors, the Belvedere Lagoon for example, served as wintering holes. Until the entrance to Belvedere Lagoon was filled in 1926, a drawbridge linked a narrow, sandy strip of Tiburon to Belvedere hill. That bridge could be raised at any time, for a fee, but there also was a time each spring when it would open for the freshly varnished fleet to pass in force to the bay. There the Belvedere fleet would join boats from elsewhere and parade the bay with all flags flying.

In 1963, the Corinthian Yacht Club began hosting the annual Blessing of the Fleet in Raccoon Strait, with a bevy of clergy doing the honors. For many people today, the Blessing is the first goal of Opening Day. The parade route leads from there across the Golden Gate to the cityfront.

Crowds have diminished in some years and boomed in other years. In the 1990s, numbers grew, and the institution was renewed. But Opening Day will always draw more than its share of once-a-year sailors. They can be spotted by the way they drop their anchors over somebody else's anchor rode at Angel Island, or sail around sporting Marina del Rey racing stripes (fenders over the side), or try to work to weather with the jib-luff tension slack and the leading edge of the sail bagging into big, ugly scallops. Racing stripes and scalloped jibs have

their good points, however. They warn everybody else to keep their distance.

Stockton Sailing Club and other freshwater locations have their own Opening Day celebrations. Parades. Bands. Flags. Balloons …

Anywhere you go, there's not that much to "open" in our year-round boating world, but, hey, any excuse for a party.

WILDLIFE

Many creatures inhabit these border regions between the land and the sea, and the best of them tend to be fragile. It's ironic, but naturalists find many wildlife problems caused by well-meaning, environmentally-concerned people in small, quiet boats. In some areas, the most frequent problems come from kayak traffic, because people "strap on" a kayak to go exploring, and when they do, they think they're part of nature. They couldn't be more wrong.

A seal in the water may tag along with a boat without concern. It has the security of a ready escape. Seals on the beach are different. Any alien craft, whether it's a kayak, a rowing boat or a sailing boat, can send a panic through a seal haul-out. If the animals are taken by surprise, the problem might be all the worse for making a quiet approach. Imagine calling "Fire!" in a crowded theater and watching the young and the weak being trampled in the stampede. Understand too that a pup separated from its mother is a candidate to become an orphan. You need to keep a distance, and it's best to pass parallel. If you see seals moving toward the water, back off.

Rookeries are just as problematic, because it's in the breeding ground that birds are most vulnerable, and birds are nervous creatures. If you scatter birds off their nests, you've opened the way for predators to get to the eggs. Usually, the people who do it are not even aware that they've done it, or they wouldn't have, because all they had in mind was to be part of something beautiful. At the Point Reyes Bird Observatory, they have a simple rule: If you're close enough to get a good look without binoculars, you're too close.

Once, white geese covered these shores like a carpet of snow. Eagles ruled the sky. Once, in the South Bay marshes, there were clapper rails in abundance. Now the clapper rails are down to 600 and counting. Why be part of the problem?

The bay is open range — almost. There are rules written and unwritten. Among the unwritten rules, good manners suggest that cruising boats give way to racers. This is common practice, the theory being that the cruiser is in no hurry while the racer is wound up tight and fighting for every inch. The preferred maneuver is to pass the racing boat to leeward, never coming between the racer and the wind. A sailing boat casts a windshadow equal to several times the height of its mast, and that windshadow interferes with other boats.

The cruiser can easily cope with one racing boat at a time, and any cruising skipper should be alert enough to avoid a patch of water soon to be occupied by a mass of racing boats. Some idiots blunder on, and we're not out to excuse the idiots. In practice, however, there are days when no matter where the intelligently-managed cruising yacht goes, no matter which way the cruiser turns, somebody comes on yelling, "Racing! Hey! We're racing!" Confronted by a wall of boats, the cruiser may be trapped. It's impossible to keep off everyone's wind. Racing sailors on a day like this ought to be courteous and understanding from their own side of the fence. San Francisco Bay is a pretty small place, and it's not often that an encounter with a cruising boat has actually cost anyone a race, much less a season championship. Life is too short for a lot of bad mouthing in what should be our finest hours.

Starting areas for races are easy to spot, and noncontestants should avoid them. Races are usually started at an imaginary line between a committee boat and a buoy. Occasionally, when there are multiple starts for multiple fleets, there will be a buoy on one side of the committee boat to mark a starting line and another buoy on the opposite side to mark a finish line. Both will be set square (perpendicular) to the wind. On the cityfront, both the Golden Gate and St. Francis Yacht Clubs have permanent buoys established in-line with their clubhouse race decks. Those start/finish lines are used for less-formal races, not for national championships. They're also the hot ticket for starting and finishing ocean races, and they are often loaned out to other organizations. These permanent lines work because the seabreeze is reliable, and the lines are square enough, considering. They can be adjusted slightly by

Just carving wind. [PHOTO BY ROB MOORE, *LATITUDE 38*]

moving the marker at the clubhouse end.

Usually, it is easy to figure which way a racing fleet will go after the start; it will go upwind. If the starting time is at all close — ten minutes or less — the fleet will gather behind the line (downwind) in a chaotic welter. Skippers at this point are measuring the length of the line (in sailing time), deciding on the favored end, shooting the bow into the wind to check the wind direction or confirm a windshift, and watching to see whether their significant opponents are setting up for a start near one end of the line or the middle. The boats will group behind the line and go from there.

Sailboat races start upwind whenever possible. Except in fluky winter weather, upwind starts are a solid rule on San Francisco Bay.

Races are started by a stopwatch-countdown to a red shape that signals the start. Guns and whistles are also used, but the official signal is the shape, not the sound. The race committee sights straight down the line. Any boat that noses over before the countdown reaches zero must return to restart. And if there are strong currents across the race area, the smart money will go for the fast water as soon after the start as possible. If you understand what the currents are doing, you can guess which way the fleet will go.

BEFORE YOU GO

EXPERIENCED SAILORS CAN TELL AT A GLANCE if they're sailing across a current that is pushing them sideways. The process of ranging is so ingrained, they don't even have to think. The beginner can see the same thing, but it takes a bit of thought. Ranging is simply the art of looking at two aligned objects and watching to see if the alignment changes. If it does change, that tells you something.

Imagine beating upwind from Southampton Shoal, with Angel Island dead ahead. For a range, you choose two objects. Let's say you choose a chimney of one of the old, red-roofed quarantine buildings and a tree rising from the hill directly behind it. Then, without turning the boat, you see that the tree (the object in the rear) appears to be moving to the left. That tells you that the boat is moving to the left — you're crossing an ebb tide current coming out of the river, setting the boat to the south.

Stop. Don't dig out the chart and look for Southampton Shoal. Instead, try this on a tabletop: Set two objects in line and watch the relationship as you move your head from side to side. Salt and pepper shakers will do. See the changes? Pay attention whenever you're on the water, and soon, ranging will become as instinctive as looking.

Ranges also reveal whether your boat will cross ahead or behind another in an encounter on the water. Simply sight across the other boat to some stationary landmark. If the other boat is moving ahead of that "range," it will pass ahead. If the other boat is falling behind the range, it will pass behind. If the range is not changing — a steady range — you're on a collision course.

Meeting large ships, it is good to give some extra room for courtesy as well as safety, even when your boat is clearly crossing ahead. A ferry boat skipper, with much more maneuverability than a big-ship captain, once commented that, "the racing sailors are easy to deal with because you can guess where they're going, but the cruising boats — you don't have a clue, and you don't have a clue whether or not they have a clue, either." Close under the bow of a ship is no place to be, and it is likely to provoke some loud, long toots — five or more, the danger signal — from the ship's master. From the bridge of a ship, the captain or pilot will often lose sight of a small boat (behind the bow or a stack of containers) before they cross. It is not only illegal but unsafe to come too close; these big ships disturb the windflow, and they create disturbances in the water, a force of suction right into the hull and propellers.

At night, the ship's range lights tell you what you need to know about its direction of travel. There's a red light to port and a green light to starboard, of course, but the range lights consist of two white lights raised above the rest of the ship, visible at a greater distance than the green and the red. The aft light is higher than the forward light, so, by watching these two and treating them like any other range, the sailor can figure the ship's course and bearing. Knowing that, you know what to give, and when.

Another group that can use a little extra space is the Predicted Log Racing Association, whose member craft (motorboats usually, but sometimes sailboats under power) can be identified by the "PLRA Racer" banners they carry. "Race" is misleading, however. PLRA contests are more like auto rallies. Predicted logging is a test of precision, with the skipper navigating between checkpoints and timing his arrival not by means of boatspeed or the clock, but by engine rpms alone. An observer aboard carries the only clock and records "mark" at checkpoints. Predicted logging is usually done at moderate speeds, with careful timing and attention to course. Champions operate within an error range of two percent, often less, and they appreciate it to the full when someone can and does offer open water.

THE BIG BOAT RULE

Ignorance of the Big Boat Rule has landed more people in trouble than any other day-in, day-out aspect of boating. Yet all it is, is common sense (plus a few chapters of Admiralty Law).

Let's start with a common sense example. The setting was the San Francisco Marina, where the westerly was coming in chill and clear and the big, 1923 yawl *Santana*, sails furled, was motoring down the channel toward open water. Under sail, *Santana* is a lively beast despite its fifty-five feet and twenty-five tons. Under power, the boat does not stop or spin on a dime.

Santana had just cleared the breakwater, motoring at about four knots, when a windsurfer doing a good fifteen came in from left field and tried to conquer the same space at the same time. And lost. There was a resounding whap on the port quarter of the big boat, then a face looked up from the water and growled, "Thaaaaanks, dammit!"

What was *Santana* to do? The helmsman had no chance of anticipating, much less avoiding, the intentions of a more maneuverable and faster-moving craft. Moreover, *Santana* had very little safe water surrounding. Sail has right of way over power? Yes, but — it is unlawful to interfere with any boat that is restricted to a narrow channel. At Yerba Buena Island, among the Coast Guard's radar watchers at Vessel Traffic Service, they still chuckle over the small boat skipper who

called up to scream about being, "almost run down by a tanker." And that brings us to International Law.

Ships and barges-under-tow cross San Francisco Bay some 22,000 times a year. Those ships measure their turning radii in the thousands of yards and their stopping distances by the mile. They are restricted to shipping lanes that make their share of the bay, in practical terms, very small. That is why:

Commercial traffic has the right of way. Pleasure craft do not.

On the open ocean, where there are no course restrictions, sailboats may indeed claim the right of way over ships. But ships are much easier to spot than boats, and we could make an argument that any small boat skipper on a collision course with a moving mountain who assumes that he has been seen, and the mountain will move around him, is less sparklingly intelligent than the skipper who takes care of himself. In cruder company, we could phrase that more briefly.

And the nearby ocean — the Gulf of the Farallones — is not the open ocean. Here, ships operate under restrictions. Since October 13, 1994, all large ship traffic, barges, ferries and large tour or charter vessels on the bay or its approaches have been required to operate under the Vessel Traffic Service (VTS), maintained round-the-clock by the Coast Guard from the top of Yerba Buena Island.

VTS San Francisco was born out of a collision between two Standard Oil tankers just west of the Golden Gate Bridge in the early hours of January 18, 1971, in heavy fog. The bow of the *Arizona Standard* drove into the hull of the *Oregon Standard* and ripped it wide open, spilling 840,000 gallons of crude. The oil spill and damage to boats and wildlife were shocking, though the volume has long since been surpassed by other disasters. (In the growing VTS industry, the captain of the *Exxon Valdez* that created the big Alaskan spill is known as "Saint Hazelwood"). Even more shocking in the San Francisco spill was the obvious avoidability of the whole mess, given a reasonable use of available means of communication. That provided the impetus to create the Vessel Traffic Service.

Few sailors will ever need direct contact with VTS San Francisco, but the system is there to help whenever and however it is needed. Everyone who uses the bay should understand what is going on with those 22,000 commercial transits a year. Implementation of the VTS system (notice how easily we adopt officialese) specifically acknowledges the rights of small boat users on our crowded waters. In other places with this much shipping, you would expect to find pleasure craft required to cross the shipping lanes quickly, at right angles only. Here, to quote from the VTS User's Manual, "The geographical constraints of San Francisco Bay make implementation of a TSS (Traffic Separation Scheme) impractical and unnecessarily restrictive on recreational and harbor tour boats. Instead, traffic flow within the Bay is guided by a series of TRMs (Traffic Routing Measures) … The recreational boating public have a legitimate expectation that ships will adhere to the traffic routing system. Therefore, particularly in central San Francisco Bay (where many boats are often present), the hazards of deviating from the routing system are very pronounced."

It follows that, if these large, unwieldy machines are locked in and limited in what they can do, we have to give them the water they need.

All power-driven vessels 131 feet or longer, all towing vessels 26 feet or longer, and all passenger-carrying vessels certificated to carry 50 people or more are required to contact VTS by radio before they leave the dock or before they enter the VTS sector. VTS closed circuit viewing is being gradually extended upriver as far as Benecia, and ships upriver all the way to Stockton and Sacramento maintain radio contact, calling in at fixed reporting points. At sea, VTS reaches beyond the Farallon Islands, north to Bodega Head, and south to Pescadero Point. This is the biggest VTS area in the country. Traffic is monitored through a combination of radar, closed circuit television and radio reports from participating vessels, with an increasing reliance on computer integration as upgrades become available.

Communication is the main function of VTS. By having one central point of intelligence, the Coast Guard can keep track of ships coming and going. It is then possible to advise their captains and pilots of the traffic and hazards they can expect to encounter, and if necessary suggest changes in speed or route to maintain separation. Unlike air traffic control, VTS does not direct the movements of the vessels under its jurisdiction unless there is a special need. It will not direct a vessel to make a specific maneuver unless that vessel has strayed out of its traffic lane or there is imminent danger. The captain (or pilot) is free to make his own decisions. By reporting the ship's plans, however, and making position updates, the master of the ship makes it possible for VTS to perform a massive amount of coordination. VTS could suggest slowing an incoming ship, for example, or speeding up an outbound ship so they don't pass in the narrow Pinole Channel of San Pablo Bay.

On the West Bay, there are two Traffic Lanes and a Deep Water Route. The designated Eastbound Traffic Lane lies between the cityfront and Alcatraz. Inbound ships arriving east of Alcatraz turn north to enter the rivers, or they turn south, for Oakland Harbor and the South Bay anchorages. The Westbound Traffic Lane lies north of Alcatraz, between Alcatraz and Harding Rock. Immediately to the north of that is the Deep Water Route, the required path for any inbound traffic 45 feet or deeper and outbound traffic 28 feet or deeper. *So: between Harding Rock and Angel Island, we have a two-way lane of ship traffic and also the biggest, most heavily-laden vessels.*

VTS RADIO

We've already said that it's rare for sailors to need to contact VTS. It is important, however, to understand the radio umbrella, which involves three channels and exempts ships inside the bay from monitoring the common calling frequency, Channel 16.

Actually, ships are exempt from monitoring Channel 16 from the time they enter the Inshore Sector, beginning at the Sea Buoy, 11.1 nautical miles west of the Golden Gate Bridge. Ships under VTS are exempt from monitoring Channel 16 because they are required to monitor VTS channels 13 and 14, and having too many radios squawking at once creates an obvious hazard.

Channel 14 was adopted in 1994 as the standard VTS operating frequency on the Bay. Channel 13, the previous standard, was turned over to bridge-to-bridge communication. Before the change, there was so much activity on poor old Channel 13 that the pilots couldn't break through to get their business done.

VTS monitors 12, 13, 14 and 16, but their Channel 16 guard is limited to central San Francisco Bay and areas nearby. Coast Guard Group

Momentum = Mass X Velocity [PHOTO BY DON HILBUN]

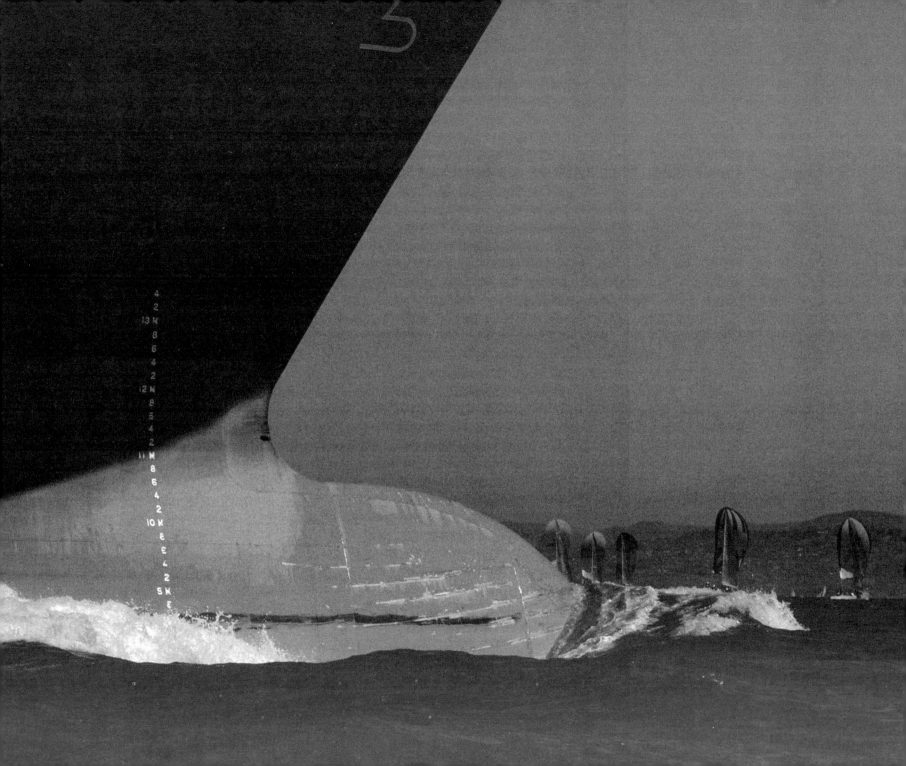

San Francisco maintains a 24-hour guard on Channel 16 covering the Bay, Delta, and offshore waters.

Here's a point to consider: If you're becalmed, with a motor that won't start, and there's a big ship aimed more or less at you that you know is expecting you to get out of the way — but you can't — calling them on Channel 16 is probably not the quickest way. Yes, Group San Francisco will hear you, and they will relay. Yes, VTS will hear you, and they will relay. But the ship that's coming on is sure to be monitoring Channel 13 (bridge to bridge) and Channel 14 (inshore VTS). The people you can reach on those channels are highly motivated to not run you down, and the quicker you let them know your problem, the better. Their careers are a mess if you commit suicide under their bow, so have pity on their families.

Offshore, when in doubt, stick to the Big Boat Rule. Commercial traffic still has the right of way in the local shipping lanes, and it's common sense to stay out of the way of moving mountains. In poor visibility, it's worth tuning into Channel 12, the offshore VTS frequency, at 15 and 45 minutes past the hour. All reporting traffic, meaning almost everything big enough to plow you under, will be identified along with position and route. If, because of possible collision, you need to report your position, VTS will take the call.

If every boat running around on the bay or the ocean tried to yak it up with VTS, the system would crash. A normal day of yachting does not include a conversation with VTS. But when there is reason to make contact, you should not hesitate. Lack of blood, gore, and headlines will add up to success for the Vessel Traffic Service. When you call, in order to do your fellow sailors proud, be prepared to describe your boat, position, and course crisply and efficiently. If you can't, do what you have to do. But work at it when you get home, and don't go back until you can get it right.

OUR COAST GUARD

Headquartered on Coast Guard Island, Alameda, the Pacific Area Command of the U.S. Coast Guard covers the 11th District (California, Nevada, Arizona and Utah), also the 13th District (Oregon, Washington, Idaho and Montana), the 17th District (Alaska) and the 14th District (Hawaii). The duty zone, commanded by a Vice Admiral, encompasses 74 million square miles. In a consolidation move accomplished in 1996, the Pacific Area Commander is now "double hatted" as they say in the service and also serves as 11th District Commander.

The service maintains five stations for Search and Rescue in the Bay and Delta, also Station Lake Tahoe. The remainder of Northern California is covered by stations and cutters based at Fort Bragg, Humboldt Bay, and Crescent City.

Prominent "SAR" stations are located on Yerba Buena Island (between San Francisco and Oakland), at Fort Baker (tucked into Horseshoe Cove at the north end of the Golden Gate Bridge), at the Cal Maritime Academy (near Carquinez Strait), and at Rio Vista (on the Sacramento River). Two 82-foot patrol boats in the region cover the fisheries and law enforcement. For crisis response, especially on the ocean, the service often calls upon the helicopter crews who stand duty around the clock at San Francisco International.

The Coast Guard does not routinely respond to non-emergency SAR. That work — the motorboat that runs out of gas, the sailboat on the sandbar and all the many variations — is given over to the Coast Guard Auxiliary or to commercial operators whenever possible. Commercial towing services arose in the late 1980s as the Coast Guard, facing severe reductions to its budget, cut back on services that had once made it something very close to a Triple A of the waterways. In the new world, you have to expect to pay. There are commercial operators who will respond to a call, and there are membership assistance companies that you can join as a matter of insurance

All Coast Guard stations monitor Channel 16 for communication and distress. Group Command at Yerba Buena Island — the coordination center for the region — can also be reached by dialing 911. The service responds to some 2,500 Search and Rescue missions a year in the Bay Area, only a few hundred of which occur on the ocean. Rio Vista gets more calls than any other station, about 600 per year. At Group Command, the explanation goes something like this: "Up the river the air is warm, the water is calm — anybody feels comfortable jumping into a boat, and anybody and everybody does. Most beginners won't go out on the bay, though. They look at it, and they can see it's not for them."

Crisis calls, especially on the ocean, are likely to go to the pilots at Coast Guard Air Station San Francisco, at the north end of SFO near the old Pan Am hangar (now a Federal Express hangar but once a home to the fabled Clippers, the seaplanes of the Pacific route). A minimum of one helicopter crew is kept in readiness around the clock: pilot, copilot, flight mechanic and medically-trained rescue swimmer. In the twelve months before press time, the crews of Air Station San Francisco were credited with saving 43 lives, and not only on the ocean. Coast Guard helicopter duty in Northern California is unusual for including inland waters as well — the Delta, for example, where all those radio towers and wires make for what one pilot called "an interesting challenge" in low visibility.

The Coast Guard's roots go back to 1790 and the commissioning of ten revenue cutters for the enforcing of tariff laws. The 11th District traces its history to 1849, when the officers of the *Revenue Cutter Lawrence* were assigned to cut through the chaos of the Gold Rush town and serve as police, judges, and customs agents.

The Coast Guard has grown in its 200 years, but it remains small compared to other branches of the military service, with only 38,000 people worldwide — roughly half the capacity of Candlestick. Those people serve from the Suez to Panama, from the Gulfstream to the Molokai Channel. They've been charged with increased duties in law enforcement at the same time that basic funds were being cut. But whatever the locale, the pride of the service is in lifesaving, and that's never routine.

We met her in San Francisco, but it was on an early spring day over the Strait of Juan de Fuca that Lieutenant Alda Siebrands first attracted attention outside her own unit. On that day, Lt. Siebrands was called upon to divert her helicopter from its assigned pollution patrol. The new mission was to rescue two men whose skiff had capsized in heavy surf.

At full throttle it took minutes — long minutes — to reach the scene. One man hauled himself into the helicopter's rescue basket and was brought up quickly, hypothermic and delirious from the 45-degree water. The second victim got one arm across the basket, took a wave, and rolled unconscious.

But the aircraft, being under orders for a pollution patrol, was shorthanded. It did not carry a rescue swimmer.

So Lieutenant Siebrands, flying as pilot in command, pulled off her helmet, told her copilot, "It's all yours, Binky," and … jumped. ◆

"Too much of a good thing can be wonderful." Mae West [PHOTO BY ROB MOORE, *LATITUDE 38*]

A TIDE IN THE AFFAIRS OF MEN

"Slack water is a state of mind."
— HARRY EASOM

THE TIDE IS A REACTION, AND THE TIDE IS A FORCE. At high tide, water bulges away from the planet, reacting to the pull of the sun and the moon. At high tide, boats go places they can't go at low tide. They can stick there too, if they stay until the tide falls.

The action of the tide, rising and falling, creates a powerful thrust of current spilling through the Golden Gate. Those currents flood and ebb through the bay and the rivers. Then tide becomes a force. You're either with it, or against it.

Tidal variables account for about 80 percent of the current variables on San Francisco Bay. That leaves 20 percent for the influence of river flow, prevailing or perverse wind, atmospheric pressure, and spirits unnameable by day. As we translate the rise and fall of tides into the flood and ebb of the currents, there are times when the science of prediction verges upon voodoo. The voodoo is up to you. The rest, we'll take a look at.

We can predict the tides because they pass in regular cycles: daily, monthly, yearly, and even a nineteen-year cycle that returns the sun and the moon to identical relations in the heavens.

The moon – smaller, but denser and closer – has the greatest influence. Its monthly orbit creates a cycle with twice-monthly spring tides and twice-monthly neap tides.

Every half-orbit, arriving at opposite sides of the planet, the moon aligns with the sun. (Figure 1) With moon and sun pulling along the same line, the water springs to its highest highs and lowest lows. The moon-sun alignment doesn't have to be perfect (as it would be in an eclipse) for tides to "spring." The moon's actual orbiting time is 27.3 days, and (to be precise) we find a new moon or a full moon – and spring tides – every 13.66 days. High highs and low lows. Then the moon's passage carries it out of alignment with the sun. Their combined pull lessens, and so does the tidal range (the height difference between high tide and low tide). Highs each day are a little lower, and lows are a little higher, until the moon reaches either first quarter (after the new moon) or third quarter (after the full moon). The earth's primordial satellite and its home star are then out of phase as far as they go. They are in quadrature, tugging almost at right angles. The tidal response is weakest, and the tidal range is least. This is the time of the neap tides as also shown in Figure 1. Afterward, hour by hour, the moon moves on, closing once again on alignment with the sun. Each day, high tides rise a little higher and low tides fall a little lower until moon and sun re-align, and the tides again spring to high highs and low lows.

As a rule of thumb, spring tides are about 20 percent greater than the mean tide, and neap tides are about 20 percent less.

There is also a point in the lunar orbit when the moon is at perigee – as near earth as it comes – and it draws high perigean tides simply by being so close. A perigean tide may temporarily interrupt a trend in the monthly cycle, as when the moon at perigee raises the level of a

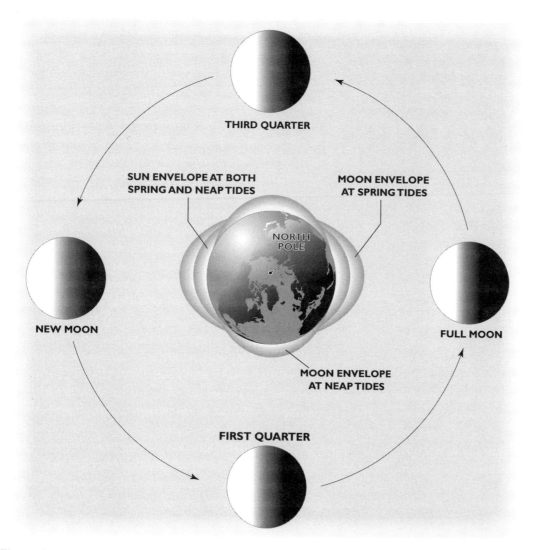

THIRD QUARTER

SUN ENVELOPE AT BOTH
SPRING AND NEAP TIDES

MOON ENVELOPE
AT SPRING TIDES

NORTH
POLE

NEW MOON

FULL MOON

MOON ENVELOPE
AT NEAP TIDES

FIRST QUARTER

Figure 1: Tides "spring" to high highs and low lows twice a month, at syzygy, when the new moon and the full moon line up with the gravitational pull of the sun. The smallest tides of the month, neap ties, occur at the quarter moons, when sun and moon pull at right angles. (The illustration ignores the lag time of inertia, which delays actual tides by a day or more.) [ART BY BRUCE KREFTING]

neap tide. Or, if perigean tides coincide with spring tides, the double whammy will produce very high highs. If a storm hits at the same time, it will be a storm to remember. Rain winds from the south will drive water out of the South Bay and pile it up on the marshlands at Larkspur and San Rafael. Richardson Bay will swell across the mud flats until it threatens to reach the gym doors at Tam High.

THE RHYTHM METHOD

Tides on San Francisco Bay have two cycles daily: two highs and two lows. These are semidiurnal tides. The two highs are usually very different, as are the lows. Thus we have higher high water and lower low water, and lower high water and higher low water occuring at Points X and Y, respectively, in Figure 2. At oceanfront locations in Northern California, the average difference between high tides on a given day is two feet. The average difference between lows is two to three feet. So: a measurement of mean lower low water is taken as the reference point for water depths printed on Pacific Coast charts. Tide books employ the same reference, indicating the height of tides as so many feet above or below mean lower low water.

At 13.66-day intervals, the moon arrives at a point overhead either the Tropic of Cancer or the Tropic of Capricorn. There, at maximum declination, it creates the maximum difference between the day's two highs and two lows: Tropic Tides. Later, passing from one Tropic to another, the moon crosses the equator, drawing as it does the least difference between highs and lows: Equatorial Tides. Occasionally, a twenty-four hour day catches only three peaks of the total cycle. Then the next tide will follow hard on the heels of midnight.

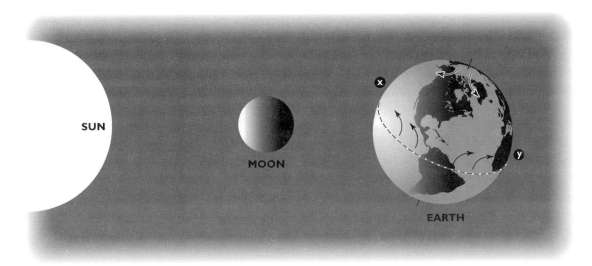

Figure 2: Tidal flow on a spinning planet: Higher high water at Point X; lower low water at Point Y. Low tide occurs at longitudes between.

[ART BY BRUCE KREFTING]

A complete tidal day is 24.84 hours. No part of the cycle is ever lost; low tide will not be followed by another low tide.

The ancients were well aware of the tides and their correlation to the stages of the moon. Pliny the Elder, for example, was a rock star of Roman science in the First Century A.D. Now he's often dismissed as a Compiler Of Other People's B.S., but Pliny is not someone to be dismissed so lightly. He cared enough about fact finding to run *toward* Vesuvius when it blew its top. Until that day, his last, one understanding Pliny shared with all the educated minds of his time was the connection between moon and tide, and one puzzle was what we now call the lunitidal interval – the lag time between the passage of the moon and the response of the tides.

So, here's a confession. Our illustrations so far have been simplified, as if spring tides, for example, occur exactly when they are generated, as the moon aligns with the sun. Instead, there is lag time, a delay. In the case of spring tides, there is a delay of a day or more before the waters spring to their highest highs and lowest lows. According to the best minds now going (2000 years behind Pliny), the main cause of the lunitidal interval is inertia: water has mass, mass has inertia, and inertia slows response time.

In lunar stages between neap tide and spring tide, there is even a period when high-tide forces are developed before the moon's passage overhead. Moon and sun pull separately, and the tidal bulge appears somewhere between their nearest points on the planet.

The moon orbits in the direction the planet rotates, making one orbit per 27.3 rotations and "catching up" with San Francisco Bay or any other point on the planet fifty minutes later each day. The mathematics of it are pure and beautiful for two more-or-less round rocks rolling around in space, and there are practical implications for small, bipedal mammals who like to sail: The tide cycle runs about fifty minutes later each day - roughly, very roughly – so if you remember low tide yesterday, or maximum flood or whatever, you can make a good guess about today. If you remember the trend over several days, you can make a very good guess.

Now we have enough pieces of the puzzle to think about tides the way a scientist would. Look again at Figure 1. Think of the moon rotating slowly through its orbit and the earth rotating relatively quickly. There is a big bulge of water following along after the moon and a corresponding bulge of water on the opposite side of the globe. Oceanographers use the term tide wave (not to be confused with the catastro-

35

ARISTOTLE, GALILEO, NEWTON AND YOUR FOREDECK

THE RELATIVE IMPORTANCE OF DIFFERENT TIDE FACTORS IS still a matter of debate among professionals. One legend has it that Aristotle died a suicide, hurling himself into the waters of the Euripe because he could not explain the action of the tides. Historians don't swallow the tale, but it must have seemed plausible once. Accustomed to waters where tidal effects were scarcely noticeable, the author of The Poetics spent the last months of his life on the island of Euboea, separated from mainland Greece by the Euripe. In this narrow channel, tidal exchanges between Aegean and Mediterranean waters generate currents as great as nine knots. Those are currents of Homeric proportions.

Babylonian philosophers, secure behind their figured walls and bronze gates, theorized that the moon in passing compressed the atmosphere, which compressed the waters, which generated tides. Long after that, no less a seventeenth-century rationalist than René Descartes carried on this notion, cogitating a space filled with ether. On the boot of Italy, Galileo Galilei's own seventeenth-century mind was focused on showing the earth to be round, and orbiting the sun, and rotating on its axis. Tidal action he blamed on the ocean's inability to keep pace. Galileo compared tides to the sloshing of waters in a big bowl. He offered this as further proof that the world turned, and he pooh-poohed anyone who suggested that maybe the moon attracted water.

Galileo died in 1642, the year Isaac Newton was born. Forty-five years later, Newton's Philosophiae naturalis principia mathematica gave us our present understanding of tidal action by way of the concept of gravity and the Equilibrium Model. From Newton we understand why the moon, being smaller (but denser and closer) exerts more tidal force upon the earth than the sun. Also from Newton, we get the basic math for high water and low water. It rains a lot in England, so Newton had time to ponder. If his picture of tidal behavior is not simple, it's at least easier to hold in the mind than anything offered in this century by Albert Einstein, who wanted to relieve us of the concept of gravity and free us to inhabit instead a space-time continuum curved around a magnetic field. That is, free to have nothing solid under our feet. Who can say what comfort curved space might

have been to Newton, rubbing the apple-bump on his head, as he wrote, "Hitherto we have explained the phenomena of the heavens and of our sea by the power of gravity, but … I have not been able to discover the cause of these properties from phenomena, and I frame no hypothesis."

Newton was well aware that his mathematics left unexplained gaps in tidal behaviors. For just one example that came into focus long after Newton's life, consider that the earth does not rotate around its core. Rather, the earth and moon revolve around a common center of gravity lying a thousand miles below the surface of the planet and some three thousand miles from the center. It is possible to think of the earth and moon as a binary planet system rather than as planet and satellite.

Recently, certain theorists introduced the notion that tides, which wouldn't be significant without the moon, were responsible for the appearance of life on earth. Take away the moon, they figure, and what you're left with is a steadily more concentrated lineup of molecular compounds, gradually accumulating and hardening in dry depressions. In other words, the primordial soup would have evaporated. It's a nice theory, but while we're out here in left field (how did we get here?), we'd better tip our hat to the even-newer proposition that life appeared first around deep-water chemical vents. Either way, getting back to the safer ground of mathematics, an important factor in stabilizing the motion of the earth is the rotation of the moon. Science figures it this way: The earth wobbles on its axis between 22 degrees and 24.6 degrees of tilt, giving us our seasons and, more importantly, the predictability of the seasons. If the planet wobbled around any more, the climate could be so changeable that higher life forms would never have evolved to achieve the recognition that $E = MC^2$, and hemlines are either going up, or they're going down.

If the moon is powerful enough to act on the whole planet, it should come as no surprise that the moon acts upon the waters. The "friction" of the tides in turn acts upon the moon, apparently, allowing it to slip farther from the earth.

Quick, run out to your foredeck, and watch.

phe-induced tsunami, or tidal wave). The oceanographer's tide waves have an apparent motion across the face of the planet, but to be more precise, the planet is turning beneath them.

The mathematics of tidal theory would have these waves traveling at a little more than a thousand miles per hour, a speed equivalent to the moon's apparent speed around a rotating planet. In the real world, ocean depths vary, and the tide waves are obstructed by islands and continents. Tidal effects accordingly vary in different oceans and in different parts of the same ocean, the actual speed of the tide wave not exceeding 750 miles per hour. The tide wave moves as a forced wave, balanced between the attractive gravities of the moon and sun, unbalanced by friction with obstacles and the ocean bottom.

VARIABLES

Sometimes you want to know how deep the water is, and that's a tide question. On San Francisco Bay, you're more often concerned with current questions: which way is the water going, and how fast is it moving? But we said before that tidal variations account for only 80 percent of current variations on the surface of San Francisco Bay. Before we tighten our focus from the Blue Planet to this green and brown and blue and often whitecapped bay, let's talk variables.

ATMOSPHERIC PRESSURE – Air pressure at sea level bears down at 14.7 pounds per square inch, on average, but that weight varies with temperature and other factors. A storm-producing low pressure system delivers exactly what the name promises — low pressure — and low pressure can allow the surface of the bay to rise by as much as a foot over a tide-book prediction. In the total tide-prism of a shallow bay, that's a big percentage. You get an opposite effect from those hot, high pressure systems of summer and autumn. They push the surface of the water down. The volume of water, in turn, affects the strength of the currents.

San FRANCISCO BAY IS A COMPLEX and variable system. Even so, the bay is relatively compact, and it's often an easier "read" than, say, Puget Sound, which runs 110 miles north to south. Seattle sailors have to deal with that much deeper, larger body of water where a strong pressure system, out of sight on one end of the Sound or the other, can throw the predictions way out of whack. The old saw is true — if you can sail San Francisco Bay you can sail anywhere — but that doesn't mean you've seen it all.

WIND DRIVEN CURRENTS – A strong, sustained wind will carry surface water with it. A booming summer westerly driving the surface of a flood tide may raise water levels by a foot over calm conditions and delay the turn of the tide by nearly half an hour. Other strong, sustained winds blow through in the southerlies advancing a (typical) low pressure system or the northerlies that come behind it. In each case, the wind is going to push surface water along, with an effect on tide height and surface current.

Ten knots of wind is likely to create a surface current of about two-tenths of a knot. Twenty knots could get you three-tenths of a knot. Given a strong seabreeze, wind-driven current is a definite factor in building that familiar ebb-tide chop.

(Any wind-driven current in the Northern Hemisphere tends to flow slightly to the right of the true wind direction. That's the Coriolis force at work. With a sustained wind blowing across open ocean, the effect is worth considering. In the confines of San Francisco Bay, there's so much else going on that it's hard to even identify a force so subtle, except at the cocktail hour.)

RIVER FLOW – Sixteen rivers join to become the Sacramento River and later the "San Francisco River," as it rolls past Alcatraz. Together, they drain 40 percent of the total surface of the state. The effect of river volume is hard to pin down. The experts don't always agree. But, there's a lesson there.

The current predictions that you find in tide books take river flow into account, averaging the seasonal rainfall variations. The book assumes that more water comes out of the river in the winter and spring than in summer and fall. A wet winter might produce 100,000 to 200,000 cubic feet per second, which is still a small component of the 5,000,000 cfs pumping in and out on a normal tide. A dry summer might reduce the river flow to 4,000 cubic feet of water per second.

It takes very high river stages to fool the tide books in a big way, with NOAA accounting for those average seasonal variations. U.S. Geological Survey findings indicate that river discharge may vary from a one-percent component of ebb-tide flow at low river stages to ten percent at radically high river stages. The theorists, when you interview them with a notepad in your hand, are not impressed by the effects of river flow on the currents of San Francisco Bay. But this is a point where there is a definite gap between theory and field experience.

From ordinary month to ordinary month, whether it's winter or summer, if you see predictions for six knots of ebb or more, you will probably find it happening when the moon at perigee corresponds to a spring tide. The arrows on the current charts don't change whether the discharge rate is five thousand cubic feet per second or twenty thousand, and your experience on the water does not change, either. But, what will get your attention is a winter approaching record rain levels and a corresponding spring runoff. Then you'll find ebb currents working when there's no ebb predicted in the book, and the speed in the channels will be astounding.

The North Bay, with the river channel running through closed confines, is more affected by a strong runoff than the rest of the system. The effects of a heavy winter can last into the summer, with fresh

Tom Blackaller and Ed Bennett in 6150, a Star they *didn't* sink. [PHOTO BY DR. JOHN E. HUTTON]

water from the rivers overriding the denser, saltier ocean water in a grand display of frothy tide lines and color differentials. At the U.S. Geological Survey offices in Menlo Park, hydrologist Ralph Cheng points to the heavy winter of 1986 as an exceptional example of river runoff. That year, the salinity of the water at the Golden Gate dropped to 10 parts per 1000 from a norm of 30 parts per 1000. At that point, it was almost fresh water. Ongoing studies found similar numbers after the heavy rains of 1997 and 1998.

PUSH COMES TO SHOVE

Tide predictions are assembled at the National Oceanic and Atmospheric Administration headquarters in Rockville, Maryland, using the Equilibrium Model as we have presented it: 1) Changes in relative position of the moon and sun. 2) Changes in declination. 3) Changes in distance from earth. The various permutations produce as many as sixty-two tidal constituents to be fed into the computers. The actual tide then equals the sum of these parts, weighed against the effect of river discharge at a particular time of the year, as predicted from the data of previous years.

At oceanfront locations where the rebound of the tide wave is simple – bouncing off the continent – the mathematical models produce excellent predictions without a lot of "ifs" and "howevers." If, however, you're sailing the San Francisco Bay and Delta, you'll find the tide wave bounding and rebounding from crooks and shallows, islands and countercurrents, and playing some pretty tricks. Tide-and-current intelligence will depend upon observation and experience.

Much of the data that still goes into the predicting of bay tides and currents was gathered in the 1920s (though that picture is changing rapidly now as the world goes digital). A more recent physical survey was conducted by a NOAA team aboard the vessel *MacArthur*. A ship's officer commented at the end of that survey that he had used the tide books for the sake of deploying instrument buoys at minimum current. The books were accurate, he believed, "Give or take half an hour."

People who spend a great deal of time on the bay will keep track of the trends, and you might hear them say, "The tides are running about twenty minutes late," or fifteen minutes early, or some such figure. If so, it won't be an erratic figure that changes day by day; it will be a trend stretched out over days, weeks, or even months. You can't make accurate tide and current predictions for a daily outing without being aware of the present trend.

One sixth of the volume of the bay flows in and out with each tide cycle. Ebb tides are reinforced with river water, so ebb currents tend to flow a little longer and stronger than flood currents. A pattern of 7s and 5s – seven hours of ebb for five hours of flood – is knocked about as a rule of thumb. On the rise, flood tides run all the way to Sacramento.

The tide wave advances with its greatest force through the deepest cuts, the shipping channels, that once were the stream beds of ancient rivers. That is also where you will find the quickest currents. In the West Bay, the North Channel between Alcatraz and Angel Island runs 100 feet deep (which is why you'll see the biggest ships using the North Channel). The South Channel, between Alcatraz and the cityfront, is only 40 feet deep. Current charts show the highest velocities near the venturi formed by the Golden Gate.

In the main body of the bay, there is a net change of water over a number of tidal cycles. Other things being equal, a raft floating on San Pablo Bay will drift out and in a bit on each cycle, but each ebb tide will carry it closer to the Gate until, eventually, the raft checks out and goes to sea. Other things not being equal, the raft will wind up at the north end of Sausalito as part of a houseboat, but that's a separate issue.

Any place where fresh and salt waters mix is called an estuary, including all of the San Francisco Bay and San Pablo Bay. About one fifth of the San Francisco Bay Estuary is fresh water, and the ways and means of its mixing dictate much of the ecology. The point of greatest saltwater penetration – the null zone – lies a few miles inland from Carquinez Strait, advancing or retreating with decreasing or increasing river flow.

In the South Bay, there is little freshwater drainage. Instead, the South Bay depends upon flow from the north for its daily and seasonal flush. For a South Bay that receives more than its share of sewage and industrial waste, this influx from the North Bay is the only effective cleansing action – reason enough to fear any further reduction of river flow into the estuary.

The South Bay-North Bay exchange is fundamental to any understanding of how our tides work: North Bay and South Bay have different characteristics, and they're out of synch.

Tides turn first in the South Bay. That is what makes it possible for South Bay ebb water to join the North Bay flood, or a half-cycle later for the North Bay ebb to mingle with the South Bay flood. Get that picture in your head, and you can bring a lot of tide events into focus. We'll study it more after we've dipped into our tide book.

THE MOST MISREAD BOOK IN TOWN

A general understanding of current and eddy, combined with predictions from the tide books and current charts, can answer most of the questions of small boat travel: Is the water deep enough? Will the currents help or hinder? Finer points matter only to the racing set, who have seen it proved over and over that when it comes to the finer points, there is no substitute for applied intelligence. Expert racing sailors from other parts of the world win championships on San Francisco Bay in spite of the "local knowledge advantage." Maybe even because of it, if the locals are driving with blinders on. Equipped with a feel for how currents flow and tides turn, the expert will check the turf, talk to as many people as he can (including the fishermen, if he's really smart), and then get down to business. Setting sail, the expert will doublecheck the tide book, then look at the water, and study the current on one or several buoys to see just where in the tide cycle the moment really fits.

All tide books share certain basics. If you just want to sail laps of the San Francisco Bay and Delta, you don't need the Department of Commerce's Tide Tables for the Pacific Coast of North America and Asia or the Tidal Current Tables for the same. For what it would cost you in quarters to park for twelve minutes on Montgomery Street, you can buy a handy pocket edition that will tell you much of what there is to know about the movements of local waters. Or, in a lot of shops, they're free.

Longtime sailors have probably noticed that their pocket editions took a turn for the better in the 1990s. Bar Pilot 37, Frank Hoburg, got fed up with the books he had been getting from printers who had no understanding of what they were printing and didn't always get it right. Hoburg decided to do his own and sell them under various in-house covers to pilots, shippers, yacht clubs and chandleries. These are the pocket-sized tide books you'll find aboard most boats and packed into the duffel bags of all who take their sailing seriously. Whatever the form, all the information comes from NOAA; the rest is a matter of intelligent packaging.

Any tide book will include a daily calendar for a given year, January 1 through December 31, and it will indicate the phases of the moon. For each day, it will state the times for high and low water. It also will list those tidal heights in feet above or below mean lower low water, with information on the strength and direction of currents. Somewhere in the book there will be a statement informing the reader in legalese that all figures are approximate, and nothing is guaranteed.

Frank Hoburg has had many opportunities to compare the bay to the book, "And I continue to be intrigued by how often you can find the water turning, right on schedule. If you use your head when you use the tables, you won't go wrong."

Here's another pro with the same message: Mik Beatie, a sailor and a ferryboat driver for Golden Gate Transit, plays and works on the bay. That's his life. "I go through the tide book at the start of my day," Beatie says. "I take numbers and times from the tables, and I write them down on a piece of paper and put them in the book next to the current charts that I'll be looking at." Beatie's book, by the end of the year, has been marked off line by line and page by page. Extraordinary rains will throw things off, he said, but, "The water gets back to the book real quick along the cityfront (at the foot of Market Street, for example, where the ferries dock). What you've got to watch out for is the North Bay and the North Channel, 'cause the river can really rip. There was one year the runoff was so strong, Harding Rock Buoy dragged under. It just plain disappeared for a while."

Your pocket edition will probably have three main parts. The largest part by far will be the calendar section, with predictions for highs and lows at the Golden Gate, also for maximum current at the Golden Gate. A corresponding section will give predictions for highs, lows, and current maximums at Carquinez Strait. (Many bay sailors go through a new book and cross out the Carquinez Strait information rather than risk looking at the wrong material some day, in haste, and coming out all wrong.) *Always use the correct correction table.*

The pocket book will also include correction tables to identify highs and lows, current maximums, and their timing at other locations. In most consumer books you will find the National Oceanic and Atmospheric Administration's charts of current flow in ebb and flood, even though NOAA officially withdrew the charts from circulation in 1991.

The current charts contain useful information. We're not going to give up, just yet, on these handy-dandy little pictures. Taken broadly, they illustrate the important hydraulic features of San Francisco Bay. NOAA pulled the charts out of distribution with the explanation that predictions obtained from them, "are not as accurate as those determined from more recent information published in the NOS Tidal Current Tables."

Gradually, we are finding a new range of computer-generated data at our fingertips. In the 1990s, the U.S. Geological Survey and the National Oceanic and Atmospheric began a joint survey of currents and winds in Northern California, coupled to and cross-corrected against the standard tide and current data coming from NOAA's facility in Rockville, Maryland. Many sailors followed the research by checking in at the USGS web site. See page 49 for more on digital currents. Here, we'll cover the little book that fits your hip pocket. Our references come from the tide tables for

November, 1998 as shown in Figure 3. Times and heights apply to the Golden Gate. In the left column of the tide tables are the phases and declination of the moon.

Bold type leads us quickly to the largest tides and the strongest currents of the month.

A full moon occurs on November 3. Simultaneously, the moon arrives at perigee, its closest approach to earth. This combination of strong-tide forces produces a textbook-perfect illustration: The highest

NOVEMBER
TIDES AT GOLDEN GATE, CALIFORNIA – 1998
Heights in feet   Pacific Standard Time

Moon	Day	Time	Ht.	Time	Ht.	Time	Ht.	Time	Ht.
		Low		**High**		**Low**		**High**	
E	1 Sun	0211	0.5	0902	5.9	1458	0.6	2125	5.2
	2 Mon	0257	0.7	0939	**6.3**	1543	-0.2	2223	5.4
PO	3 Tue	0343	1.0	1018	**6.5**	1629	**-0.7**	2320	5.4
	4 Wed	0429	1.3	1057	**6.7**	1716	**-1.1**		
		High		**Low**		**High**		**Low**	
	5 Thu	0017	5.4	0515	1.8	1139	**6.8**	1805	**-1.2**
	6 Fri	0115	5.3	0604	2.2	1224	**6.7**	1855	**-1.1**
N	7 Sat	0214	5.2	0658	2.6	1312	**6.4**	1949	**-0.8**
	8 Sun	0317	5.2	0801	2.9	1405	6.0	2046	-0.4
	9 Mon	0422	5.2	0916	3.0	1505	5.6	2147	0.0
◐	10 Tue	0525	5.2	1039	3.0	1613	5.1	2250	0.4
	11 Wed	0624	5.3	1157	2.6	1728	4.8	2351	0.7
	12 Thu	0714	5.5	1302	2.2	1844	4.6		
		Low		**High**		**Low**		**High**	
	13 Fri	0047	0.9	0757	5.6	1355	1.7	1954	4.5
E	14 Sat	0136	1.2	0833	5.7	1440	1.2	2055	4.5
A	15 Sun	0219	1.4	0906	5.8	1519	0.7	2148	4.5
	16 Mon	0259	1.7	0935	5.8	1554	0.4	2236	4.6
	17 Tue	0336	1.9	1002	5.9	1627	0.1	2321	4.6
●	18 Wed	0411	2.2	1029	5.9	1659	-0.1		
		High		**Low**		**High**		**Low**	
	19 Thu	0004	4.6	0446	2.5	1058	5.9	1731	-0.2
	20 Fri	0045	4.6	0519	2.8	1128	5.9	1804	-0.2
	21 Sat	0128	4.6	0554	3.0	1200	5.8	1840	-0.2
S	22 Sun	0212	4.7	0633	3.3	1236	5.7	1919	**-0.1**
	23 Mon	0259	4.7	0719	3.4	1316	5.5	2003	0.0
	24 Tue	0349	4.7	0818	3.5	1405	5.2	2052	0.1
	25 Wed	0440	4.9	0932	3.4	1504	4.9	2146	0.3
◑	26 Thu	0529	5.1	1051	3.0	1615	4.6	2244	0.5
	27 Fri	0615	5.3	1201	2.4	1737	4.5	2344	0.7
	28 Sat	0659	5.7	1301	1.7	1859	4.4		
		Low		**High**		**Low**		**High**	
E	29 Sun	0041	1.0	0741	**6.0**	1354	0.9	2016	4.6
	30 Mon	0135	1.2	0823	**6.4**	1443	0.0	2124	4.8

LUNAR DATA

● = NEW MOON	◑ = LAST QUARTER	N = FARTHEST NORTH OF EQUATOR
◑ = FIRST QUARTER	A = IN APOGEE	E = ON EQUATOR
○ = FULL MOON	P = IN PERIGEE	S = FARTHEST SOUTH OF EQUATOR

32

NOVEMBER
CURRENTS AT GOLDEN GATE, SAN FRANCISCO 1998
Currents in knots   Pacific Standard Time

Day	Slack	MAX Current Time H.M.	Vel Knots	Slack	MAX Current Time	Vel Knots	Slack	MAX Current Time	Vel Knots	Slack	MAX Current Time H.M.	Vel Knots	Slack
1 Sun		0100	3.9E	0436	0735	3.7F	1043	1332	4.2E	1715	2007	3.6F	2313
2 Mon		0154	3.9E	0524	0820	3.8F	1123	1420	**4.9E**	1803	2059	4.1F	
3 Tue	0011	0246	3.9E	0611	0905	3.9F	1204	1507	**5.4E**	1852	2150	**4.5F**	
4 Wed	0107	0337	3.7E	0658	0950	3.8F	1245	1555	**5.7E**	1941	2242	**4.7F**	
5 Thr	0203	0428	3.5E	0746	1036	3.6F	1329	1643	**5.7E**	2032	2334	4.6F	
6 Fri	0259	0519	3.2E	0836	1125	3.3F	1415	1732	**5.5E**	2125			
7 Sat	0029 4.4F	0356	0612	2.8E	0931	1217	2.9F	1505	1823	**5.2E**	2221		
8 Sun	0126 4.1F	0454	0708	2.5E	1033	1313	2.5F	1601	1917	**4.7E**	2320		
9 Mon	0228 3.7F	0553	0808	2.2E	1141	1417	2.1F	1703	2015	4.1E			
10 Tue	0020	0333 3.5F	0651	0914	2.2E	1254	1528	2.0F	1810	2116	3.6E	
11 Wed	0120	0437 3.3F	0746	1027	2.3E	1403	1645	2.0F	1921	2220	3.2E	
12 Thr	0218	0536 3.2F	0836	1139	2.5E	1506	1756	2.2F	2028	2325	3.0E	
13 Fri	0312	0627 3.1F	0921	1232	2.9E	1600	1856	2.4F	2131			
14 Sat	0025 2.8E	0402	0711	3.1F	1003	1311	3.2E	1648	1947	2.7F	2228		
15 Sun	0115 2.7E	0447	0750	3.0F	1040	1344	3.5E	1730	2031	3.0F	2321		
16 Mon	0158 2.6E	0528	0824	2.9F	1115	1416	3.8E	1810	2111	3.2F			
17 Tue	0009	0237 2.6E	0606	0856	2.8F	1148	1450	4.1E	1848	2148	3.3F	
18 Wed	0054	0314 2.5E	0642	0928	2.6F	1220	1525	4.3E	1924	2223	3.4F	
19 Thr	0138	0353 2.4E	0717	1001	2.5F	1252	1603	4.4E	2001	2258	3.3F	
20 Fri	0222	0433 2.3E	0750	1037	2.4F	1323	1642	4.4E	2038	2336	3.3F	
21 Sat	0305	0514 2.2E	0825	1116	2.2F	1357	1723	4.4E	2116			
22 Sun	0016 3.2F	0350	0558	2.1E	0904	1157	2.0F	1433	1807	4.3E	2157		
23 Mon	0100 3.2F	0437	0645	2.1E	0951	1244	1.9F	1515	1853	4.1E	2241		
24 Tue	0147 3.1F	0525	0736	2.1E	1050	1336	1.7F	1606	1944	3.9E	2329		
25 Wed	0238 3.1F	0615	0830	2.2E	1158	1435	1.7F	1708	2038	3.7E			
26 Thr	0021	0331 3.1F	0704	0926	2.5E	1308	1539	1.8F	1820	2135	3.6E	
27 Fri	0116	0425 3.2F	0751	1023	2.9E	1413	1646	2.1F	1937	2234	3.4E	
28 Sat	0211	0518 3.3F	0837	1119	3.5E	1512	1751	2.6F	2050	2334	3.4E	
29 Sun	0306	0610 3.4F	0921	1213	4.1E	1606	1853	3.1F	2159			
30 Mon	0033 3.3E	0359	0659	3.6F	1004	1305	**4.7E**	1657	1951	3.7F	2302		

33

Figure 3

high tide of the month, 6.8 feet above mean lower low, occurs two days later at 11:39 a.m. (1139), neatly illustrating lag time. The lowest low tide, 1.2 feet below mean lower low (-1.2), follows at 6:05 p.m. (1805).

Now look at the current tables and observe that the strongest flood and ebb currents of the month also follow the full moon/perigee combination. Lag time enters the equation, so we see 4.7-knot and 4.6-knot floods on the 4th and 5th, respectively. Ebbs run stronger, peaking at 5.7 knots on the 4th and again on the 5th.

So we find the highest highs, the lowest lows, and the strongest currents associated with the spring tides of a full moon near perigee. Step ahead in time (scanning down the page), and we see spring tides of the new moon rising nearly as high (a maximum of 5.9 feet above MLL) and falling to -0.2 feet below MLL. Flood currents top out at 3.4 knots, and ebbs reach 4.4 knots.

By definition, a neap tide has to come along about one week after a spring tide, and the left side of the tide table leads us quickly to the symbol for a first quarter moon on November 10. Three days later, the moon passes over the equator. This combination should produce modest tide differences and mild currents, and it does. Looking at the tables we find low higher-highs (5.6 feet above mean lower low water on Friday the 13th, for example), soon after the New Moon and as the moon simultaneously approaches its farthest point from earth, apogee. Compare the predictions for lower-lows here with the numbers around the third-quarter moon that occurs on the 26th. Then, scan across the page to the current tables for similar comparisons, and you will recognize the neap tide trends. If the examples are not perfectly tidy, that's good. One goal here is to inspire you to develop street smarts, not stick you with book smarts.

While we're on that note: We said earlier that tides run about 50 minutes later each day. That's the best rule of thumb we know. But, look at the higher high tide figures for November 3rd and 4th and note that higher high tide on the 4th is forecast only 39 minutes later than high-

WE DON'T HAVE TO CURE our habit of saying, "The tide is coming in," or, "The tide is going out," but we should be aware that, technically, we're all wet. Tides rise and fall. A rising tide is a flood tide. a falling tide is an ebb tide. Horizontal movements of water are called currents. Flood currents flow into the bay. Ebb currents flow out.

er high tide on the 3rd. The difference between lower lows is 47 minutes. These numbers do get around, don't they? Drop down to the higher highs of the 11th and 12th, and you'll find a predicted difference of exactly 50 minutes; think of that wondrous precision as an accident.

Tides fluctuate through a range of 24 percent, a large portion of the total volume of a bay averaging only eighteen feet deep at mean lower low water. The mean tidal range at the Golden Gate – the average difference between high-water and low-water marks – is four feet. The maximum range is about twelve feet, and that would occur only during a winter storm.

As the rising tide crests, it behaves differently in the North Bay and South Bay. This is related to the tidal exchanges we mentioned on page 39.

The flood tide propagates a progressive wave through the West Bay and North Bay, turning back the ebb tide and damming the river flow. Because of that river flow, tide levels at high water are slightly higher in the North Bay than elsewhere, and low tides on average do not fall as far. The tidal range is the least in the estuary. The progressive wave drives upriver beyond Sacramento. Then it disappears, and the waters ebb until the next flood tide.

South Bay tides act as a standing wave that sloshes back and forth, north and south, like water in a bowl. High tides top out and low tides bottom out sooner than they do in the North Bay, even at points equally distant from the Golden Gate. Oscillation is probably a better term than "sloshes back and forth," but either way, it's just one more way of giving a name to what we might as well call a flebb.

Let's imagine, for example, a time late in the ebb tide cycle. To imagine it better, take a look at the tide-book chart of currents three hours after maximum ebb, Figure 4. In the Golden Gate, flood tide forces are building, slowing the last of the ebb. The South Bay has already (previously) reached low water. It's ready to rise. In the North Bay, backed by river flow, the current is still ebbing strongly, so North

Bay ebb – a mix of fresh and salt water – floods into the South Bay.

Now let's jump ahead six hours to the next transition, seen in Figure 4. It's three hours after maximum flood, and the South Bay has topped out. South Bay water is already ebbing, flowing north, and joining flood currents still coming in from the Golden Gate.

The Tidal Differences From the Golden Gate, Figure 6, shows the traveling time for the tide wave as it arrives on the California coast.

Ocean front locations see the flood tide crest sooner than Fort Point, but inside the bay, the minus signs become pluses. It takes 14 minutes for the crest to travel from the Golden Gate to Alcatraz. The book gives that as a reading of +0.14. In the South Bay, there are separate readings for the east end of the San Mateo Bridge (+48 minutes) and the west end (+52 minutes). At Sacramento, 81 nautical miles upriver, the delay is seven hours, 34 minutes for high tide or nine hours, 34 minutes for low tide. It would be convenient if the time differences for high water matched the differences for low water, and so would a lot of other things that will never happen.

In the column for height differences, we find that high tide at Alcatraz is the same height as high tide at the Golden Gate, a difference of 0.0. At Yerba Buena Island, however, a tidal difference of +0.3 indicates that the flood tide piles up an additional three tenths of a foot of water above the height at the Golden Gate. (These ratios are easy arithmetic, but keep an eye out for the asterisks, which indicate a ratio. The *1.04 figure for high tide at Pinole Point in San Pablo Bay indi-

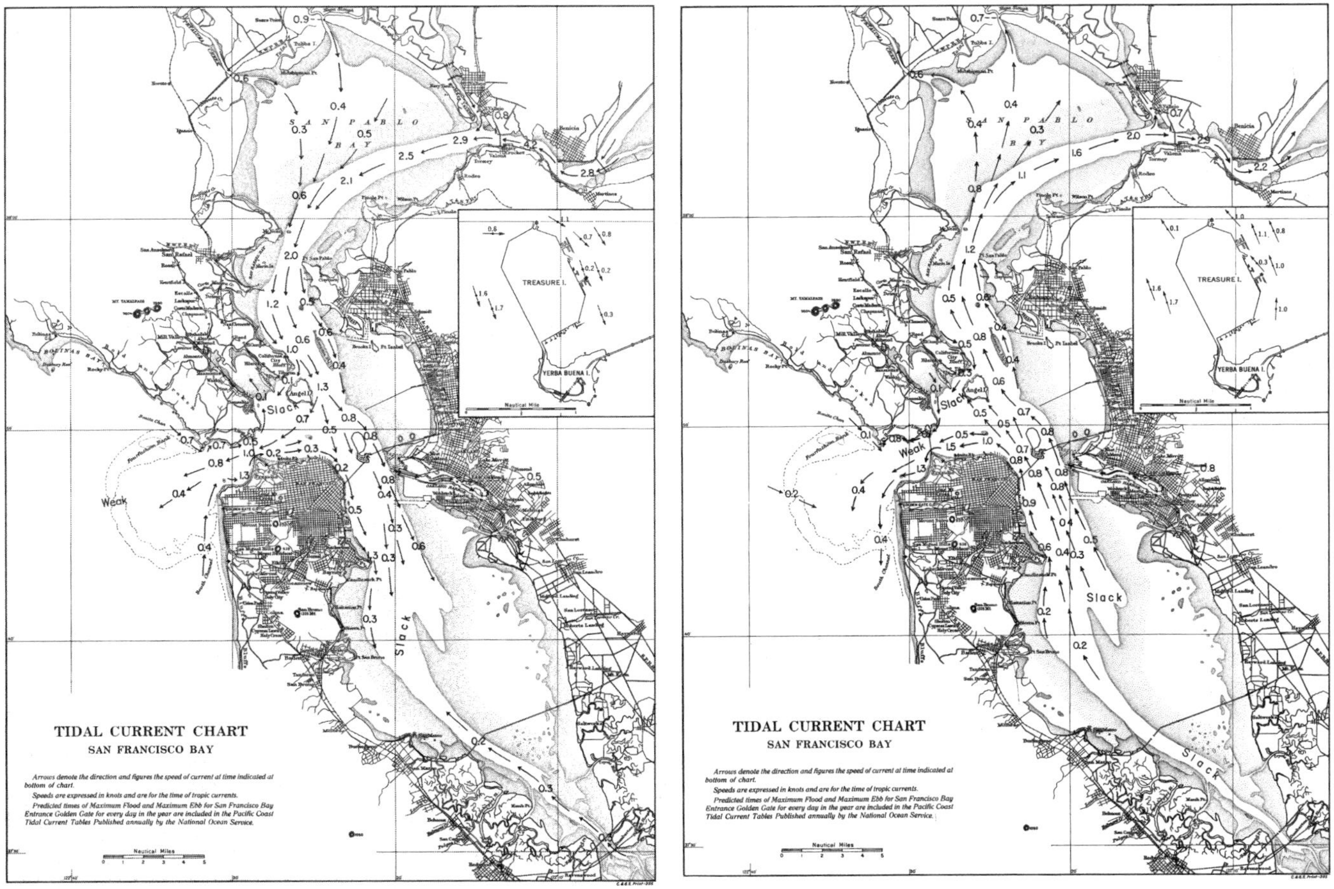

Figure 4: At each change of the tide, there is an exchange of water between the North Bay and the South Bay. Current charts show this clearly, though without a hint of how we should name a current that is ebbing from here and flooding to there. A flebb?

cates that high water there is a ratio of the height of the tide at the Golden Gate. For example, with a four-foot tide in the Golden Gate, 1.04 X 4 yields a high water at Point Pinole of 4.16 feet. In this book, that's the same thing as four feet.

"FROM THERE TO HERE, FROM HERE TO THERE, FUNNY THINGS ARE EVERYWHERE"
[Dr. Seuess said that]

When San Francisco Bay sailors say, "Check the tide book," they usually mean, check the current. Maximum flood and maximum ebb are the benchmarks for nearly all the figuring we do on how to sail the bay, but let's admit there are other ways to go. One of the great sailors of the post-World War II period, Jake Wosser, referenced his race planning off the highs and lows, and well into retirement age, he was still winning races and still a skipper of choice whenever the San Francisco Yacht Club had to put up a boat for an important trophy. Asked why he didn't get out of the way for the younger guys, Wosser said, "If they want it, let them come and take it."

You can't quarrel with success. This book is going with the majority, however. We'll focus on the current tables, where you're likely to spend most of your real-world time (and going digital, currents are where you'll spend all your time unless you're faced with a specific channel-depth, anchoring-depth question).

Maximum flood does not coincide with high water, and maximum ebb does not coincide with low water – or even with the most rapid change in vertical height – so we are blessed with separate tables for currents, also for current differences and constants. Maximum current precedes maximum high or maximum low by an hour or more, typically, and sometimes by nearly two hours.

Figure 5 shows the Current Differences From the Golden Gate for slack water after ebb, maximum flood, slack water after high, and maximum ebb. There is also a column of speed ratios with separate figures

READING THE WATER

TIDE LINES MARK CURRENT BOUNDARIES, and they help us read the water. Tide lines form wherever currents run side by side in opposing directions, as they do at the change of tide. They also form between two streams of water going the same direction at different speeds, between a current and an eddy, and between bodies of water with different density. One of our most consistent and conspicuous tide lines develops twice a day in the North Channel, where the South Bay ebb collides with the North Bay ebb. It is violent and frothy enough to be called a tide rip.

A tide line can be a subtle thing. It might show no more evidence than a different texture on the water's surface. When neither wind nor currents are strong, a long, meandering line between flood and ebb may appear as a narrow, smooth band reflecting light differently. A tide line will also collect more flotsam than the water surrounding it.

Usually, the water on one side of the tide line will look different from the water on the other side. Even a mild breeze will form different patterns on the surfaces of flood and ebb. The essential difference lies in whether the wind blows in the same direction as the current flow, against the current flow, or across it.

On San Francisco Bay, it makes sense to pose tide line questions in terms of a "normal" summer westerly, where flood currents go with the wind flow. Down-current equals downwind, so flood currents smooth the wave pattern. By contrast, ebb currents fight their way upwind, so an ebb-tide surface is choppier. Ebb-tide whitecaps form with less wind, and the waves are close together and steep. (In a big wind and a big tide, near Alcatraz, they're humongous.)

Color is also a great indicator. In the tide transitions in the West Bay — at three hours after maximum ebb, for example — light green or brownish ebb water flows out through the channels and out through the center of the bay. Meanwhile, incoming sea water floods blue and dark along the shorelines. It's easy to tell which is which. But watch out for the sucker punch. When the flood tide turns back ebb water, you can have a brown flood current.

for flood and ebb. Raccoon Strait has ripping currents, so let's take that for an example and check the listing for Raccoon Strait off Point Stuart. Say we do Sunday brunch on August 9 at Sam's in Tiburon and slip the lines at about noon to head back out to the Bay. There's a hint of fog building at the Gate, but we're still inside the Belvedere heat bubble as we motor slowly out to the channel, coiling the dock lines and unfurling the main. The skipper, meanwhile, pulls out the tide book and checks the listing for August 9, Currents at the Golden Gate. (Obviously, if s/he's just starting on the book, this must be a casual sail.) The prediction calls for a maximum flood of 4.3 knots at the Golden Gate at 12:22 p.m. — pretty soon — and the current chart shows a flood tide moving through Raccoon Strait. But how strong is that flood?

First, checking the flood tide column in Tidal Differences from the Golden Gate, Figure 6, we find two listings for Angel Island: "west side" and "East Garrison." Neither of those locations matches our own, but the corrections show only a three-minute difference from the west side to the east side of the island, so we're splitting hairs to worry that they're not spot-on for Tiburon Cove. The tables indicate that high tide crests at the west side of Angel Island 13 minutes after high tide at the Golden Gate, so let's use that figure and expect high tide to reach Raccoon Strait at 12:22 plus 13 minutes, or 12:35 p.m. In the Speed Ratio corrections column of Figure 5, we find that maximum flood here runs at four tenths (0.4) the

strength of maximum flood in the Golden Gate. The computation of .4 X 4.3 yields a maximum flood in Raccoon Strait of 1.72 knots, more accurately understood as, "not quite two."

If you want to sail from here to there, or there to here (though funny things are everywhere) the charts give you a reasonable picture of what to expect. For a cruise or a quick joyride, there's nothing more to ask. Those who luxuriate in traveling without a schedule might even

Current Differences from the Golden Gate

Low Slack H M	Flood H M	LOCATION	High Slack H M	Ebb H M	Speed Ratio Fld/Ebb
		OUTER COAST			
-1.01	-1.01	Point Pinos	-1.01	-1.01	0.2/0.2
W V	W V	Point Santa Cruz	W V	W V	
W V	W V	Point Montara	W V	W V	
-1.12	-1.12	Point Reyes	-1.12	-1.12	0.3/0.3
-1.20	-1.20	Salt Point	-1.20	-1.20	0.3/0.3
-1.29	-1.29	Point Arena	-1.29	-1.29	0.3/0.3
-1.38	-1.38	Point Cabrillo	-1.38	-1.38	0.3/0.3
-1.36	-1.36	Punta Gorda	-1.36	-1.36	0.3/0.3
		GOLDEN GATE & APPROACHES			
-0.30	-0.30	Sea Buoy – "SF"	-0.30	-0.30	0.1/0.1
-1.52	-1.41	Main Ship Bar Channel #1/#2	-1.41	-1.19	0.2/0.2
-1.29	-1.27	South Channel	-1.04	-1.10	0.4/0.4
-0.28	-0.38	Pt Bonita/Mile Rk (midchannel)	-0.28	-0.51	0.7/0.8
		SAN FRANCISCO BAY ENTRANCE			
-0.20	-0.01	Golden Gate Bridge .5 mi E	-0.28	-0.36	0.9/0.7
-0.02	-0.03	Golden Gate Bridge .8 mi E	-0.05	+0.12	0.9/0.7
		SAN FRANCISCO BAY SOUTH			
-0.30	-0.30	Alcatraz Island W	-0.08	-0.12	0.8/0.6
-0.29	-0.15	Alcatraz Island S	-0.25	-0.29	0.5/0.6
-0.10	—	St Francis Yacht Club B/W	-1.50	—	—
-1.35	—	Pier #27	-2.20	—	—
-1.10	—	Pier #29	-2.20	—	—
-0.55	—	Pier #7	-2.05	—	—
-0.55	—	Pier #14	-3.00	—	—
-1.40	—	Pier #26	-1.50	—	—
-0.25	—	Pier #38	-2.25	—	—
-1.40	—	Pier #50	-2.20	—	—
-1.20	—	Pier #70	-1.55	—	—
-1.50	—	Pier #94	-2.05	—	—
-1.25	—	Point Avisadero	-0.40	—	—
-1.30	—	Point Avisadero .8 mi S	-3.25	—	—
-0.57	-1.21	Alcatraz Island .8 mi E	-1.13	-0.25	0.4/0.6
-1.39	-1.11	Treasure Island .8 mi NW	-1.00	-1.55	0.4/0.3
-0.45	-0.49	Anchorage #7 Outer	-1.11	-0.32	0.4/0.7
-1.38	-1.02	Anchorage #7 Inner	-1.04	-1.01	0.5/0.6
-1.12	-0.47	Treasure Island .5 mi N	-0.45	-0.36	0.4/0.4
-0.31	-0.36	Treasure Island .3 mi E	-1.07	-0.26	0.5/0.4
-0.32	-0.52	Yerba Buena Is. W of	-1.06	-0.21	0.5/0.7
-1.12	-0.44	Yerba Buena Is. .3 mi SE	-1.00	-1.07	0.2/0.3
-1.47	-0.56	Oakland Outer Harbor Entrance	-0.45	-1.19	0.6/0.5
-1.54	-1.01	Oakland Inner Harbor Entrance	-1.08	-1.37	0.3/0.4
-1.18	-1.10	Oakland Channel NAS Lt #4	-1.02	-0.57	0.2/0.2
-2.38	-0.48	Oakland Channel Berth #68	-1.12	-1.40	0.1/0.1
-1.35	-1.21	Oakland Harbor Webster St	-1.25	-1.31	0.3/0.3
-1.21	-1.36	Oakland Harbor High St Bridge	-1.25	-1.42	0.5/0.4
-1.44	-0.22	Anchorage #8 NE part	-1.09	-1.25	0.4/0.2
-0.50	-0.44	Rincon Point .6 mi E of	-0.52	-0.43	0.7/0.6
-1.05	-0.45	Rincon Point Midbay	-1.10	-0.55	0.7/0.6
-0.53	-0.33	Mission Rock .6 mi E	-0.40	-0.25	0.9/0.7
-0.43	-0.43	Mission Rock 1.3 mi E	-0.34	-0.17	0.7/0.6
-1.33	-1.03	NAS Entrance Buoy #1	-0.50	-0.51	0.6/0.7
-0.52	-0.37	Potrero Point 1.1 mi E	-0.38	-0.35	0.6/0.6
-0.52	-0.56	Anchorage #9 (middle)	-0.29	-0.33	0.6/0.5

W V – Weak & Variable

9

Current Differences from the Golden Gate

Low Slack H M	Flood H M	LOCATION	High Slack H M	Ebb H M	Speed Ratio Fld/Ebb
-1.39	-1.26	Alameda Radar Tower, .9 SSW of	-1.50	-1.43	0.2/0.2
-0.45	-0.39	Point Avisadero .3 mi E	-0.35	-0.11	0.6/0.6
-0.47	-0.16	Point Avisadero 1.0 mi E	+0.03	+0.02	0.6/0.4
-0.47	-0.24	Point Avisadero 3.1 mi E	-0.32	-0.15	0.5/0.5
-0.47	-0.43	Point Avisadero .6 mi ESE	-0.36	-0.30	0.5/0.4
-1.00	-0.33	Anchorage #14 NW part	-0.51	-0.43	0.4/0.3
-1.20	-1.04	Oakland Airport SW	-1.01	-1.09	0.2/0.2
-1.02	-0.52	Sierra Point 1.3 mi ENE	-0.47	-0.31	0.3/0.3
-0.57	-0.48	Sierra Point 1.2 mi E	-0.48	-0.13	0.3/0.2
-0.44	-0.38	Oyster Point 2.8 mi E	-0.35	-0.07	0.3/0.4
-1.03	-0.52	Sierra Point 4.4 mi E	-0.31	-0.24	0.3/0.2
-1.31	-0.45	Point San Bruno .5 mi E	-0.43	-0.58	0.2/0.1
-1.30	-1.10	Mulford Gardens Channel #2 SSW	-1.12	-1.04	0.3/0.2
-1.12	-1.12	Little Coyote Pt 3.4 mi NNE	-1.12	-0.52	0.2/0.2
-2.07	-1.52	Little Coyote Pt 3.1 mi ENE	-1.20	-1.40	0.2/0.2
-0.24	-0.44	Little Coyote Pt 1.2 mi NE	-0.33	-0.02	0.5/0.4
-0.05	-0.15	San Mateo Bridge	+0.03	+0.24	0.5/0.4
-0.19	-0.39	Redwood Pt, Blair Is 1.2 mi SE	-0.24	+0.03	0.5/0.4
-0.12	-0.01	Dumbarton Hwy Bridge	-0.10	+0.17	0.5/0.3
-0.36	-0.12	Dumbarton Hwy Bridge .3 mi SE	-0.20	-0.28	0.4/0.3
-0.27	-0.38	Dumbarton Point 1.2 mi SE	-0.10	+1.03	0.4/0.3
-0.07	-0.24	Dumbarton Point 2.3 mi NE	-0.22	+1.05	0.4/0.3
		SAN FRANCISCO BAY NORTH			
-0.42	-0.46	Yellow Bluff .8 mi NE	-0.59	-0.50	0.6/0.5
-0.20	+0.04	Yellow Bluff .8 mi E	-0.10	+0.13	1.0/0.7
-0.13	+0.14	Point Cavallo 1.3 mi E	+0.10	+0.13	0.8/0.8
+0.29	+0.27	Alcatraz Is .5 mi N	-0.41	+0.02	0.6/0.7
+0.12	-0.03	Point Blunt .5 mi SW	-0.29	+0.02	0.4/0.5
-0.32	-0.01	Point Blunt .3 mi S	-0.08	+0.37	0.6/0.7
	-0.10	Point Blunt .8 mi SE	-0.11	-0.43	0.3/0.4
+1.01	-0.18	Point Blunt .3 mi E	-0.15	+1.52	0.3/0.5
+1.27	+0.10	Angel Island off Quarry Point	-1.42	+1.16	0.2/0.3
+0.46	+0.58	Angel Island .8 mi E	+1.03	+1.28	0.4/0.3
+0.09	+0.56	Point Simpton 1.1 mi E	+0.31	+0.02	0.5/0.2
-3.45	-4.22	Richardson Bay Entrance	-3.59	-2.56	0.3/0.2
-0.33	-0.04	Raccoon Strait off Point Stuart	-0.34	-0.27	0.4/0.6
-0.33	-0.51	Raccoon Strait	-0.50	-0.41	0.6/0.5
—	-0.50	Raccoon Strait off Hospital Cove	-0.38	-0.29	0.5/0.5
+0.20	-0.38	Bluff Point .1 mi E	-0.14	+0.19	0.6/0.6
+0.11	+0.34	Bluff Point 1.2 mi E	+0.26	+0.02	0.4/0.3
+0.20	+0.43	Southampton Shoal Light .2 mi E	+0.21	-0.06	0.3/0.3
-0.03	+0.30	Point Chauncey 1.3 mi E	+0.45	+0.11	0.4/0.4
-0.01	-0.38	Point Chauncey .8 mi NW	+0.13	+0.02	0.4/0.3
+0.16	-0.03	Point Chauncey 1.3 mi N	+0.20	+0.14	0.6/0.5
-2.00	-1.01	Berkeley Yacht Harbor .9 mi S	-0.40	-0.58	0.1/0.1
-1.48	-1.14	Fleming Point 1.7 mi SW	-0.56	-1.18	0.2/0.1
-0.25	+0.09	Point Richmond 1 mi E	+0.13	-0.01	0.3/0.3
-1.57	-1.47	Point Richmond .8 mi NNW	-1.11	-1.51	0.1/0.1
-0.03	+0.11	Red Rock .1 E	+0.31	+0.18	0.4/0.4
-0.27	-0.29	Red Rock .6 mi E	+0.13	-0.22	0.6/0.4
-0.18	+0.10	Point San Quentin .8 mi E	+0.05	-0.35	0.2/0.2
+0.11	+0.27	Point San Quentin 1.3 mi E	+0.38	+0.34	0.4/0.4
+0.43	+0.34	Point San Quentin 1.9 mi E	+0.31	+0.48	0.5/0.6

10

Figure 5

find transcendent moods in deliberately stemming a foul current, since the day is all there is, and the sailing is all there will be.

But there are the racers too. Racing sailors really do want to know whether to take that extra fifty-yard tack in protected water – and perhaps deliberately sail extra distance – before hazarding countercurrents near the mark. They want to know now, and they want to know forty-five minutes from now on the next go-round, when the wind might be different, the current is sure to be different, and their opponents, probably, have been shuffled. It is one of the magical, contrary, addictive attributes of yacht racing that the game is played on a shifting surface, with a variable power supply, and part of the necessary odds-computing intelligence is stored only in the seat of the pants. Nobody can be right all the time.

AS THE TIDE TURNS

Newcomers to the game often expect the tide to turn first in the middle of the bay, but that's backwards.

The tide turns first on the beach.

Whether the tide is flooding or ebbing, the first fingers of the new tide currents will form in a narrow band along the San Francisco cityfront. Later, thin bands of current will form along the Marin shore. These threads will broaden and strengthen gradually, until they take over the entire bay.

There is no substitute for spending time thinking about these problems, or better than that, sailing the bay with an active mind and eye. No chart can

tell you everything you need to know, not even the digital images that are replacing the outdated tide book pictures.

But, *Sailing The Bay* retains a nostalgic fondness for the simple-minded utility of the pictures and arrows in those good ol' tide books. We thought about reprinting all 12 here, but it seemed a bit much. Most people already have more than one tide book floating around in drawers, glove compartments, or the bilge, and the easiest way to use

TIDAL DIFFERENCES FROM THE GOLDEN GATE

HIGH WATER		LOCATION	LOW WATER	
TIME	HEIGHT		TIME	HEIGHT
		OUTER COAST		
-1.08	-0.5	Monterey, Monterey Bay	-0.47	0.0
-1.08	-0.6	General Fish Company Pier	-0.46	-0.1
-1.10	-0.7	Moss Landing, Ocean Pier	-0.48	-0.1
-1.06	-0.7	Elkhorn Slough, Highway 1 Bridge	-0.49	-0.1
-0.54	-0.5	Pacific Mariculture Dock	-0.40	0.0
-0.43	-0.4	Kirby Park, Elkhorn Slough	-0.39	-0.1
-0.36	-0.4	Elkhorn Slough Railroad Bridge	-0.39	-0.1
-1.15	-0.6	Santa Cruz, Monterey Bay	-0.58	0.0
-1.06	-0.3	Princeton, Halfmoon Bay	-0.50	0.0
-0.49	+0.1	Ocean Beach, Outer Coast	-0.35	0.0
-0.11	-1.6	Bolinas Lagoon	+0.37	-0.4
-0.50	-0.1	Point Reyes	-0.26	0.0
-0.12	*0.87	Tomales Bay Entrance	+0.20	*0.91
+0.32	-0.7	Blakes Landing, Tomales Bay	+1.15	-0.2
+0.38	-0.6	Marshall, Tomales Bay	+1.16	-0.1
+0.40	-0.6	Inverness, Tomales Bay	+1.24	-0.2
-0.38	-0.2	Bodega Harbor Entrance	-0.16	+0.1
-0.51	-0.2	Fort Ross	-0.30	0.0
-0.40	0.0	Arena Cove	-0.17	0.0
-0.42	-0.1	Point Arena	-0.21	0.0
-0.31	-0.1	Albion	-0.19	0.0
-0.31	-0.1	Little River Harbor	-0.19	0.0
-0.38	-0.1	Mendocino, Mendocino Bay	-0.21	0.0
-0.30	0.0	Fort Bragg Landing	-0.20	0.0
-0.31	+0.1	Noyo River	-0.12	+0.1
-0.31	-0.1	Westport	-0.22	0.0
-0.39	+0.2	Shelter Cove	-0.17	+0.1
-0.28	-0.1	Cape Mendocino	+0.01	0.0
		SAN FRANCISCO BAY (Central)		
-0.17	+0.3	Point Bonita, Cove	-0.10	0.0
+0.14	0.0	Alcatraz Island	+0.18	0.0
+0.13	+0.2	San Francisco, North Point, Pier #41	+0.11	0.0
+0.23	+0.4	Rincon Point, Pier #22½	+0.25	0.0
+0.32	+0.3	Yerba Buena Island	+0.40	0.0
+0.28	+0.3	Oakland, Matson Wharf	+0.36	0.0
+0.33	+0.2	Oakland Pier	+0.48	0.0
+0.37	+0.5	Oakland Inner Harbor	+0.41	0.0
+0.32	+0.6	Alameda	+0.41	0.0
+0.33	+0.4	Oakland Harbor, Grove Street	+0.42	0.0
+0.38	+0.6	Oakland Harbor, Park Street Bridge	+0.44	0.0
+0.49	+0.8	Bay Farm Island, San Leandro Bay	+0.59	0.0
+0.47	+0.8	Oakland Airport	+0.52	0.0
+0.33	+0.5	Potrero Point	+0.46	0.0
+0.25	+0.9	Hunters Point	+0.39	0.0

NOTE: When an asterisk (*) precedes a difference, that difference given is a ratio, and the height of high or low water at the Golden Gate is multiplied by the ratio to determine the height at the station.

6

TIDAL DIFFERENCES FROM THE GOLDEN GATE

HIGH WATER		LOCATION	LOW WATER	
TIME	HEIGHT		TIME	HEIGHT
		SAN FRANCISCO BAY (South)		
+1.01	+1.4	San Leandro Channel	+1.29	0.0
+0.22	+1.4	Roberts Landing, 1.3 mi West of	+1.28	+0.1
+0.38	+1.2	South San Francisco	+0.56	0.0
+0.48	+1.1	Oyster Point Marina	+1.07	0.0
+0.38	+1.1	Point San Bruno	+1.10	+0.1
+0.42	+1.4	Seaplane Harbor	+1.03	0.0
+0.42	+1.5	Coyote Point Marina	+1.08	0.0
+0.52	+1.8	San Mateo Bridge, west end	+1.20	+0.1
+0.48	+1.8	San Mateo Bridge, east end	+1.19	0.0
+1.03	+0.3	Alameda Creek	+2.31	-0.8
+1.02	+0.9	Coyote Hills Slough entrance	+2.28	-0.6
+1.06	+2.1	Redwood Creek, entrance (inside)	+1.38	+0.1
+0.53	*1.41	Redwood Creek Marker #8	+1.28	*1.05
+1.02	+2.2	South Bay Wreck	+1.37	+0.1
+1.03	+2.2	Corkscrew Slough	+1.42	+0.1
+0.58	+2.2	Redwood City, Wharf #5	+1.32	+0.1
+1.03	+2.2	West Point Slough	+1.36	+0.1
+1.15	+2.2	Smith Slough	+1.58	0.0
+1.11	+2.6	Newark Slough	+1.58	+0.1
+1.03	+2.2	Granite Rock	+1.38	+0.1
+1.09	+2.5	Palo Alto Yacht Harbor	+2.09	0.0
+1.12	+2.6	Mowry Slough	+2.07	0.0
+1.05	+2.8	Calaveras Point, west of	+1.49	+0.1
+1.19	+1.7	Mud Slough Railroad Bridge	+2.59	-0.1
+1.14	+2.7	Guadalupe Slough	+2.15	0.0
+1.23	+3.4	Upper Guadalupe Slough	+2.21	+0.2
+1.13	+3.1	Coyote Creek, Alviso Slough	+2.08	+0.2
+1.15	+3.4	Gold Street Bridge, Alviso Slough	+2.34	+0.1
+1.21	+2.6	Coyote Creek, Tributary #1	+2.45	-0.3
		SAN FRANCISCO BAY (North)		
+0.10	-0.3	Sausalito	+0.14	0.0
+0.11	-0.2	Sausalito, Corps of Engineers Dock	+0.21	0.0
+0.13	-0.2	Angel Island, west side	+0.21	0.0
+0.16	+0.1	Angel Island, East Garrison	+0.20	0.0
+0.21	+0.1	Berkeley	+0.38	0.0
+0.23	+0.1	Point Isabel	+0.33	0.0
+0.25	0.0	Richmond Inner Harbor	+0.36	0.0
+0.29	0.0	Chevron Oil Company Pier	+0.36	0.0
+0.47	0.0	Point Orient	+0.52	0.0
+0.37	-0.1	Corte Madera Creek	+0.52	0.0
		SAN PABLO BAY		
+0.59	+0.1	Point San Pedro	+1.01	0.0
+1.12	*1.04	Pinole Point	+1.26	*0.92
+1.25	-0.1	Hercules	+1.49	0.0
+1.22	+0.1	Petaluma River Entrance	+2.11	-0.1
+1.59	*1.11	Lakeville, Petaluma River	+2.50	*.81
+2.10	*1.16	Upper Drawbridge, Petaluma River	+3.10	*.81
+1.11	+0.1	Gallinas Creek	+1.30	-0.1

*See note, page 6.   7

Figure 6

this information now, if your noodle is seriously noodling, is to pull out a tide book, open it to the charts, and lay it alongside *Sailing The Bay*. The charts show the broad strokes, and it's worthwhile to take a highlights tour. So, if you'll please keep your hands and feet inside the ride at all times ...

Let's start with the diagram for Maximum Flood at the Golden Gate. Almost all the arrows are inbound – into the bay from the ocean, into the South Bay, into the North Bay and even into the river at Carquinez Strait. Not shown, farther upriver and out of the picture, are the fresh-water currents that, at the same moment, are ebbing, flowing toward the sea with a slack water zone between them and the flood.

Note that the biggest numbers (the strongest currents) occur in the deep channels. The smallest numbers (the weakest currents) occur in the shallows. Note, too, that these figures have to be corrected through the Table of Current Differences before you know the actual current on any given day. But the numbers are obsolete. We're just looking at the arrows.

At Maximum Flood at the Golden Gate, the only countercurrent in the picture operates west of the Golden Gate Bridge, on both sides of the strait. To the south, at Baker Beach, water squeezed out of the venturi forms an eddy. (The promontory where Fort Point stands, and which launches the deck of the Golden Gate Bridge, projects into the choke point of the strait and cuts off part of the flood-tide stream.) On the north side of the strait, an eddy is indicated in the bight between Point Bonita and Point Diablo. Outbound small craft will sail close to one shoreline or the other to seek relief from the current.

Anyone who spends time on the bay, and pays attention, will recognize that there are smaller, more subtle movements of water that are not accounted for in the NOAA diagrams. On the eastern side of Angel Island, around the corner behind Point Blunt, flood water tends to swirl around in a small eddy at and after maximum flood. It's nothing complicated to figure: Flood tide currents can't make a sharp turn to fill that small area, so the water swirls. Throughout the bay and the rivers, wherever there are obstructions, there are similar, predictable effects on water flow. In some cases, they come and go very quickly. It was not the purpose of these charts to put the bay under a microscope, and even as this data is updated, improved, and superseded by other work, the finer points will still be up to you.

At one hour after maximum flood, we find the numbers on the diagram decreasing. The only exceptions occur in the Golden Gate, where the eddies on the north and south shores are gaining strength. And then — at two hours after maximum flood — we find a first small finger of ebb forming on the cityfront. At first, it is narrow and weak as it slips out and around Fort Point to join the eddy at Baker Beach. The turning moments along the cityfront are definitely early, even dramatically early.

At three hours after maximum flood, there are big changes. Now the South Bay has crested and begun to ebb, strengthening the ebb tide flow that is taking over the Central Bay and joining a continuing flood tide flow into the North Bay. Separately, on the Marin shore, ebb tide has begun to stream out of Raccoon Strait, across the face of Sausalito's Yellow Bluff, and out the Golden Gate. This ebb stream is one of the great visual dramas of the bay. It is easy to recognize from the hills, or the bridge, or even a boat.

We switch to referencing Maximum Ebb at the Golden Gate at two hours before "max ebb," a time when ebb currents have taken over the entire bay. Outside the bay, in the Bonita Channel (the northern route through the bar), currents now flow north and will continue to flow north until maximum ebb and probably a bit beyond. This relatively

HERE'S A CURIOSITY YOU CAN CARRY around without including it in your course planning — the Coriolis force — which can pile up the flood tide on the San Francisco shore several centimeters higher than on the Marin shore. The Coriolis force is a product of the earth's rotation, bending all forces in the Northern Hemisphere to the right. The flood flows in, and the Coriolis force piles it up at Crissy Field and Aquatic Park. The ebb flows out, and the Coriolis force piles it up at Tiburon and Horseshoe Cove. Go ahead. Tell your friends you can feel the difference.

brief period (approaching maximum ebb) is the only time in the 12-hour cycle when currents in the Bonita Channel flow north. Most of the time they flow to the south, either as flood currents or as an eddy to the late ebb.

Entering the ebb tide cycle, flood currents continue in the river channel beyond Point San Pablo, and they don't disappear from Carquinez Strait until almost maximum ebb. A boat bound upriver that left early enough, riding the flood, can still be riding a flood tide at this point, if it made good time and is now well into the rivers. Flood tide won't crest at Sacramento for seven and a half hours after the crest at the Golden Gate. But a skipper hitting Carquinez Strait at Maximum Ebb at the Golden Gate had best add a few hours to the E.T.A.

At maximum ebb, we see the beginnings of back-eddies on both shores of the Golden Gate. These strengthen throughout the ebb tide cycle until, at two hours after maximum ebb, the prevailing north-south flow through the Bonita Channel has re-formed, and we find it sneaking around Point Bonita. There it joins the back-current as the first finger of a new flood tide.

At three hours after maximum ebb, the bay is alive with current and countercurrent – flood along the shorelines, and the late ebb rolling out through "the middle." It's a beautiful, complicated picture. Boats racing upwind on the cityfront face a classic dilemma late in the transition, when the ebb tide in the middle is too attractive to pass up, and the flood stream on the beach is powerful. Skippers have to decide when to bite the bullet and go "back in." Hit the beach too soon – start short-tacking the beach while your competitors are romping away in a fast stream of ebb tide – and the price is devastating. Stay out too long, get caught in the middle stemming a solid flood, and you'll be left with a good view of the leaders as they tack out from the beach to round the mark ahead of you. Only the lucky, and those who really, really, really do their homework will get it right.

We could talk the current diagrams to death without making anyone a whole lot smarter. Living with the tide books (and the USGS data), thinking through the problems before you go out, paying attention while you sail, reflecting on your experiences later — these are the keys to competence. Keeping a journal of your sailing is the route to supreme competence.

And don't forget, we've focused so far on the current charts, with their pretty pictures and admittedly bogus numbers. In the world of mostly-powerboating – where Berkeley architect Haluk Akol once became the first Predicted Log Racer ever to win the national championship on his home waters – the current charts never were the bottom line. "Compared to the charts, the current tables take a little digging into," Akol said, "They're not pictorial, but they're better. For someone who's serious, they offer many more reference points than the charts. One problem they have, though, those points are defined to the nearest mile. I got frustrated and wrote to Maryland (to the National Oceanic and Atmospheric Administration headquarters) and got the locations to the nearest quarter mile."

And that's the way it was. These days, Akol could have saved himself a lot of work by going digital ...

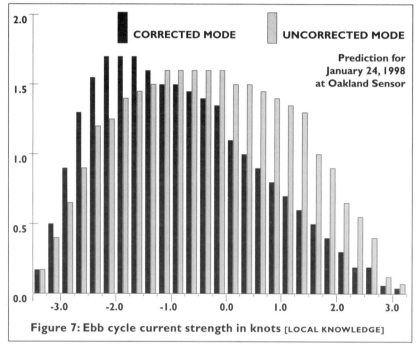

Figure 7: Ebb cycle current strength in knots [LOCAL KNOWLEDGE]

CORRECTED MODE UNCORRECTED MODE

Prediction for January 24, 1998 at Oakland Sensor

RESOURCES

sfports.wr.usgs.gov/sfports.html In the mid-1990s, the U.S. Geological Survey and the National Oceanic and Atmospheric Administration teamed up to develop more-accurate readings and predictions of San Francisco Bay currents, regional winds, and the interactions between water and wind.

The Current Pattern Analysis for Oil Spill Response was funded, no surprises here, on fears of future oil spills. It grew out of NOAA's nationwide PORTS project — Physical Oceanography Real-Time System — to provide real-time tide and current data for the ports of Tampa, Houston, New York/New Jersey, and San Francisco. However, our body of water is the only location where real-time sensor data is used to cross-check and improve a numerical model. Better yet, the results are posted on the internet for all to see. The model, an ongoing electronic tide book, was implemented in the Menlo Park office by Dr. Ralph Cheng, a U.S.G.S. project chief with decades of experience in San Francisco Bay hydrodynamics. As *Sailing The Bay* went to press, the tide/current web site was expected to be transferred to the administration of the San Francisco Marine Exchange.

Combining water-current data with wind-current data is a first, but for those interested in wind, and who isn't, there is also a wind page (see page 57 for a sample) getting hundreds of thousands of hits, many of those from sailors. To create the wind page, observed data from many points are combined with a numerical model. You see a picture of what's happening right now on the ocean, the bay, and the surrounding hills, or you can search through a history of your favorite moments. The work is based on collaborations between Professor Douglas Sinton at San Jose State University and Dr. Frank Ludwig of SRI International.

Wind currents didn't come easy, but water currents posed an even tougher challenge. Water is water, and this being San Francisco Bay water, it does not give up its mysteries lightly. The transition from theory to real-time data was delayed more than once.

Compared to the ample locations where wind is measured on a routine basis, currents in the Bay are expensive and difficult to sample.

Lifting to the weather mark. [PHOTO BY DR. JOHN E. HUTTON, JR.]

NOAA's newest devices are called ADCPs — Acoustic Doppler Current Profilers — and they are a large improvement over the old surface buoys that had a bad habit of being run down or dragged away. ADCPs sit on the bottom and use echo differentials (echo returns) to measure the movement of currents at different depths above them. For a hydrologist like Cheng, it was like turning on the lights. "The percentage of data return increased dramatically," he said.

The first ADCP placed in the Golden Gate lasted only three months, still an attractive figure compared to certain past failures with surface buoys, but the ADCPs have one weakness from a sailor's point of view. They fail to measure the top 10-15 percent of the water column, which is where we spend our time. Also, ADCPs monitoring the Golden Gate are placed south and north — to monitor the inbound and outbound shipping lanes, respectively — so they are not to be interpreted as mid-span. But from the outset this serious, long term effort improved and extended our knowledge of the Bay, and ADCP data can be incorporated into personal use software, as we will see below. (Real-time sensor data can be obtained online or from a voice line recording at 707-642-4337.)

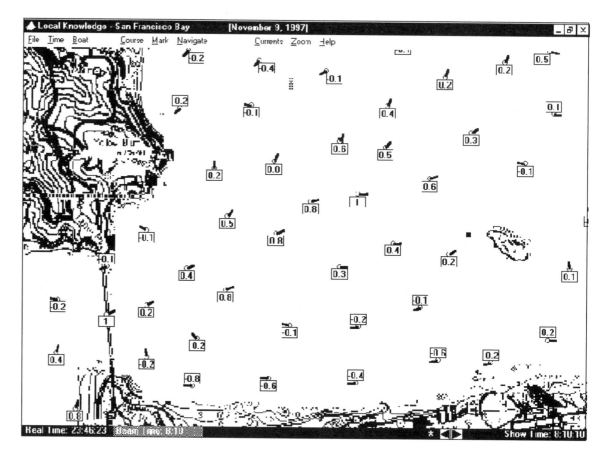

It was clear from Day One of the Digital Age that tide-and-current study had entered a new era. The use of real-time data to correct NOAA tide and current predictions is dazzling to anyone who grew up on hip shots. Winds, current, and wind-current interaction can be quantified now and presented visually. Even the behavior of the current column is there to be seen at depth and in depth.

LOCAL KNOWLEDGE: THE COMPUTER MODEL Current behavior is complicated, but predictable. If you get the tiger by the tail, you know something about the tiger. Identify the essential behavior of the tide and current at any point in the system, and you have a grip on the whole system. You might find it easier to get a grip, however, with a little Local Knowledge ...

Dave Brayshaw probably didn't know how much he was getting into when he set out to create software that would not only portray San Francisco Bay currents, but allow the user to "sail" one or more boats from point to point, testing different choices along the way. But, Brayshaw's Local Knowledge does exactly that.

Unlike the U.S.G.S. study, Local Knowledge is not a research project for anyone except its author. As a computer program, it takes the existing NOAA data as a given - just as a tide book does - and plugs the numbers into a mathematical model. Then it puts them on the computer screen with information between NOAA data points provided by interpolation. As a result, if you use Local Knowledge for making predictions, you have to consider all the usual caveats. Is it, for example, one of those seasons when, "The book is off," because the river is really high? Not to worry. Brayshaw has built in a system to cover that and more. With a little research on your part — acquiring and entering publicly available real-time data from the PORTS sensors - you can develop amazingly accurate portrayals of current events (pun intended).

There's a lot to learn from this software. You can manipulate it — speed it up, slow it down, zoom in, drop markers and watch them disperse — and ask your own questions and develop your own answers. With the opportunity to place one or more "boats" on the screen and set them off on different courses toward a mark, you can simulate a racing leg or even an entire race.

Here, in paraphrase, are some of Dave Brayshaw's thoughts looking back over the development process:

It is rare that all ADCPs are working and reporting at the same time, but data from just one can be used to fine-tune the program's display. The number of sensors and their precise locations have changed somewhat since the original installation in 1996, but they continue to be placed to maximize benefit to commercial ships transiting the Golden Gate, Oakland Harbor, or the channels leading to San Pablo Bay. Users should remember that currents are not measured mid-span, in the deepest water, so the numbers are often different from predictions read from tide charts and tables for a corresponding hour. In the first year of available comparisons, for example, the Golden Gate sensor near the South Tower gave readings that were very close to tide book predictions for the timing of slack water and the timing of maximum current, but speed readings typically registered about one half the predicted value (because the prediction was telling us what velocity to expect in deep waters mid-channel).

Local Knowledge includes an input screen for real-time sensor data. The user has to get this information from the PORTS web site or the call-in number. The program then will use this real-time data input to adjust its parameters and alter its predictions for the entire Bay and current cycle. With this feature, the program takes into account the measured seasonal variations and becomes extremely accurate in comparison to tide-book predictions, which are averages based on historical data. For an example, look back to Figure 7 to see the difference between the actual ebb current and the predictions at the Oakland Bridge sensor on January 24, 1998. This data shows the ebb current rising much earlier and more sharply than predicted, then tapering off over the remainder of the cycle. On this day, the maximum flood current and the timing of the turn to ebb were very close to their predicted values, but the rainy season can cause these figures to also vary widely. Since these variations cannot be predicted in advance, they are not reflected in the tide books. They can be identified and displayed only through a combination of numerical modeling and real-time correction.

THE BIG PHYSICAL MODEL A capsule study of tides and currents is available in Sausalito at the U.S. Army Corps of Engineers Bay Model. Built originally to study a proposal to dam the entrance to San Francisco Bay – a very bad idea, as it turned out – the model has since been used for studies of currents, toxic dispersions, and the effects of changes caused by river volume and landfill. The model runs 400 feet on its longest dimension. It is operated, with tides pumped in and out, only when studies are under way, which is rare, or for special occasions. There's been talk of establishing a regular schedule, so call ahead (415-332-3871) to see if there's progress on that. You won't learn any of the fine points about upwind racing legs on the Olympic Circle – the model isn't perfect, and East Bay windshifts play a big role that obviously isn't being modeled – but you can see clearly and quickly the ebb and flow of the major current lines in the deep water channels in the Golden Gate, the West Bay and the rivers. There's something to be learned from studying a tide cycle that takes minutes instead of hours and happens all within view. It's just like real life: The tide rises, the tide falls, and the currents run every which way. ⬥

THE WIND IS FREE

FOR MANY A SAILOR FROM LOS ANGELES or other South Of Market climes, a trip to the San Francisco Bay is a pilgrimage. Wind, always (or almost always) reliable wind is the theme. There's scarcely another sailing spot on the globe that delivers so much to so many so often. That said, it's only fair to add that, for many a Bay sailor, sailing in the southland also has the character of a pilgrimage. Eventually, you just want to get warm.

Aboard the Blue Planet, seabreeze is a global given. You may confidently predict a seabreeze, an onshore flow of air, wherever warm land adjoins a large body of water, and that's us all over. That's California from the shining strand at Coronado to the rollers of Crescent City.

But San Francisco Bay … well … what you get here is a seabreeze of heroic proportions.

BOOMTOWN

Imagine a still summer morning. Spinnakers have been hung out to dry, or they're already dried and ready hands are banding them with yarn to make them controllable at the set. Meanwhile, there is scarcely a breeze to stir them. Duffel bags and ice supplies pass from dock to deck. There is a mood of quiet expectancy. A rowing shell passes beyond the harbor entrance, and it might as well be crossing a pond. The surface of the bay beneath it is mirror-smooth, blinding in the eastern light. We can hear the heavy drumming of a fishing boat's diesels, the cry of gulls across the water, and, if it's a race day, the buzz of mark-set crews roaring around in fast little boats, enjoying smooth water thrills while they last. Maybe there's even a northerly working over the North Bay, and dissipating. No one needs to be told that's not the breeze of the day.

In Golden Gate Park, the first roller skaters are strapping on their wheels and trying out their moves, but significant events are under way far to the east, where the early rays of the sun are beating down on the roof of Lucky's in Lodi, on the parking lot of the DairyQueen in Stockton, on the lined-up metal rooftops around the Ford dealership in Tracy, and every bean field upriver to Sacramento and beyond.

The valley is heating up.

Only a tiny portion of the sun's total energy strikes the earth, and only 43 percent of that tiny portion penetrates the atmosphere to reach the surface of the planet. However, when it gets here it quickly warms the soil, which warms the air in turn.

Let's say that again: air is heated primarily by contact with the ground, which takes its warmth from solar radiation that passed through the air to get there.

Heated air expands, becomes less dense, and rises. Rising, it tries to create a vacuum below it, which it won't, because the resulting area of low atmospheric pressure draws in something to replace it. In this case, what comes in is air from the ocean, where the air is cool and dense, and air pressure is high. We speak of a pressure gradient between the interior and the coastline. The greater the gradient the stronger the wind. And between the valley and the sea there is one —

count it, one — sealevel opening, the Golden Gate.

You know what happens next.

On rare occasions the gradient seabreeze will bust in like a wall of stormtroopers, and the wind on the bay will go from zero to fifteen faster than you can say, "Oops, I left my raincoat downstairs." The norm, however, is a gradual building. By the time the first, darkening ripples appear under the Golden Gate, that rowing shell should be home or close to home. The wind may hang in the Gate for a time, but eventually it will fill in, steadily, increasing and moving eastward until it takes over all of the bay, the passes, and the interior.

Waiting for the breeze of the day, the educated eye will keep a lookout to the west for the sudden heeling of boats and darkening ruffles on the surface. Those are the telltale signs that the wind is coming.

ON SHORE FLOW DOMINATES local sailing from March through October. The onshore gradient is so powerful that a nighttime land breeze — wind blowing from the land, a perfectly normal phenomenon along temperate coastlines elsewhere — is a rare phenomenon here. Only the far southern shores of the South Bay develop a land breeze often enough to merit mention in the Coast Pilot, "and even here it is an infrequent occurrence."

The onshore flow of cool air moves in beneath hot, dry continental air, so our typical summer weather condition is an inversion. In most places the air gets cooler as you go to higher elevations. Here, between the marine layer and the dry air above it, temperatures rise.

Statistically, the nighttime breeze over the bay remains westerly, with local quirks. If we looked only at statistics, in fact, we'd think the seabreeze never quits. Statistically, the summertime westerly flows in at three to ten knots between 11 p.m. and 9 a.m., increasing later in the morning to six to fifteen knots and building in the afternoon to a velocity of fourteen to twenty. In the evening, as the sun sets and the valley cools, the westerly tends to subside. But these are averages taken from a daily cycle including calms and gales.

Cycles in the strength of the seabreeze also take place over a week or more. These longer cycles are bound up with yet another cyclical phenomenon, the summer fog, as it cools the valley enough to equalize the pressure gradient, which turns down the seabreeze, which allows the valley to warm, which turns on the seabreeze, which cools the valley and turns down the seabreeze, allowing the valley to warm …

THE GOD OF THE FOG SMILES UPON US

Fog is a cloud that forms at water level, or ground level, or close. What people call "a San Francisco fog" is caused by the horizontal movement of air — wet, heavy ocean air — blowing across cold-water currents near the coast. The coastal water cools the air (below its dew point), and then the air, which has soaked up moisture across thousands of miles of open ocean, can no longer hold that moisture. A myriad minuscule water droplets drop into the air, clinging to myriad floating particles of salt. We look at the result and say, "What's this myriad stuff?" and call it fog.

Mark Twain never said, "I spent the coldest winter of my life one summer in San Francisco," but he should have. Whoever

THE NATIONAL WEATHER SERVICE

IN NORTHERN CALIFORNIA, the National Weather Service is headquartered in Monterey, where powerful computer modeling mixes information gathered from satellites, offshore buoys and reports from shipping. Subcontractors launch weather balloons out of the Oakland Airport, but their data, which is especially useful for the aviation report, goes to Monterey for processing.

Marine forecasts rely heavily on satellites, which provide full Pacific coverage. Without the satellites, fog forecasts would be hit or miss. Almost as important are the six buoys operating 24 hours a day off the coast, transmitting information on air and sea temperatures, barometric pressure, wind speed, wave direction and wave height.

Satellites and buoys both provide up-to-the-minute data.

said it first knew a bit about fog.

The coastal fog bank is a semipermanent feature of summer weather in Northern California. The band of fog may be wide, a hundred miles or so. It may be narrow. It may retreat from the coast for a while, then return as the pressure gradient steepens, penetrating all the way to the valley itself and burying the Bay Area under a thick marine layer of cool air. That's as good a time as any for an excursion to Tahoe, Whiskeytown or Block Island. Ocean winds are often lighter than winds on the bay, especially if the ocean is covered by fog. Piloting is difficult then; boat handling is not.

PACIFIC WEATHER PATTERNS

Local weather is a product of local conditions interacting with broad weather patterns on the ocean. To get that picture, we have to look at what drives the prevailing summer wind, and with it, the prevailing current.

Somewhere about mid-Pacific, due west or a little south of our latitude, air is flowing outward from a zone of high pressure. We call it the Pacific High. The air flowing out, influenced by the rotation of the earth, develops a clockwise rotation that becomes a prevailing northwesterly as it blows along the California coast. FIG.8

The Pacific High Pressure Zone is one of a belt of highs ringing the northern hemisphere at about the same latitude. As highs go, the Pacific High is exceptionally stable, but not foolproof. Like other stable high pressure systems, it is a product of descending air (that is, the weight of descending air). In this case, air that first rose with the heat of the tropics, and flowed north, cools and comes down near mid-Pacific with more air arriving

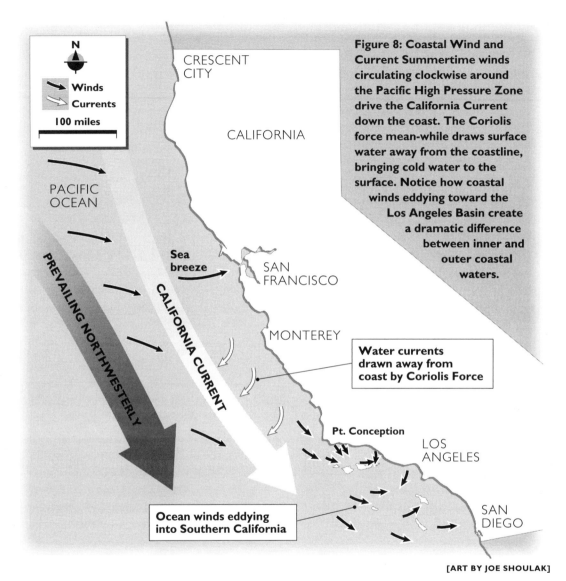

Winds
Currents
100 miles

Figure 8: Coastal Wind and Current Summertime winds circulating clockwise around the Pacific High Pressure Zone drive the California Current down the coast. The Coriolis force mean-while draws surface water away from the coastline, bringing cold water to the surface. Notice how coastal winds eddying toward the Los Angeles Basin create a dramatic difference between inner and outer coastal waters.

Water currents drawn away from coast by Coriolis Force

Ocean winds eddying into Southern California

[ART BY JOE SHOULAK]

above it and pressing down in turn. The air driven outward from the center of the High is influenced by the Coriolis force, bending motion to the right in the Northern Hemisphere, which creates that clockwise flow of air we introduced above: northwesterlies along the coast, southeasterly tradewinds blowing toward Hawaii, southerlies and westerlies blowing "over the top" and back toward the coast.

We tend to think of the California coast as running north-south, and when we look out through the Golden Gate, we think we're looking west. More precisely, the view from Alcatraz to the ocean runs south of west — about 240 degrees — and the coastline runs from northwest to southeast. The prevailing wind, as it circles the Pacific High, follows this path down the coast, becoming our familiar northwesterly wind and driving a southeasterly current with it.

Note again that we name a wind for where it's coming from. We name a current for where it's going to. And we dangle our participles with glee.

The northwesterlies push a surface current down the coast, the California Current, some 500 miles wide and moving at about two-tenths of a knot. But wind and water alike are affected by the earth's rotation. Both tend to curl to the right, away from the coast. Or perhaps we should say that, in the rotation, the harder parts of the planet are leaving the softer parts behind. Either way, this curling force draws the surface current away from the coast, calling up cold water from the depths to replace it (and creating a vast algae bloom as the deep-water nutrients reach the sunlit upper levels of the sea). Coastal ocean temperatures drop ten to fifteen degrees below temperatures in mid-Pacific. Meanwhile, the northwesterlies deliver an enormous mass of relatively warm, water-saturated air from mid-ocean. That warm, water-saturated air cools in crossing the coastal waters, and the fog machine is born. With the interior valleys heating up and drawing in the seabreeze through six major gaps in the coastal range (the Golden Gate above all), the Bay Area benefits from natural air conditioning.

Summer ocean temperatures near the coast can sometimes be colder than winter ocean temperatures, if there is strong upwelling. Typically, you would see a high water-temperature reading at the Farallones of about 55 degrees in November and a low of 52 degrees

in April. Note the narrow spread. South of here, the strong ocean winds keep driving on, and so do the coastal currents. Point Sur and Point Conception are famous for wind, and the stream roars right down the coast past Southern California.

Los Angeles has a warmer climate in small part because it is farther south, mostly because it is tucked away from the ocean wind and current (see Figure 8). The Los Angeles basin sits in a coastal indentation protected by mountains and miles from the coastal northwesterlies and the cold, deep-water currents they produce. Much of the weather near L.A. is governed by the Catalina Eddy, a swirling sidecurrent from

YOUR OWN FORECAST

RICHARD LAY, FORMERLY A METEOROLOGIST with the National Weather Service, once drew up a rough wind-prediction guide for his friends at the Coyote Point Yacht Club. The idea is to estimate the strength of the seabreeze from the onshore-inshore pressure differential. Lay's suggestion is to compare the San Francisco Airport barometric reading to the Sacramento barometric reading.

You subtract Sacramento barometric pressure from SFO barometric pressure and multiply by 30 to arrive at a reading in millibars. For example: 30.00 inches (SFO) - 29.92 (SAC) = .08 X 30 = 2.4. Then you take that figure into the table below to arrive at an estimated peak for the seabreeze of the day.

Lay cautions that this approach is useful but rough. In an office of professionals, he would not make a prediction without also accounting for the depth and strength of the inversion layer; pressure gradients to the north and south; any weakening, strengthening, or movement of the Pacific High; diurnal change in barometric pressure; changes to the thermal low pressure in Southern California, and Delphic chickens speaking in tongues. That said, here's the table.

PRESSURE GRADIENT   SAN FRANCISCO-SACRAMENTO
0.0 - 0.5 millibars: light/variable to 15 knots
0.5 - 1.5 millibars: westerly 5 to 15 with stronger gusts
1.5 - 3.0 millibars: westerly 15 to 30
3.0 - 4.5 millibars: westerly 20 to 35
4.5 - 6.5 millibars: westerly 25 to 40 (probably gale)

the prevailing northwesterlies that continue down the coast past Mexico. Southern California marine forecasts will refer to the "outer coastal waters," where it might be blowing 20 knots while the wind is a mere eight knots in the "inner coastal waters" near the Santa Monica Pier.

Off San Francisco, the fog bank typically reaches elevations of 500 to 1,500 feet, where it is held back by an inversion layer of hot, dry air subsiding from the eastern zone of the High. Again, we speak of an inversion layer wherever a layer of warm air rides above a layer of cooler air. It is this inversion that blesses the peaks of Mount Tamalpais with sunshine on most of the days when the ocean and bay are fogged out. Viewed globally, San Francisco's prevailing summer inversion is a rare case, but so are local politics. In the spring or fall, you can often see the inversion layer splitting the towers of the Golden Gate Bridge, with the fog line riding below it. As the weekly (more or less) cycle builds, and the fog increases, the marine layer pushes the inversion up.

There are many variations in the fog. During an ebb tide, it is common to see an incoming fog breaking up and turning patchy as it hits the warmer water coming out of the bay. Summertime ebb tides are often ten degrees warmer than flood tides — and along the edge of that fog line, look for big, man-eating gusts.

Or, you might see a bay that is crystal clear on the ebb tide suddenly develop a thin blanket of sea-level fog as the tide turns and cold ocean water floods in. This is most common in the spring or fall, when the inversion layer is low. These are the fogs that cause white-out on the west bay. Fog may also form as air rises up the slopes of the coastal hills. At other times an upper level trough may pass through — a low pressure system in the upper atmosphere — allowing the fog deck to lift higher than the peak Mount Tam.

In summer, especially in July or August, air close to water level may cool enough to eliminate the critical temperature difference between air and water. This cool marine layer then spreads over the region, dropping temperatures to summer minimums, and the fog-forming conditions move aloft — to the contact level between the cold layer and warmer air above. Now we have that familiar height-of-summer high fog, the kind that can penetrate all the way to the valley. Visibility

| 0 - 4.9 | 5 - 9.9 | 10 - 14.9 | 15 - 19.9 | 20 - 24.9 | +25 |

Wind speeds are in knots and are color coded according to the key. All speeds are for the wind at 10 meters above the surface elevation.

A seabreeze afternoon as shown by the wind sensors at sfports.wr.usgs.gov/sfports.html. Sailors will experience many shifts not shown here as the breeze bends around land masses, or turns to follow the river channels.

is good on the water, but the skies are gloomy, and if the condition persists too long, even fog-loving natives get to grumbling.

Harold Gilliam, environmentalist and writer, estimated that a million gallons of water an hour float through the Golden Gate as vapor at Maximum Fog. People who have sailed only in hot, dry places won't understand what San Francisco Bay sailors mean by heavy heavy air until they've inhaled a bit of that density, or taken it on the chin.

You will notice a difference between a wet, drippy fog and a dry fog, though both carry moisture. What we call a wet fog can penetrate clothing in a hurry and drop a lot of water. Fog drip in the Berkeley Hills can reach ten inches over a summer. A wet fog was probably formed far at sea, leaving time for a great deal of moisture to accumulate and the drops to grow big, or it may be wet because the temperature is low, and the air is losing water quickly, or both. A dry fog is formed over the land, or close in, or it forms in warm air, which can hold more moisture.

The Golden Gate is the main opening for the penetration of wind and fog, but there are other openings as well. On the peninsula south of San Francisco, the San Bruno Gap feeds wind into the airport area and Coyote Point; the Crystal Springs Gap (the San Andreas Fault channel) feeds wind into Redwood City with a cooling effect that can reach all the way to San Jose. To the north, the great opening is the Estero Gap, which draws ocean air from Bodega Bay into the Petaluma Valley.

August is our foggiest month. Fog signals operate 40 to 50 percent of the time in the ocean approaches and 15 to 20 percent of the time in the Golden Gate. At other times, perhaps, visibility is good and the signals are not operating, but high fog rolls over the hills and the bay. In a hard summer, veterans will tell you, the sun never breaks through.

A true San Franciscan loves the fog. As one ace real estate salesman said, showing a house in the Sea Cliff, "My dears, we're having one of our silver days." But San Franciscans dream of golden days, too, especially during those hard summers when it seems the fog will never quit. Here's the philosophy of it: Shirtsleeve sailing on the bay is wonderful, but if it were like that all the time, the bay would be so crowded we couldn't sail at all.

The strength of the seabreeze and the depth of the fog depend in part on the strength and integrity of the Pacific High. The summer wind of the bay is a product of two forces — the high pressure of the ocean wind pushing from behind and the low pressure of the valley pulling the wind ahead. So it's not really true, as people say, that, "The ocean doesn't blow, the valley sucks." You can see the importance of the ocean winds whenever the High weakens, and with it, the coastal northwesterlies. Without that strong push from behind, the fog will not penetrate the valley. Instead, it will settle over the coast and the bay, perhaps for weeks at a time, while valley temperatures soar. The "cycle" de-cycles, producing one of those hard summers we were talking about. If the High remains weak, the decline of the coastal winds will slow the current and the upwelling of cold water. As coastal waters warm, albacore fishermen find themselves hauling in warm water fish on the order of barracuda and yellowtail.

In a "normal" summer weather pattern, the High is positioned to the west of San Francisco, effectively blocking any storms arriving from the ocean and redirecting them to the Pacific Northwest. That gives Seattle its famous wet summers, while California goes dry. Occasionally, a fragment of a Pacific storm may slip through and drop a little summer rain. Significant summer rains, however, will probably come in a rogue system that has escaped its rightful stomping grounds in the Gulf of Mexico and galloped across the continent with a load of warm rain and crackling bolts of lightning. If we figure that occasional abnormalities are normal, we can say that summer rain is normal. Rarely does a summer pass without at least one wet day, but — how quickly we forget. No sooner does the wet stuff begin to fall from the sky than perplexed citizens will gather under shelters at Port Sonoma or the piers at Mission Rock, knitting their brows and agreeing, "I never saw anything like *this* before."

Heat waves represent another normal and usually welcome abnormality. There may be mild episodes, almost heat wave-warm, at the bottom of the fog cycle. Then you can sail the bay without Klondike gear, but the opportunity won't last long. The cycle will crank up again. We reserve the honorable title of Heat Wave for those occasions when a high pressure cell takes over the weather and shuts down or greatly tempers the seabreeze. One record-setting heat wave lasted five days.

Temperatures in San Francisco soared to 105 degrees, enough to make the deck of the Bay Bridge sag ten feet. Flags hung limp. Automobile exhausts and factory fumes turned the sky dirty brown, and the air was obnoxiously noxious. The Bay Area is an effective smog trap if the wind machine is switched off.

A two-day or three-day heat wave is more typical. If it comes with a morning calm and a mild seabreeze, that is also typical. The breeze may come late in the day, but usually it will come.

Another heat wave condition develops when a high pressure cell, perhaps a renegade spur from the Pacific High, settles over the Pacific Northwest. The clockwise flow of air around the high will cross us as an easterly wind, flowing hot and dry. It may come as a violent "fire wind," with the Forest Service posting signs advising, "Fire Danger 100%" at park entrances. Land breezes figured in the destructive Berkeley fire of September, 1924, which claimed hundreds of homes, and the Mill Valley fire of July, 1928, which took out houses and threatened downtown before the seabreeze revived and firefighters gained the upper hand. The fearsome Oakland Hills fire of 1991 was also driven by hot, dry winds blowing out of the valley.

High pressure incursions are a regular feature of autumn weather, and so is the mildness of Indian Summer.

Even without a heat wave, October and November generally bring an increase of air pressure over the region and a moderating of the seabreeze. With the earth moving through its orbit, we are experiencing then what we call the southward migration of the sun. The valley cools. The Pacific High weakens and follows the sun south. Ocean temperatures, already warmed by summer heat, rise a bit more as a declining northwesterly drives a declining current.

In autumn as in spring, the inversion layer rides low. These are the conditions that produce spectacular fog-sculptures over Alcatraz and Angel Island. Or, if the seabreeze falters and starts again, you might see a layering of haze, clear air, haze, and clear air again. (You probably won't see this phenomenon in summer, because then the breeze builds steadily and tops out high.)

During periods of high heat — probably in the fall — the Petaluma and Napa Valleys can act as miniature high pressure zones, forcing air out and creating a northerly flow through San Pablo Bay and the North Bay. Usually, this flow will break up somewhere between Richmond and Angel Island, leaving a strip of calm between itself and the westerly that continues through the Golden Gate.

In the Oslofyorden, they pronounce the K. [PHOTO BY DR. JOHN E. HUTTON, JR.]

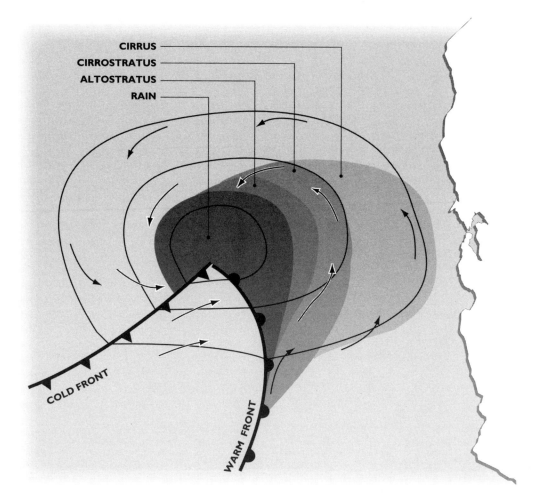

CIRRUS
CIRROSTRATUS
ALTOSTRATUS
RAIN

COLD FRONT

WARM FRONT

Figure 9: A textbook case of a winter storm, the familiar extra-tropical cyclone of the North Pacific. High cirrus clouds and a windshift to the south announce the arriving storm. Then clouds lower, delivering rain just ahead of the frontal system and along the cold front — the squall line. As the storm passes, clearing skies bring windshifts to the west and north and a cooling breeze. Occasionally, winter storms really are this "pure." More often, the elements are mixed.

[ART BY BRUCE KREFTING]

There's really not a great deal to say about autumn except how fine it is. We get some of our best sailing in this time of transition, as the pressure gradient moderates and the High moves south, gradually opening the door to winter storms.

WINTER

Winter in Northern California is our most variable season, but we don't look at the official calendar to define winter. It's better to say that winter is what happens, November through February. Essentially, this is a time of quiet, with the lowest winds of the year. The Coast Pilot for the Pacific Coast reports calms in winter 15 to 40 percent of the time inside the bay and 10 to 12 percent of the time on the ocean. Unless storms are passing through, winds are likely to be gentle (averaging eight to nine knots, according to the Pilot), and sailors like to joke that winter is the true season for warm sailing on the bay. Even in cool temperatures, ghosting along on a hint of a northerly, with the decks dry in bright sunshine, can be a balm, an honest balm, compared to the wind chill of a spray-faced, fogbound howler in July.

Winter is also the rainy season. Three-fourths of the precipitation in Northern California falls between December and March. We've said that rains occasionally sneak in during the summer, but the meat-and-potatoes storms that swell the rivers and fill the reservoirs wait for changes far to the west. With the Pacific High Pressure Zone following the sun, moving south from our latitude, it is no longer positioned to block frontal systems or push them up Portland way. The storm track is open.

In the winter, the Bay Area is exposed to the jet stream and with it, to the warm fronts, cold fronts and occluded fronts that work through other parts of the country all year long. For present purposes — since

In the days of reaching legs [PHOTO BY DR. JOHN E. HUTTON, JR.]

there are plenty of sources that treat weather in detail — we're going to limit ourselves to the basics of what meteorologists call extra-tropical cyclones. We call them winter storms. They arrive by way of the north or the west. If winter storms descend from the north, they tend to come on cold, dumping a good feed for the Sierra snowpack. When they come from the west, we may speak of them as "Hawaii storms." Temperatures are warmer, and the energy and moisture may be intense, but they leave the mountains with slushy slopes, and the skiing's for lousy.

An extra-tropical cyclone may form, far at sea, wherever a cold air mass from the polar region rushes southward alongside a mass of moist, warm, northbound tropical air. The boundary will be unstable. Friction eventually is sure to disturb some region along that boundary, and cold air will begin to press under the warm air. At the same time, warm air will rise over the cold. Where that warm air rises, barometric pressure will drop. Meteorologists note this zone of decreased pressure on their weather charts as a Low.

In Figure 9, we see a sketch of a storm. Where moist, warm air rises, it cools and loses its moisture; water vapor condenses to form clouds and rain.

Where cold air displaces warm, we speak of a cold front. Where warm air displaces cold, we speak of a warm front. At maturity, an extra-tropical cyclone consists of a cold front linked to a warm front, with winds rotating counter-clockwise around the low and the entire system moving east or north-of-east at a likely speed of seven hundred miles per day.

A practiced eye can often spot the approach of a low pressure system by watching the sky. Wispy, high ice clouds (cirrus) typically precede the low by five hundred miles, or a little less than a day's traveling time for the storm. In a textbook case, barometers begin falling at about the time that cirrus appear in the sky (if it's not a textbook case, the cirrus may come as remnants from a dissipating storm or one passing to the north). Some three hundred miles ahead of the low, cloud formations will lower and thicken into altostratus at eight thousand to twenty thousand feet; these translucent sheets often show dark bands at the lower elevations. Behind the altostratus come the puffy cumulus, flat-bottomed stratocumulus, and eventually the nimbostratus that

reach almost to the ground and deliver the rain.

Variations of the Latin nimbus are applied to any cloud that produces rain, though science hasn't officially recognized our local specialty, nimbofog.

Elsewhere in the world, weather fronts are a year-round threat, and skywatching as amateur meteorology — accurate amateur meteorology — is more prized than here. West coast sailors tend to be lackadaisical about watching the sky, the more so since the conditions that produce one storm will often spin off several storms close together, and the sky will be filled with a mixture of cloud types that defy a simple interpretation. The rainy season in Northern California, only a few months per annum, is an emphatically unpopular time for ocean cruising and not a peak time for Bay sailing. Cloud study is blissfully ignored by many sailors who get along quite well, thank you, until they go sailing somewhere else. But those who sail through the winter cannot ignore that direct indicator of arriving weather, the abrupt and auspicious change in wind direction.

A whipping southerly is the surest sign of an approaching storm, and a glance back at Figure 9 will show the cause. The counterclockwise flow of air around a low pressure system means that a storm passing to the north of San Francisco — the most frequent case — will be felt first as a southwesterly wind. A storm centered to the south will be felt first as a southeasterly. A storm passing with its centerline directly overhead will first bring winds from a southerly direction along its eastern edge. Rain and rising temperatures will come later at the arrival of the warm front, followed by a period of clearing skies and southwesterly winds. After that, the cold front will arrive, pushing a nimbostratus wall of cloud, and lastly, clearing skies and a windshift to the west or north.

As a rule of thumb, we find southerly winds at the approach of the storm and cold, northerly winds at the departure.

Many of the real-life storms that pelt the coastline have already reached an advanced age. Late in the life of such a storm, the cold front may catch up with the warm front, lifting the warm air mass entirely away from the earth's surface to create an Occluded Front. The warm front is blocked, or occluded, from reaching the ground. A similar cycle of windshifts will occur, but the rain will come all at once, as the single front passes through, and without a period of clearing.

The strong winds of winter never fail to catch a few negligent residents of the anchorages off guard, and the cause is not always a storm. Less frequently, but often enough to be part of the winter weather picture, powerful northerlies sweep the interior valley and the Bay Area. It happens whenever the great currents of polar continental air "skip their banks." Pressed outward from northern latitudes in the frigid, high-pressure interiors of the continent, these dry, cold currents usually follow paths east of the Sierra, chilling the deserts of Nevada and the plains of the Midwest. When polar air hops over the mountains to play the interloper along the coast, it brings a bitter winter wind that sings loud in the rigging. It's a hectic time in the anchorages. Radar watchers at the Vessel Traffic Service on Yerba Buena Island keep a close check on the positions of tankers riding to the south of them in Anchorage 8. Elsewhere, poorly tethered pleasure craft break loose from their moorings or drag anchor, presenting a danger to themselves and innocent bystanders. The Coast Guard may be drawn into the act of rescuing these boats. More often, the owners of neighboring craft are to be found rowing across troubled waters, playing Good Samaritan to a mess caused by sloppy anchoring and inattention to lines and chafe points.

The Sausalito anchorage has problems with both northern and southern exposure. Around the corner, in Belvedere, the south is the only unsheltered direction, but there is enough open water to fetch formidable waves. Wise skippers will check their equipment ahead of time and take extra precautions before storms approach. There are several harbors around the bay that have some level of exposure, but these are the only two areas where a significant number of boats ride to moorings outside a breakwater.

Calm weather presents hazards of its own, especially in low temperatures. Summer is the foggy season along the coast, but winter is the time of fog in the inland valleys.

Tule fog is our local name for a ground fog or radiation fog created when the ground is colder than the air above. We're used to seeing it in the Delta, where the waterways are edged by those bulrush-like plants we call tules. Hence the name.

On clear, cold nights, the ground and the marshes radiate heat to the atmosphere. If the air is calm or winds are less than, say, five knots, the ground quickly becomes colder than the air. A ten-degree drop is common. That relatively warm air then radiates its own heat to the ground, and it cools. The cooled air loses moisture. Droplets condense, and we have fog. In a near-perfect calm, a tule fog may float shin high, like the dry-ice fog of a Busby Berkeley musical. Too much wind will kill the process, but a mild breeze can actually circulate the fog as it forms, lifting it higher. During a long spell of quiet, cold weather, the entire northern valley may get into the act of radiating fog to depths of hundreds of feet.

Just as water is forever seeking its own level, air seeks always to equalize its pressure, flowing from a cold area to a warm area. Thus there may be episodes in the winter when an ocean-warmed Bay Area develops a land breeze, blowing from the land to the sea, calling out the tule fog in a grand march through the Carquinez Strait and the gaps in the eastern hills. Over the bay, it may be reinforced by fog radiated from the bay's own marshland. This is a tule fog on the grand scale, and it can reduce visibility to dangerous minimums on the rivers, the bay and the approaches. Tule fog is more likely to close the airports than a rainstorm or ocean fog.

Again: From November through January, and despite occasional storms and high winds, the Bay Area has its lowest average wind strength. In February the average begins to climb, and the trend continues to build throughout the spring, while major changes take place in the atmosphere.

The bay has only two seasons, really, winter and summer. Spring and autumn are distinguished mainly in the statistics they generate. Spring is often windy and cold, with a continuing threat of storms. But you as a sailor are not a creature of statistics. Sooner or later you will look to the Golden Gate, and you'll see a bright beret of fog cocked on the headland. The calendar may say it's spring, but once you put on that hat, it's summer. ☙

CRUISING THE BAY

ON CROWDED DAYS ON THE BAY REGATTA CROSSES regatta, weaving the warp and woof of a fleeting fabric — and a metaphor like that is not for the faint of heart any more than the dodge'em-scare'em on the water. Fishing cadres stake out their territory, ferries snort around, and you might encounter anything from a deep-V Scarab running seventy miles an hour to a mid-bay swimmer wearing nothing but a red cap, a pearl necklace, and a big, oblivious smile.

Once upon a time a magazine editor from New York took a ride on the bay with a local newspaperman, and the visitor got pretty worked up. He loved the crazy spires and gingerbread of the city-that-sometimes-knows-how. He admired the hawk-hunted hills rising toward Tamalpais, and he gazed off toward Grizzly Peak, where it takes a bite out of the sky behind the Campanile at Berkeley. "This is gorgeous," he enthused. "It's alive, and the colors are strong, and it's nature, and it's a big slice of nature. In New York, we have to travel so far to see something like this. But you live here. You probably don't even notice."

"Wrong," said the local. "Every morning I wake up and I walk to the window. I just stand there and stare."

There's plenty around here that's worth a good stare. What the California coast lacks in easy cruising it makes up in San Francisco Bay and the Sacramento-San Joaquin River Delta. Northern California doesn't need the gunkhole magic of Maine or the neon glow of tropical waters. This is a different world. From out at sea, the entrance to the bay can be tricky to spot, but that simple fact bought the Ohlone and Miwok tribes an extra 200 years of privacy.

Fog frequently takes the blame (or credit) for the two centuries in which Spanish ships explored the coast without discovering San Francisco Bay. Sailors know better, once they've looked at the Golden Gate from the ocean and discovered that, even with a city built around it, the entrance can be hard to pick out on an average "clear" day. The East Bay hills fill the background, and the Golden Gate doesn't stand out until one is close enough to identify the bridge across it. Spanish sailors standing off to clear points north and south wouldn't have noticed a thing.

Sausalito, just north of the Golden Gate Bridge, is a popular first call for cruising boats entering San Francisco Bay. Ayala launched the tradition in 1775 when he made it his first stop. Sausalito is relatively sheltered, with a deep-rooted sailing culture and scads of locals who speak the language of long distance sailing. Some arriving boats go to the San Francisco cityfront, where there are marinas and yacht clubs but fewer marine services, Other parts of the bay will also beckon — the Oakland "Estuary," for example, is a major marine center — but they are less often a first port of call.

In this chapter, we'll tour the cruising grounds and take a look at what they offer. We won't try to cover everything. That's worth a book and maybe two. The nuts and bolts of it - anchoring depths, marinas and facilities, chandleries, boatyards, and phone numbers for all of them — can be found elsewhere. Recreation Publications in Alameda,

Map labels:
MARIN COUNTY
SAN FRANCISCO BAY
St. Francis Yacht Club
Treasure Island Yacht Club
ALCATRAZ ISLAND
Golden Gate Yacht Club
TREASURE ISLAND
San Francisco Marina
GOLDEN GATE BRIDGE
Aquatic Park
Fort Point
Crissy Field
Fisherman's Wharf
Pier 39 Marina
National Maritime Museum
Pt. Rincon Anchorage
YERBA BUENA ISLAND
Palace of Fine Arts
Gas House Cove
Ferry Bldg.
PRESIDIO
Marina Green
South Beach Harbor
SAN FRANCISCO-OAKLAND BAY BRIDGE
China Basin
Mission Rock
The Ramp
SAN FRANCISCO
Central Basin
India Basin
Islais Channel
HUNTERS POINT
3COM PARK
N
1 mile
SAN FRANCISCO BAY

[MAP BY JOE SHOULAK]

publisher of the monthly magazine *Bay & Delta Yachtsman*, also puts out an annual *Marina Guide* with marina information and more. The *MPC Boaters Directory*, published in regional editions out of Newport Beach, covers marina facilities and includes harbor charts, navigation references, and a yellow pages section for services ranging from acupuncture to engine repair. Both are free and widely available in chandleries and marina offices.

THE WEST BAY

The San Francisco cityfront runs from bay to breakers, just like our big, crazy cross-town foot race. Sailors speaking of "the cityfront," however, are usually talking about the stretch from the Golden Gate Bridge to Fisherman's Wharf. This area includes the windsurfing beach at Crissy Field, the San Francisco Yacht Harbor, the St. Francis and Golden Gate yacht clubs, and the Fort Mason piers. It fronts the West Bay, the focal point of the region. Since we've already said a lot about the West Bay, we'll take a look here at San Francisco and the city's four very different marinas.

Exploring San Francisco with the Golden Gate as a starting point, we come first to the Presidio, the still-developing Golden Gate National Recreation Area, a national park created from a former U.S. Army base. There's been a military presence here since the Spanish deployed a permanent force in 1776 and constructed a traditional walled fortress, a presidio. Civilians attached to the Presidio soon moved east across the hills to establish a suburb in the warm zone we now know as the Mission District. This was Spain's most remote outpost in the new world, and when things went badly in Madrid, the supply ships simply failed to show, sometimes for years at a time.

The Presidio rolled over from Spanish rule to Mexican rule in 1821. In 1847, during the U.S.-Mexico War, it was occupied by the New York Volunteers, and with the treaty that ended the war it began its long career under the U.S. Army. The oldest U.S. Army building still standing in the Presidio was built in 1857, and many more are nearly that old. Bare sand dunes were planted with trees in the 1880s, and the Presidio is now as forested as Golden Gate Park. A level area near the water marks Crissy Field, an important early center of military aviation. One of its fliers, Major Dana Crissy, was killed in 1919 in a cross-country endurance test, and the field was given his name. The sand beach at Crissy Field is a windsurfers' mecca, and it is sometimes used for off-the-beach dinghies and catamarans.

Our first docking opportunity is the San Francisco Yacht Harbor, a stunning setting in the maw of the wind funnel, some two miles east of the bridge. Just inland from the harbor is the Palace of Fine Arts, an extravagantly-columned relic of the 1915 Panama-Pacific Exposition, when this neighborhood was covered with architectural fantasies that were not built to last. The harbor was dug to its original limits at that time, carved from wetlands that, in 1915, had no known ecological value. Across Marina Boulevard from the harbor, you enter the quiet, winding streets of the Marina District, now covering the site of the Exposition. Climb the hill that rises to the south, and you come to Pacific Heights, where the silver kings built bigger replacement houses after they were burned out of Nob Hill in the '06 shake and bake.

Being city-operated, the 700 berths of the San Francisco Yacht Harbor tend to be under-budgeted compared to other harbors in the area. The good news about old wooden docks, however, is they're a lot homier than the modern stuff, and this harbor is a good place to be. If you don't believe it, check the waiting list. Out of respect for tradition, the harbor master's office still flies its red gale warning pennants — even though the Coast Guard has discontinued their use, and even though they have to fly them nearly every day in the summer. During our peak wind months, the usual question is, "One pennant or two?" There is a supermarket near the eastern end of the harbor, but it's a long hike from the guest docks and an even longer way around from the guest docks of the St. Francis and Golden Gate yacht clubs. The clubs occupy a finger of land with access via the west end. Coffee shops and snack shops can be found near the supermarket, but the closest shopping area is

Chestnut Street, six blocks in, which made an amazing sociological shift circa 1993, from frumpy to cool, almost overnight.

There are long-term problems with silting near the entrance here, and the harbor was nearly choked off in the early 1990s with sand swept down from Crissy Field Beach. More than once, the largest boats in the St. Francis Yacht Club's annual Big Boat Series have been blocked from the club docks by shallow water, berthing instead at South Beach Harbor, some four sailing miles away. The entrance has since been dredged to depths of ten feet and more, with promises (promises) to keep the problem from recurring. Big boats have returned to the San Francisco Yacht Harbor, but deep-draft Maxis might be locked in or locked out at low tide.

The only diesel source in San Francisco is the fuel dock at Gas House Cove, tucked into the eastern subsection of the San Francisco Yacht Harbor alongside the massive piers of Fort Mason. (Gas House Cove lies directly across from the supermarket, which sounds convenient, but there is too much surge here for long-term guest berthing.) Fort Mason, with its red-tiled roofs, was once a staging area for troop shipments to the far Pacific. It has been converted to a center for museums, small theaters, galleries, non-profit offices and a good vegetarian restaurant, Greens, that overlooks Gas House Cove.

The St. Francis Yacht Club and the Golden Gate Yacht Club sit on the north side of the marina, with views to the bay on one side and the city on the other. Both are active racing clubs, the more so for having start/finish lines right in the "front yard."

East of Fort Mason, behind a curved cement breakwater and backed by a pair of curved high-rise apartment buildings that make it easy to spot, Aquatic Park offers access to sailing boats and overnight anchoring. There are two active swimming clubs on the beach, so no motoring is allowed. There is easy access to Fisherman's Wharf. The anchorage is bordered on the west side by a Sea Scout station and on

> **A**LONG THE SAN FRANCISCO cityfront, there are many days when there is less wind close to the beach. Downwind against an ebb tide, or upwind against a flood tide, cityfront racing will pose the dilemma of going "out for the wind, or in for the tide." It's one thing to see the problem, but you're not likely to be right all the time.

the east by the Hyde Street Pier, home to the historic ships of the National Maritime Museum. The skyscraper spars of the barkentine *Balclutha* tower over the scene, which is beautiful and yet not often visited, even by local boats. Dinghy landing on the pier is not allowed; this is museum territory. Take the dinghy to the beach instead and chain it to a lamppost, or, as the rangers say, "It *will* be stolen." Anchoring is limited to 24 hours. To stay longer, talk to the rangers ashore, and whether your stay is long or short, anchor with a special thought for strong currents.

Alcatraz lies across the channel from Aquatic Park, but there's no docking at Alcatraz. Access to the prison tour is via the excursion boats that leave from Fisherman's Wharf. An Alcatraz tour is highly recommended. It's a nice place to visit, but you wouldn't want to live there.

Fisherman's Wharf, 2.8 miles east of the Golden Gate Bridge, is more of a tourist stop than a fisherman's stop these days, but there is an active movement to preserve as much as possible of the original life of the place. Most fish delivery takes place at Pier 45, overhauled and re-opened in 1995, and most of that activity goes on early in the day, before the tourists are out to see it. Locals tend to avoid the famous restaurants of Fisherman's Wharf, but when they go, they emerge saying things like, "Gee, that was actually rather good." Dock space is very limited, and it's rare to take a boat there. Call ahead, if you're determined to try. Don't pass up the crab in season.

Pier 39, a tourist destination at the foot of Telegraph Hill, has a marina that welcomes travelers. Restaurants are no problem to find here. You'll never make it through all of them at Pier 39, much less Fisherman's Wharf next door. For less touristy experiences, you'll have to go deeper into the city. The Italian flavor of North Beach, the bohemian cafes of the area, and the eateries of Chinatown are within walking distance if you're ambitious and don't mind a bit of inspirational scenery.

Sea lions have taken over the west-side piers. Harbor management tried to run them off at first, then saw they were a tourist draw and turned to encouraging them. Pier 39 is busy and sometimes noisy. Like other San Francisco harbors, it is likely to be windy in the afternoon, and it has problems with surge, but it provides ready access to enter-tainment areas and to downtown San Francisco. Your kids will approve. The cable cars of the nearby Hyde Street Line have long queues most of the time (locals wouldn't think of it), but if you gut it out, or go very early, it's a memorable ride up and over Russian Hill and down, through the saddle, and up again to the crest of Nob Hill and then down yet again to the upscale shopping around Union Square. The Hyde Street Line crosses Lombard (the crooked street) and brushes Chinatown, with views for days.

Pier 39 has supermarkets, drug stores and a post office conveniently close by, also municipal bus services. But the Muni is no treat unless you're looking for a cultural experience. If you just want to get somewhere, take a cab.

Around the corner and south of the Bay Bridge is South Beach Harbor, with 700 slips and views across the bay toward Oakland. It is more sheltered than the San Francisco Yacht Harbor or Pier 39, with minimal surge and good docking for large craft. The South Beach YC is stationed here, and you can shop for necessities close by.

South Beach sits near the southern end of the San Francisco Embarcadero, which was being overhauled and revitalized in the mid-1990s, an opportunity provided by the removal of an earthquake-damaged, double-decker freeway that had overwhelmed and esthetically destroyed the shoreline in the 1960s. For too long this area was an outpost in the post-industrial landscape of a dying port. Now the South Beach neighborhood is characterized by condominiums, restaurants, and night life. SOMA — the South of Market Area — lies inland, the city's neighborhood of lofts, galleries and all-night rock & roll. For an anthropological experience, go to a hardware store and watch the natives try on the chains.

China Basin, farther south, has berthing inside an area bordered by two drawbridges. The gargantuan machinery of the Fourth Street Bridge is popular with moviemakers looking for a place to hang a hero out to dry before a last-minute escape. James Bond survived, for one. Most of the activity in China Basin is commercial. The berthing is so limited and the services so few that they do not fit our purpose here. Even farther south, however, Mission Rock has the attraction of being a place, and a character, unto itself. Located in a neighborhood that is downscale and industrial, Mission Rock tempts a writer to throw in adjectives on the order of "funky" and "atmospheric." More to the point, Mission Rock reminds us of a time when there was a Frisco in San Francisco, and the city was better off for it. The San Francisco Yacht Club was initially headquartered here (not the first SFYC, but the one that came later, and endured), and the restaurants now are popular with downtown executives and city politicians who seek them out for open air power lunches over burgers and beer. Guest berths are available. The Mariposa Yacht Club is close by, also the Bay View Boat Club (host of the annual Plastic Classic, a concours and regatta for older fiberglass boats) and the busy San Francisco Boatworks.

THE NORTH BAY

The North Bay is our most popular sailing destination. People come here for the warm and usually sunny skies, the sheltered anchorages, and vistas of open hills. Long distance travelers will want to rent a car and go beyond the North Bay to explore Marin County. There you will find hiking trails, spring waterfalls, small inns, the beginning of the redwood forest, and coastal mountains towering above rocky surf. Far-

Yes, silting can be a problem on the cityfront. [PHOTO BY ROB MOORE, *LATITUDE 38*]

ther north and inland, about an hour's drive from the Golden Gate Bridge, is the wine country, a region of vistas and gracious living. Pinots and Chardonnays are favored close to the coastline and the bay, where temperatures are relatively cool. Premium Cabernets often come from the heart of the Napa Valley, which is sheltered and hotter.

On North Bay waters, much of the fog and seabreeze are blocked or moderated by the coastal hills. Mount Tamalpais rises to an elevation of 2,571 feet, tempering the cool summer northwesterlies and the rainy winter southwesterlies. It's the strongest influence, but not the only influence, on the microclimates that abound here.

In Sausalito, the town closest to the Gate, it is not uncommon to sit in the harbor in summer sunshine and watch a thick wave of fog roll over Wolfback Ridge, trail into streamers, and dissipate before it reaches the harbor. The Sausalito waterfront is not necessarily shirtsleeve-warm on a day like that. One more hill to the east, however, tucked into the cove behind Belvedere Island, there will be people enjoying life in a warm and toasty little sun bubble, with a view across the bay toward skyscrapers half-obscured by a wind-driven fog. Take one more jump east — to the East Bay — and you'll be in Richmond. Then you'll understand why locals call it the Richmond Riviera.

Sausalito is where Ayala started, and that's good enough for us. The town has large, deepwater marinas, boatyards, and a federally-designated anchorage. A selection of California's yachtiest yachts berth here, and so does an aquatic counterculture. One of the high points of the counterculture took place a generation back, when Alan Watts was living on a houseboat at the north end of town. The artist Jean Varda's converted lifeboat went out often, flying its painted sails, and Anais Nin was on hand to capture vignettes for her diaries. The Red Legs played renegade rock & roll concerts on World War

Strawberry Pt.

Kappas Marina

Clipper Marina

Cass Marina Marina Plaza

Schoonmaker

RICHARDSON BAY

TIBURON PENINSULA

San Francisco Yacht Club

Corinthian Yacht Club

TIBURON

Sam's

Belevedere Cove

RACCOON STRAIT

Ayala Cove

N

1/2 mile

Pelican Yacht Harbor

Sausalito Yacht Harbor

SAUSALITO

MARIN PENINSULA

Hurricane Gulch

ANGEL ISLAND

Pt. Knox

Pt. Blunt

Presidio Yacht Club

Coast Guard Station

Yellow Bluff

Horseshoe Cove

SAN FRANCISCO BAY

GOLDEN GATE

GOLDEN GATE BRIDGE

ALCATRAZ ISLAND

[MAP BY JOE SHOULAK]

II dry docks now gone, and rock singer David Crosby, before the drugs got to him, would always take a turn by the Trident restaurant when he was outbound in his Alden schooner *Mayan*. The Trident (in the former S.F. Yacht Club) was the jetset scene of the moment. From this distance, it's not important to know whether Crosby was waving to millionaire record producers, or the dealer-waitresses in their gossamer gowns, or both. Many years later, coming off his Texas jail term, Crosby tracked down and re-purchased the *Mayan*. An Alden is an Alden.

Sausalito was once the site of a Miwok village called Liwanelowa. Later, it was a Spanish land grant held by the Richardson of Richard-son Bay, and later still it was a whaling port and a source of fresh water for the boomtown across the way. Today Sausalito is a hill town with a village feel, and Americans think of it as Mediterranean. The downtown district close to the Sausalito Yacht Harbor was surrendered to the tourist industry decades ago. You can't buy a screwdriver on Bridgeway, but you can buy one of those Official San Francisco Sweatshirts they sell to goosebumped tourists who assumed that, if its 95 degrees in Tulsa, it's 95 in Frisco. Caledonia Street, one block inland along the Pelican Harbor stretch of the waterfront, is the locals' refuge for now.

SAUSALITO

FOR A TOWN THAT IS VERY IMPORTANT to the sailing community, Sausalito lags in amenities for cruising yachts. Few marinas set aside space for guest berthing, but anchoring is legal along most of the waterfront. Buoys mark the areas where it is not (off Dunphy Park and close to the Army Corps of Engineers docks). Sausalito does have a city-owned, officially-sanctioned dinghy landing at the restaurant called Margaritaville, and don't stress yourself over the sign that advertises a 15-minute limit. There is also a free launch ramp on the site.

Richardson Bay is a no-discharge zone, and boats that are going to hang on a hook for very long will have to prove there is nothing going overboard. There is a pumpout service provided for the anchorage. There is also a 72-hour anchoring limit, but cruisers are welcome to apply for a permit for more time. To get it, they should register with the Richardson Bay Harbor Administrator at 289-4143. Getting the permit is not a problem, and you might also get some tips: how to avoid certain unmarked wrecks, for example, and why to prefer a Danforth anchor over a plow in the "liquid mud" and often strong winds of Richardson Bay.

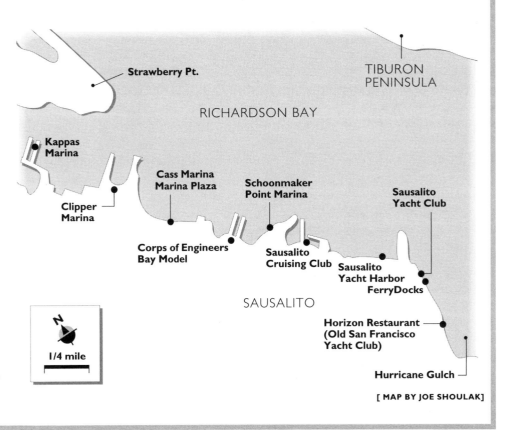

[MAP BY JOE SHOULAK]

The southern end of Sausalito is the mouth of Hurricane Gulch, a canyon exposed to big blasts of the seabreeze. There's a story that a 19th century developer tried to bill it as Shelter Bay, and the locals laughed him down. A few pilings left abandoned in the shallows here mark the remains of the Nunes Brothers Boatworks, builders of the classic Bears, also of Templeton Crocker's mighty, 118-foot *Zaca*, later and more notoriously owned by Errol Flynn. The shingled restaurant on the boardwalk once belonged to San Francisco's most famous madame, Sally Stanford, after she adopted a career as a Sausalito politician that culminated in a stint as mayor. The ridges on either side of the canyon have been home to many a sailor, including actor and author Sterling Hayden.

North of Hurricane Gulch, higher ground creates the Banana Belt in its lee and the first of the anchorages used by visiting boats. There is a long stretch of the town's main street, Bridgeway, that fronts the water along a rock embankment. The waters here don't attract great numbers of boats, but they do seem to attract very large yachts that travel in some estate, with crews and quick shoreboats that dash around the corner to land.

A short distance up the steepest face of the hill above Bridgeway is a modern house that seems to be sitting on the foundations of a castle. Trees have grown up and made the foundation hard to see, but this is where William Randolph Hearst intended to build Hearst Castle, with arched bridges leading across Bridgeway to a private dock. He laid this much of the foundation before the citizenry caught wind of his plans and blocked construction. Hearst moved on to San Simeon.

Two restaurants stand on pilings and reach out from Bridgeway. The larger, two-story building was home to the San Francisco Yacht Club from 1898 (replacing an older structure that burned) until 1926. By that time, heavy traffic ashore, lack of parking, and constant ferry traffic that kept their moored craft rocking and rolling convinced the membership to move to a new site in a protected lee in Belvedere Cove. The move triggered events that might otherwise have taken years: As of the 1920s, most San Francisco YC members (and Corinthian YC members, for that matter) lived and worked in San Francisco. They wanted a city club that could run seven days a week and make yachting some-

Ayala Cove [PHOTO BY PATRICK SHORT]

thing more than a weekend game at the end of a ferry ride. This group included the owners of some of the largest boats in the SFYC and CYC registries. SFYC members added the objection that Belvedere Cove, without dredging, was too shallow for their craft. Calling themselves the Forty-Niners, this group found land at a commanding site in San Francisco, formed a new club, and called it the St. Francis.

A little farther north, Sausalito Yacht Club rests on pilings in a fortunate spot next to the ferry landing, with some half dozen moorings set just off the clubhouse. In the summer, Sausalito YC sponsors a popular Tuesday night "beer can" series, one of many casual events that can be found in every corner of the bay. Just beyond SYC and also on pilings, the Spinnaker Restaurant is a landmark by virtue of its position, jutting east beyond any other point and marking a slight left turn for boats bound upchannel (and marking a point where deep-draft boats should begin to take care to stay in the channel). The most southerly of the town's marinas, Sausalito Yacht Harbor, lies just around the corner, directly off downtown and the tourist industry. It's booked solid by locals. Nothing is set aside for guest berthing, but the harbor is worth a tour for its collection of museum-quality yachts.

Farther north, Sausalito Cruising Club occupies a barge tied up off Dunphy Park, close to Galilee Harbor. Both Pelican Harbor and Marina Plaza have guest slips, though not a lot. Schoonmaker Point Marina, between Pelican Harbor and Marina Plaza, is the one harbor that is conspicuous in accommodating traveling boats. A beach and palm trees provide the landmarks. Many cruisers anchor off Schoonmaker's, where the beach is often used for small boat launching and swimming. The waters off Marina Plaza are also a tempting place to drop a hook, but here the channel is very wide and humming with fishing boats and party boats. Think it through before you pick a spot. One more click to the north, Clipper Yacht Harbor is closest to the town's one big supermarket and two chandleries, Bay Riggers and West Marine, but Clipper sets nothing aside for guest berthing. It's strictly space-available, with a 50-foot maximum. Clipper is also home to the big one among Sausalito boat yards, Anderson's.

Overnighting locals might enjoy going all the way out to the middle of Richardson Bay to drop a hook, and that can be a beautiful thing. Before you go, however, know that the beauty is sometimes compromised by music from waterfront hangouts. Richardson Bay also has shallows, unmarked wrecks, and the occasional flying midnight speedboat. I like it out there, but shine that light.

The far northern end of town, where the water goes shallow, is home to the houseboat marinas, now hooked up to services and not quite the outlaw community of yore. Much of the northeastern end of Richardson Bay belongs to a wildlife sanctuary managed by the Audubon Society from a headquarters on the Tiburon peninsula. That territory is off limits to boats from October to April 1.

The rugged Tiburon peninsula, across Richardson Bay from Sausalito, has been carved into landscaped, gentrified communities reaching south toward Belvedere Cove and, arguably, the most blessed of all the tucked away harbors on San Francisco Bay. Certainly the most rarified. There are no public marinas in Belvedere Cove, but there are two yacht clubs and the ever-popular Sam's Anchor Cafe, famous for burgers al fresco and recognizable from the water by a sign that says, yep, SAM'S. Sam's offers docking for sailors with a hunger or a thirst. Eight boats would be about the max, however, and you could face a crunch on a summer weekend. If you draw more than four feet, you won't fit at the dock at low water, but that's why boats have anchors and dinghies.

A few boats ride to moorings off Belvedere Cove, tempting strangers to make a beeline straight in. Not a good idea. Anyone taking a keelboat to the San Francisco Yacht Club, tucked into the most protected corner of the cove, should take the long way around. The smart route starts at the entry channel to the east, at a green buoy near the downtown ferry dock. From there the channel passes close under the windows of the Corinthian Yacht Club, a grand, white Georgian that conjures up the days when ladies wore white gloves because that's the way things were supposed to be. Note the "basement" of the Corinthian clubhouse, now used for storage and maintenance. That was the original building, but, the members had ambitions. At the end of the channel, the San Francisco YC occupies an unpretentious modern building, with a registry befitting the oldest yacht club on the West Coast.

From the Corinthian YC or Sam's next door, the visiting yachtsman has direct access to Main Street, Tiburon, with shops, restaurants and art galleries. It gets busy here, but not on the scale of downtown Sausalito. The walk from SFYC is longer but pleasant, leading past the China Cabin, a structure that began its life as the social saloon of the SS China, which first docked in San Francisco in 1867. The China Cabin spent part of its history as an "ark," one of the houseboats in which the area's elite families summered in the belle epoche. It has since been removed to a foundation on pilings, and it is open to the public as a maritime museum featuring walnut woodwork, cut-glass floral windows, and chandeliers hung with crystal prisms. Another piece of local history is St. Hilary's, an 1888 Catholic church located up Tiburon hill and visible from most of the town. St. Hilary's is a rare survivor of Carpenter Gothic in its original setting — a small, white, frame structure surrounded by a wildflower garden. Two flowers, the Black Jewel and the Tiburon Paintbrush, grow nowhere else in the world.

The bay views from Tiburon are unsurpassed, and just across Raccoon Strait lies Ayala's second stop, Isla de Nuestra Señora de los Angeles, Angel Island. The island is a state park and a former military installation (a Nike missile site) like so many of the Bay Area's open-space treasures. There are trails for hiking and biking and nine hike-in campsites. Most visitors arrive by ferry. Typically, the island is crowded

"The fog came in on little cat's feet." Nope. The whole cat. [PHOTO BY JOHN RIISE, *LATITUDE 38*]

near the dock and almost empty elsewhere. There are Civil War-era buildings along the trails and reminders of the days when Angel Island was a quarantine and detention center for immigrants, the Ellis Island of the West. The island was stripped of its native trees early in the "American" settlement and later replenished with a variety of stock. And there's enough poison oak to ruin all of next week, so beware. Stay on the trails.

Angel Island is the most popular destination for locals in boats, whether they sail a lap around it, pick up a wind-protected mooring in Ayala Cove, or anchor to the east of the island in what is usually a comfortable lee. You can moor or anchor overnight inside Ayala Cove for a fee. You can also tie up at the docks for a fee, but space is limited. It's first come, first served. Expect strong currents throughout the cove. The docks close at sunset, but there's a glorious interval in the evening, after the last ferry departs, when yachties have the island all to themselves.

Moving "up" the chart, or upriver, as we might better express it, we advance along the Marin shore and enter the lee of the Tiburon Peninsula. Local boats sometimes anchor here in the daytime, especially on holidays when once-a-year sailors are merrily tying granny knots in their anchor rodes at Ayala Cove.

A shallow draft boat can poke into Corte Madera Creek, but freeway bridges cut off access to most sailing craft. Except for private docks lining a marshy shoreline, there is no place to land. The Larkspur Ferry has a terminus here, and windsurfing is popular along the shoreline east of San Quentin. From a windsurfer's point of view, the seabreeze is generally strong and almost warm. Even San Quentin broke into the yachting scene once. A pair of prisoners managed to construct a small boat and paint it (business side only) with letters that read, "San Rafael Yacht Club." They paddled out the channel smiling and waving to the guards. San Quentin can be visited, by the way — by car. Check out the museum and contemplate the lives of people who really, really, really would rather be sailing.

SAN PABLO BAY

San Pablo Bay lost some three feet of depth during the 19th century mining rush in the Sierra. The process went on until 1884, when farmers in the Central Valley obtained a court order that blocked hydraulic mining. They had economic motives to be sure, but — irony or no — we have to note that the first political act that protected the environment of the bay came from those Central Valley farmers.

HOW THE WEST WAS WON
© San Francisco Chronicle, by Kimball Livingston

CALL IT THE AGE OF IRON MEN AND WOODEN SHIPS. Call it the age of romance. But there weren't any iron men, not really. Aboard those graceful, killer contraptions known as sailing ships, there were only creatures of flesh and blood and fortitude, idling through hours of boredom or leaping to a sudden, terror-stricken call of, "All hands!"

They were men who rubbed salt sores in the morning and climbed at midnight to face oblivion — one hand for yourself and one for the ship — clinging to a yardarm, stiff with cold, whipped blue by canvas beating out of control two hundred feet above the sea. The clipper ships could have carried taller masts and more sail, but you couldn't pay men to work any higher than that.

The West wasn't built by cowboys. The West was built by men who wore wet socks for weeks at a stretch. They sailed through the Golden Gate sideways when the wind quit. They hauled in miners and gamblers, lumber and calico, schoolmarms and the mail long before the first railroad spike was laid west of Wichita.

Not much of that heritage is left. Not one clipper ship remains here of the many that collapsed into the mud along the Barbary Coast. The cargo-hauling barkentine, schooner and scow of the San Francisco Maritime National Historical Park — by tonnage, the largest collection in the world — are the neglected stepchildren of a world that moves too fast and a city that won't go near Fisherman's Wharf unless the cousins hit town from Iowa.

But we have those ships. For how long, is yet to be seen.

Sources from the time claim that it took a half century for the rivers to clear out the debris from hydraulic mining, and ebb tides then were browner than they are now. (Hydraulic mining in the 1800s and landfill in the 1900s combined to reduce the overall surface area of the San Francisco estuary from 700 square miles to 400 square miles. Like 'em or not, that's how we got the Bay Conservation and Development Commission.)

The deepwater route through San Pablo Strait is the river channel leading eventually to the Sacramento River and the Delta. About a mile and a half inland from the Richmond-San Rafael Bridge is a scattering of exposed rocks including The Brothers, a onetime lighthouse now operated as a bed and breakfast. Across the bay on the "western" side, a long, staked channel leads past the tiny Marin Islands into San Rafael Creek (locals pronounce it san ruh fel'). Loch Lomond Yacht Club, founded in 1962, and Loch Lomond Marina stand at the entrance to the creek, with a beauty parlor and a bait shop in the bargain. If that's not enough to do you, add a market, a laundry, a chandlery, a marine mechanic, and diesel fuel.

San Rafael Creek, or San Rafael Canal as people call it, is narrow and bordered by houses and apartment buildings, many with docks. Lowrie's Yacht Harbor, about halfway up, has guest slips and marine repairs close by. The creek is navigable for a total distance of about two miles. Then it dead ends against the freeway near the San Rafael Yacht Harbor and Marin County Boat Works. Restaurants and a minor mall are close, and downtown San Rafael can be reached by walking under the elevated portion of the freeway. A landmark civic center designed by Frank Lloyd Wright lies beyond the hills to the north, but the way this stretch of Marin County is laid out, it's clear the planners expected the real people to go there by car. A bicycle-equipped cruising yachtsman can bike from San Rafael to the Marin Civic Center, but you'd better be seriously interested in the architecture. Getting there on the frontage roads is not half the fun. The same biking distance would take you inland to the town of San Anselmo, a better ride, but there's still heavy traffic. San Anselmo is neither overwhelmed by boutiques nor exactly untouched, but the town somehow captures the essence of Marin County — affluent, liberal in its habits though not always liberal in its politics, and blessed with natural surroundings that are unsurpassed in any urban setting anywhere.

San Pablo Bay offers large open expanses, but not all of it is deep enough for a sailboat. The eastern shoreline is industrial, and it's easy to go aground outside the channel at low tide. Anyone bound up-channel is headed for the rivers, whether through Vallejo or the Carquinez Strait.

On the Marin side of San Pablo Bay the shoreline is residential until you get to the large San Rafael Rock Quarry, an unmistakable landmark. The tiny, guano-covered Sisters lie just off the quarry, often with barges anchored nearby, waiting for a load of gravel or rock. Immediately to the east is McNears Beach, a county park with trees and green lawns, a swimming pool, and a long, concrete pier extending into the bay. The anchorage is comfortable in normal summer weather, and world cruisers Jim and Diana Jessie have often sent their cruising students to the McNears Beach-China Camp stretch to simply anchor, ride to the hook, and get the feel of it. "We tell them to not go ashore," Diana said. "They get the full cycle of the tide hauling them in a circle on the hook, and they're around the corner from 'civilization,' so it's an easy, controlled way to get a feel for traveling, and arriving, and being there."

China Camp State Park, just beyond McNears, is a popular stopover, with its rough-hewn shrimping and fishing village preserved from the 1880s. The wooden buildings of the village house a museum, a bait shop and a sandwich shop. Visitors can take a dinghy ashore to enjoy the village, a small beach, and the 1,640-acre park with trails for hiking and biking.

China Camp was one of a number of Chinese shrimping villages on Point San Pedro in the 1880s, when Chinese immigrants were the leading shrimpers of the Bay. The others villages have since disappeared, and only a part of China Camp remains. These were factory towns where whole families lived and worked in isolation. Nowadays you're welcome to anchor overnight off China Camp, but overnight parking of automobiles in the park is not allowed. If you invite friends to meet you, plan accordingly.

A staked channel leads off to the east. A shallow-draft boat can

FASTER HORSES, OLDER WHISKEY, YOUNGER WOMEN, AND SHORTER BOARDS

WINDSURFING WAS BORN IN SOUTHERN California, but it came of age here and in Hawaii, where adventurous spirits developed gear and techniques for high-wind sailing and wave jumping. The original Windsurfer Inc. one-design board was "totally inappropriate up here," recalls sailor/windsurfer/journalist/author Shimon-Craig Van Collie. The original Windsurfer wasn't happy at all in 25 knots. It didn't have foot straps to keep a body aboard, the center of effort in the sail shifted around, and the small fin with the center-board down would flip the board without warning when it developed too much lift.

Van Collie has lived the full development of San Francisco Bay windsurfing, and he's given a writer's thought to the subject, so we turned to him for a look at how the sport grew. What he said went like this:

"Ted McKeown and Glenn Taylor were the pioneers at introduc-

Airtime [PHOTO BY DON HILBUN]

ing boards in the 1970s and building enthusiasm, but right away you had people like Steve Silvester and Bard Chrisman and Bill Hansen and Barbara Ockel who started experimenting with rigs, fins, sails, everything. For one thing, they started chopping off the ends of the boards, and of course they found out right away that short boards were easier to sail in high winds. Maybe we should say they were possible to sail in high winds. Northern California was a fertile area for development; it still is. You've got Larry Tuttle down in Santa Cruz who's a world leader in making fins. You've got Bard who can build anything. And you could argue that Hansen invented the fully-battened sail. He did it to make it easier for people to learn, so the center of effort wouldn't be shifting around, but of course it turned out to be a better sail, period.

"Ockel led the way in building cut-down sails. People called them storm sails, and she and Diane Green were important in inspiring other people to get out on boards. We had a lot of crossovers, too. I remember Roger Hall going from a $500,000 battlewagon that went eight knots to a $5,000 rack of boards and sails that went 25 knots.

"Berkeley was always a good place for boards," Van Collie said. "Crissy Field was prime, but Crissy got more and more crowded, and then you saw people looking around for 'the next place,' which turned out to be Larkspur, Crown Beach at Alameda, Coyote Point, Lake Del Valle, Rio Vista …

"People are still searching for the next undiscovered spot, but at this point, frankly, we've picked it pretty clean. If you want to do slalom, or just get warm, you go to the Delta. If you want to jump waves you go to Waddell Creek or the Lighthouse at Santa Cruz. We have people on the bay who treat this sport like boat sailing — they start out at Crissy Field and cruise over to Angel Island and around and around. Other people are just like downhill skiers; they go back and forth in the same spot all day."

Van Collie once set out to circumnavigate the Farallones on a board. He wasn't yet a father, so it seemed like a good idea at the time, and yes, he had an escort boat. Unfortunately, the God of the Fog was smiling broadly that day upon the Gulf of the Farallones (not that you could see his face), and on the outbound leg, Van Collie recalls, "I was going on instruments until I saw the breakers on the Farallones. That's when I said, `Okaaay, that's enough for me.' "

Six hours out; four back. You shouldn't have asked.

SUMMER IN AMERICA: THE DELTA

THE RIVERS AND SLOUGHS of the California River Delta offer another one thousand miles of navigable waters. Upriver on the San Joaquin or the Sacramento, halfway between the surf and the snow, you will find a region of crops, fisheries, and water wars, the breadbasket of the country's most populous state. Here you will find narrow cuts that connect narrow rivers where sailing craft slip through in a hush. The only sounds are the buzzing of bees in blackberry vines or birds rushing to a twilight feeding. At other times your boat might ride between rock levees, high above the surrounding farmland, the air rich with the scent of plowed fields. And, you will cross intersections near the resorts where sailors share the water with skiers, jetskiers, drift fishermen, and houseboats loaded with kids, waterguns, and maybe a cherrybomb or two. Even without a paddle-wheeler whistling 'round the bend, this is the essence of summer in America.

It takes determination to be a "ditch sailor," but there are plenty of them here, visitors as well as locals sailing out of places such as Martinez, Antioch, or Stockton. They ghost along in the light breezes of the morning, and they barrel along when the breeze howls in the afternoon. Windsurfers who want to be warm while they go fast make a pilgrimage to Rio Vista. Keelboaters meanwhile go aground and get themselves off (a basic maneuver in the Delta), and they time their travels by the tide. In these narrow channels,

going with it or against it can make a difference worth half a day. Heading upriver from the bay, if you time your departure to "catch the tide," you can probably ride flood currents all the way.

For 19th century sailors, the Delta was a winter destination too. They'd moor in some favorite place, build a blind on the deck, and bag ducks until they heard the call of the office. It's not hard to imagine a warm fire in the salon in the evening, and something thirst-quenching and barrel-aged from Tennessee or Scotland, and a story about a traveling salesman, of course.

Good Delta guides already exist. If you're serious about the rivers, look to them. Here, we have a few tips.

Visitors will find marinas and restaurants along many of the waterways. Most cruisers most of the time will stay clear of all that, anchoring in a quiet spot or tying to a tree ashore. It doesn't take a lot of equipment or special planning, but there are a few basics. First, the mosquitoes are voracious, and they want *you*. Take full precautions. Also, carry at least two anchors (and expect them to become muddy in the extreme). You will need two anchors to get a grip fore and aft alongside other boats in popular spots, Potato Slough for example, or by yourself in remote places where there's not enough room to swing to the tide, which is almost everywhere. You'll need a small boat as well, for carrying out the second anchor and dropping it where

you want it, or rowing to a bank to tie a line to a tree in lieu of a second anchor. Arriving at a new anchorage, it's best to tie up or anchor in the fashion of boats already there. And when you're there, you'll want an awning or some other protection from the sun you're there to worship. The summertime heat is serious.

Swimmers — be cautious. The current might take you by surprise. And here's one more caution for those going and coming: Open stretches such as Suisun Bay, just inland from the Benecia-Martinez Bridge, build up an incredibly nasty chop on a windy day. Otherwise, there's not much to worry about in a Delta cruise. Sure, you might have to open some bridges. To do that, just use Channel 9 or blast out the good old one-long, one-short on the air horn. Then, it requires only a little luck to find a private patch of water surrounded by tules, with a meadowlark darting across a blue sky and perhaps, in the distance, a view of a freighter that seems to be plowing through fields of corn.

Take your kids to Central California by boat, and they'll think they've really gone somewhere. One Marin County stockbroker who sailed his kids to Sacramento, "Stayed there two days," as he recalled it. "We walked around Old Town, toured the Capitol building, and learned about the government. The kids ate it up. But if we'd driven there in an hour and a half it might not have meant a thing."

poke into Gallinas Creek, beyond Buck's Launch (with a ramp, boat maintenance and a bit of rustic boatbuilding) and on toward the back door of the Marin Civic Center. The route is swampy, quiet, and a bit adventurous. A more likely and more popular expedition would look toward the Petaluma River, one of the under-appreciated treasures of Northern California. This 14-mile stretch of tidal estuary became officially a "river" in the 1960s and in that stroke of the pen became eligible for dredging with federal dollars. A voyage up the Petaluma River faces few hazards, and it's never far from civilization, but it has that around- the-corner feel.

To get to the corner, however, you start right in "the middle" of San Pablo Bay. Red and green markers funnel you into a channel 100 feet wide and eight feet deep while you're still surrounded by a broad expanse of water on both sides (a broad expanse of very shallow water where egrets feed and no boats sail). Obviously, going on the rising tide has more to recommend it than merely catching a push from the current.

The marsh rises up before you reach Port Sonoma. Now you're in the tules, and you can believe in the river. A railroad swing bridge and a high, arcing Blackpoint highway bridge make Port Sonoma easy to spot on the approach. There are 282 slips, including guest slips, gas, the only diesel on the river, showers and a pumpout station. The Port Sonoma YC is here, and the setting is comfortable, but the roar of Highway 37 robs it of serenity. For that, you'll have to keep going.

But, if you really want to keep going, you'll want that rising tide even if it means waiting around. If you've missed the tide and don't want to stop at the marina, you can find a good anchorage on the east side of the channel close to the highway bridge.

Going on, you're entering the Petaluma Marsh, which surrounds the navigable channel and covers 3,000 acres. This is what you came for. It's said to be the largest tidal marsh on the west coast outside Alaska. It shelters a wealth of vegetation and wildlife. Egret and heron hunt the shoreline. Clapper rails haunt the shallows, and eagles appear from time to time. The vast reach of tule rushes formed a basis of life for the Coast Miwok. The Miwok included tules in their diet, and they wove them into daily necessities: clothing, baskets, thatched houses,

and double-ended boats propelled by paddles or poles.

Pay attention to the tides. Currents run strong. It's easy to run aground in the shallows, but there is plenty of water in the channel even when it feels tight. The river is dredged every four years, 1996 being the most recent excavation. According to the riverman's lore, the river changes course 95 times between the mouth of the river and Petaluma. Sailing scows, the National Maritime Museum's *Alma* among them, once hauled produce downriver from farm country to city markets. Steamboats plied these waters until 1950. If they can make it, so can you, and there are places to anchor out of traffic. Contact the Petaluma visitors' bureau for detailed river information including magnetic headings.

When a highway closes in from the east/north, that's your clue that you are approaching tiny Lakeville, with its lively Greek taverna. Lakeville has overnight docking for a fee. This is the first "destination" beyond Port Sonoma, and by the time you get here, you're well away from the bay. On many a summer day, you'll be able to look over your shoulder and see the fog line far behind you, where it belongs. Beyond Lakeville, the highway turns away from the river again, leaving the channel in peace.

Here's another piece of the riverman's lore, an upriver cruise on a seabreeze day can expect a wind over the transom until Port Sonoma. That wind is the bay seabreeze bending to follow the topography as it works its way inland. Then, expect the wind to clock and come from ahead, from the northwest. You get your downwind payback on the return, if you're lucky and you've been good.

In Petaluma, the Petaluma Marina is a comfortable, modern facility alongside Highway 101. Most visitors, however, will want to continue under the Highway 101 bridge to the Petaluma Turning Basin, where there are guest docks close to the Petaluma Yacht Club, and a half-block walk takes you to the historic buildings of downtown. Enroute to the Turning Basin, your way is blocked by the D Street Bridge — a classic drawbridge — and the operators request a minimum of four hours' notice to open it (between 6 p.m. and 6 a.m., 24 hours). Visitors are welcome at the Turning Basin, but berthing is competitive, so call ahead. You can also anchor out. Docents from the Petaluma Historical Museum lead walking tours of downtown every Saturday and Sunday morning, and you won't use up all the restaurants in one visit.

THE EAST BAY

The East Bay is big, thriving, and diverse. Richmond lies at the northern extreme, at the head of Contra Costa ("the opposite coast") County. To the south lie Berkeley and Oakland, part of Alameda County.

The central sailing feature in the East Bay is the wind slot, the windy zone directly downwind from the Golden Gate. Berkeley sits squarely in the path, making it the coolest and foggiest of the East Bay harbors. Points north and south are all protected to some degree, and that sets the tone of things.

Richmond and Point Richmond blossomed in the 1970s and 1980s, but the sailing roots had already grown deep. The Richmond Yacht Club, organized in 1932, is a power on the racing scene, and the residential community around it is rich in sailing talent. The village of Point Richmond lies about a mile and a half away beyond a tunnel that cuts through the hill. You will find restaurants and shops, good people, an easygoing ambiance, and almost nothing in the way of tourist traffic. To get there from the harbor, however, you need a plan. It's not a great walk.

Sailors of many stripes think of Richmond as their home on the water, but the area is especially good for youth sailing and dinghy racing. The harbor and the nearby waters are well north of the wind slot, and they're protected by Angel Island, so conditions are mild. Richmond Yacht Club has a consistently top-ranked junior program, and the yard is always full of dinghies and dry-sailed keelboats. The late Bob "Big Daddy" Klein, twice an RYC commodore, mentored the sailing program for decades and reinforced the message of the sign that hangs in the clubhouse, "This club was built for fun."

Richmond is also rich in marina berthing, especially since the addition of the 750-slip Marina Bay on the Inner Harbor. Up the Santa Fe Channel from there you will find the Richmond Yacht Harbor, Channel Marina, instant powerhouse Keefe-Kaplan Maritime, and the San Pablo Yacht Club. Richmond in the summer is protected by Angel Island from the full force of the seabreeze, and people who headquarter here, or live here, like to call it the Richmond Riviera. A lot of the time, it deserves the name. Sailors from other parts of the bay have been known to cruise through, with or without a stop, simply for the sake of good sailing.

Leaving Richmond for San Pablo Bay, you find refineries dotting the Contra Costa shoreline. The tankers that service the industry, hauling bulk liquids, make up by far the greatest volume of Richmond's commercial shipping. Annual traffic of more than 1,500 vessels is the norm. Going the other way — sailing south from Richmond on a seabreeze day — you leave the "riviera" behind.

Berkeley is windy on most summer days, with the breeze coming directly from the Golden Gate. Sailors returning from West Bay races enjoy coming home, "downwind all the way." But of course, there's no lee when they get here.

The Berkeley Yacht Club dominates the harbor entrance, with sweeping views of the bay across a rock jetty that protects the channel. BYC sponsors a full calendar of events including the Nimitz Regatta, a popular midwinter series on the Circle co-hosted with Metropolitan YC, and evening races.

The Berkeley Marina has 1000 slips, and the Berkeley Marine Center adds another 60. Both offer gas and diesel. The Marina has a pumpout station, and it has ample guest berthing with the best facilities in the harbor.

Windsurfers come to Berkeley to make sailing a high-velocity event. The waters south of the marina, semi-enclosed by the Emeryville Marina (one more hop down the beach), loom large in the lore of the pioneers. On the north-south axis, it's a great reach, and if everything goes to the dogs, you're surrounded by a lee shore. For the same reason, Berkeley is a productive dinghy training ground for the Cal sailing team. The University operates an aquatic adventures program here, and the welcoming Cal Sailing Club next door (not a part of UC) grows good sailors on low dues and shared work.

There are waterview restaurants in the harbor, and just a taxi ride away, the city of Berkeley offers a cultural extravaganza. The Fourth

Street neighborhood, just beyond the I-80 Freeway, is the closest scene, with a variety of shopping and restaurants.

Set in the hills to the east, the UC campus can be recognized by the Campanile set off from the larger buildings around it. Cal, as its devotees call it, has an enrollment of 30,000. Higher up the hill is U.C.'s Botanical Garden, a 32-acre facility recalling John Muir's words that, "When California was wild, it was the floweriest part of the continent." Berkeley has museums, parkland, and a city character unduplicated elsewhere, even among the great university towns. No place in North America is farther to the left than "Berzerkeley," and at the same time it's a mecca for science and the arts and the art of good living, a place where Alice Waters could start a restaurant in a woodframe building and build it into a revolution in cuisine — Chez Panisse — with international repercussions.

Sailing south from Berkeley, you have to take pains to avoid the Berkeley Pier, half a mile of used and useful fishing pier in its current edition — plus a derelict ex-ferry landing extending nearly two miles farther into the bay. The Berkeley City Council has been dithering for years about the falling-down parts, and you could figure they would have done something by now if they were going to do anything at all. Opinion is divided as to whether the crumbling pier is forming fish habitat or a tidal dam. Ironically, the pier was finished just in time to be made obsolete by the opening of the Bay Bridge. You'll find it marked on the chart as "ruins."

Emeryville is the next stop south, an industry-and-condo community with Emeryville City Marina and Emery Cove Marina offering more than 400 slips apiece, gas and diesel, and restaurants. Pay attention to the narrow entry channel, because the water outside the channel is seriously shallow. In the 1990s, Emeryville-east-of-the-freeway achieved a new life, attracting loft-living artists and trendy eateries. The weather here is about what you find at Berkeley, meaning that it gets straight-shot seabreeze from the Golden Gate, but the berthing can be good.

Treasure Island is a place with a future yet to take shape. Built as landfill for the 1939 Golden Gate International Exposition, it once housed a fantasy world of "Mayan" pyramids and a 400-foot-tall Tower

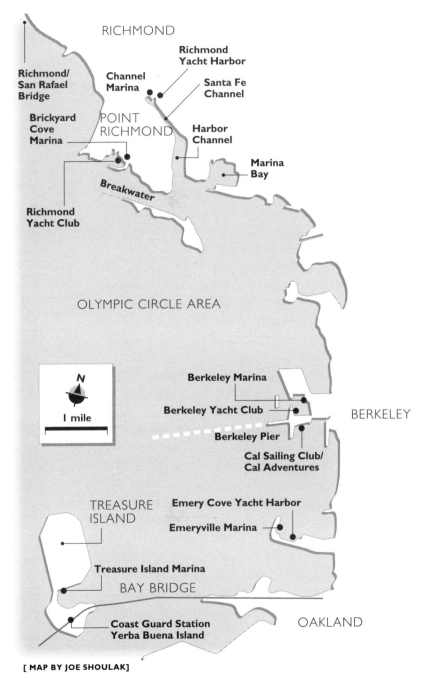

[MAP BY JOE SHOULAK]

of the Sun. The island was formed, all 400 acres of it, from an outline of quarried rock that was then filled with 20 million cubic feet of sand and mud dredged from the bottom of the bay. With World War II, it was quickly converted to use by the Navy. However, that soft fill and the earthquake perils associated with it were still haunting the place in the 1990s as the Navy returned the island to the city of San Francisco, and the city studied how to use it. One of the largest structures on the island was put to work as a sound stage for film production even before the Navy started packing, but the larger future of the island was still in debate as *Sailing the Bay* went to press.

Technically, TI was built as a peninsula extending north from Yerba Buena Island, the 345-foot tall rock with the tunnel connecting the east and west spans of the Bay Bridge. Technically, they're one island, but the promoters of the 1939 Exposition saw some sense in having their own island, at least in name, and "Treasure Island" had a certain ring. Freudian perhaps?

Clipper Cove, sheltered between Treasure Island and the wooded rise of Yerba Buena, holds a formerly all-military small-boat harbor and the Treasure Island Yacht Club, recognized (for one thing) for its popular small-boat regattas in the waters just east of the harbor. Yerba Buena — Goat Island, if you're really an old goat — remains military. Yerba Buena is headquarters to Coast Guard Group San Francisco and to shoreside maintenance for buoys and buoy tenders. The handsome house on the south side of the island, above the lighthouse, is home to the Commander of the Pacific Area.

O AKLAND AND ALAMEDA TOGETHER FORMED one of the earliest, powerful sailing centers in the bay. Boating was popular here even before 1902, when a channel was opened to extend the Oakland Slough and transform Alameda from a peninsula to an island. The dig produced the Oakland Inner Harbor, or "estuary" as it's doomed to be known, some 33 years after a different part of the

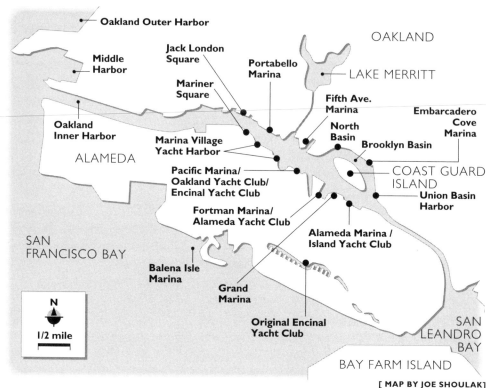

[MAP BY JOE SHOULAK]

slough was dammed off to form Lake Merritt, a small-boat haven now marked by parkland and high rise towers.

Approaching the estuary from the bay, coming in from the west or the north, it can be hard to pick out the relevant buoys and landmarks against a background of industrial flatlands and populated hills. You'll want to use a proper chart, but there's a handy rule of thumb — steer to put the big, white container cranes on your port side. Supposedly, those white container movers inspired the Imperial Walkers of *Star Wars*. Certainly, they provide your handiest reference, and they're 15 stories high, so you can spot them if you can see anything at all. The Seventh Avenue Terminal is the port's farthest reach into the bay. Its artificial, angular corners make it instantly recognizable on the chart (to the north of the Middle Harbor). There are four white cranes on the long side and one white crane on the short side, between the Outer Harbor Channel and the Inner Harbor Channel. It's the Inner Harbor Channel that you will be following, and when you're there looking at it, the next moves are obvious.

Once you've cleared the Oakland Outer Harbor and entered the confines on the Inner Harbor Channel, the former Alameda Naval Air Station will be on your starboard side — a low lying stretch, except for the hangars — and a low-lying railyard area will be on your port side. There are more white cranes ahead, and they'll appear to port, so the rule of thumb still works, though now we have plenty of other clues.

The Oakland Channel is the most industrialized of the popular boating areas in the bay. It doesn't have the nature-magic of Marin or the physical drama of the San Francisco cityscape, but this is a fascinating cruise. It's an economics lesson when the container docks are busy. It's also a peaceful retreat in the upper reaches, and well clear of the wind slot. Native legends tell of people who went sailing without getting cold, or even wet. The Port of Oakland ranks fifth in volume among U.S. container ports. It sits at a hub of railroad lines. The port has invested heavily in its intermodal role and in its ties to Asia. As much as 88 percent of the Port of Oakland's annual volume is containerized, and nearly fourth-fifths of the total volume is in Asian trade.

Besides industry and shipping, the Oakland Channel has condos and houseboats, marine repair, and 14 marinas with 3,900 slips plus end ties and dry storage.There also are some eight haulout facilities, a like number of chandleries, more than a dozen sailmakers and canvas makers, and scads of shops offering specialized services. Svendsen's, Grand, and Stone's all do fine work; Stone's can accommodate very large boats, and the yard maintains ties to a history that goes back to the beginnings of yachting on the bay. What sailors remember along here, however, is the weather. On a "normal" summer day, sailors headed home along this route shed layers of foulies and sweaters as they go, leaving the chill of the bay behind. This is a Warm Zone (it's south of

> THE SO-CALLED OAKLAND ESTUARY has carried that name so long that it's hopeless to try to change it, but, just for the record, this is really the Oakland Shipping Channel or Oakland Inner Harbor, and it's one more component of the estuarine system. The Oakland Shipping Channel began its life long ago as a shallow inlet with tricky sandbars and a marshy border. The forested peninsula to the south of it became an island, Alameda, in 1902, when a canal was opened to enhance tidal flow.

the wind slot), and that's part of the draw.

The Naval Air Station began to convert to civilian use in 1997. First up was Nelson's Boat Yard, which moved from the channel to a hangar opposite the former seaplane lagoon (and the moored ships of the Ready Reserve Fleet). You won't spot Nelson's from the channel, but you will find the channel bending to the right, inbound, just about where the Naval Air Station quits. On the opposite shore, to port, lies the heart of Oakland's waterfront, Jack London Square. The Square stands at the foot of Broadway, an important connector that runs north-south across the city. Restaurants, shops, and history are close at hand here, including Heinold's First and Last Chance Saloon, where the author of *The Call of the Wild* and *The Sea Wolf* drank whiskey, traded jokes and did some early writing. Owned by the Port of Oakland, Jack London Square has 193 slips and a guest dock with gas and diesel. There's plenty to do close by, but if you want to get into the city itself, you'll want a cab. There's the Oakland Museum, with its California collection, and Chinatown, which is smaller than San Francisco's Chinatown but not the tourist trap the larger one has become.

The Posey Tube crosses under the channel just east of Jack London Square, linking Alameda to the "mainland" with two lanes of auto traffic each way. From the water, you won't see it, but you can make out the stucco towers that mark the entrance at each end.

On the Alameda side, the first marina you will come to is Mariner Square, which led the charge in a 1970s-80s yachting boom along the estuary. More development followed elsewhere and stole the momentum, but this is still a lively place with 100 slips, a guest dock, and marine services including yacht sales, yardwork and a sail loft. Farther east, also on the Alameda side, is the large Marina Village Yacht Harbor, occupying the site of the former Bethlehem Shipyard . At Bethlehem, working heroes forged steel and fashioned it into complete transports — doubletime — during World War II. Marina Village has 750 slips, guest docking, restaurants, laundry, and a pumpout. It's the kind of place that will take out ads in the fall to congratulate "the Marina Village cruising class," listing all its boats that are headed south with the season. Pacific Marina, adjoining, belongs to the vigorous Oakland Yacht Club, once home territory to everybody's favorite local, Jack London. And no, you're not the first person to notice that the Oakland Yacht Club has packed up and left Oakland. But the San Francisco Yacht Club is no longer in Sausalito, much less San Francisco, and Cape Canaveral became Cape Kennedy became Canaveral again, and Lagerfeld designed for Chanel, and …

Forget it.

Almost next door is the Encinal Yacht Club, which moved across the island, to this site, when its property on the south shore and the waters around it were swallowed by a landfill development in the mid-1950s. A swimming pool next to a grassy lawn maintains a link with an earlier time, when EYC's clubhouse at the end of a long south shore pier made it a swimming club as well as a sailing club.

For a mind-twisting experience, pick up an Alameda streetmap and take an excursion across the island to the south end of Grand Street, which once led straight to the EYC pier. Now, instead of stopping at the original shoreline, the pavement keeps right on going, leading into a landfill neighborhood of ranch houses and squared-off lagoons. But don't go there yet. First, turn off into the old Gold Coast neighborhood that is still rich in big houses, green lawns, and tall shade trees. Except, there's no coast there (which is not to be confused with reports of Oakland, of which Gertrude Stein may or may not have meant to say, "There's no there there"). Once, the movers and shakers built their waterfront houses on the Gold Coast. Now those houses are almost in the middle of town.

Continuing, we follow the big fill that pushed the shoreline southward. There is a long beach with extended shallows and sun-warmed water. Temperatures of 69 degrees Fahrenheit are not unheard of. Usually, you can let a toddler wade around without fearing the little nipper's ankles will freeze off — and the south shore is one of the mildest places to learn windsurfing in San Francisco Bay.

Around Alameda, they capitalize South Shore. The beach lies east of Grand Street, and it's a good place to wet your toes. While we're on this side of the island, we should also travel west of Grand and take a look at Ballena Bay, a combination of land development and harbor development dating to the 1960s . It occupies a hook of filled land to the west of the 1950s fill. Ballena Bay has waterfront homes, 455 slips, and 3,000 feet of end ties with guest slips, gas and diesel, laundry and all that goes with the above. Also the Ballena Bay YC, which boldly launched the Pacific Cup race to Hawaii (and that was a good idea).

Now let's cross the island again and pick up our estuary tour where we left off. Leaving Marina Village Yacht Harbor and Pacific Marina, keeping our attention on the Alameda side for the moment, we continue eastish to a high-energy center, the Fortman Marina (since 1904), with 495 slips and the Alameda Yacht Club. After that comes Grand Marina with 384 slips, gas, and diesel. And that leaves — one more, Alameda Marina with 520 slips and dry storage. The comprehensive Svendsen's Boat Yard is here, and so is the productive Island Yacht Club, sponsor of the Silver Eagle race.

On the Oakland side of the channel, we find the Portobello and Fifth Avenue Marinas, with some 200 slips between them. Just a little farther along, Coast Guard Island guards the horseshoe-shaped Brooklyn Basin, with the North Basin (104 slips and a pumpout) and Embarcadero Cove Marina (119 slips and the Metropolitan Yacht Club). MYCO, as Metropolitan is widely known, has been a strong supporter of ocean racing, and for many years it ran the popular midwinter races on the Olympic Circle. Now MYCO shares the midwinters with Berkeley YC. Next door is Quinn's Lighthouse Restaurant, a functioning lighthouse at a spot farther west until it was barged to this location. Limited overnight berthing is possible through MYCO. Overnighters could also anchor in Brooklyn Basin, close to the fixed bridge that runs to Coast Guard Island.

Coast Guard Island houses the headquarters of the Pacific Area Command. Full-sized cutters tie up here, and military operations are planned here on a scale that would amaze you if you think the Coast Guard is just the people running around in inflatables on Opening Day. That is, if you don't think of the Coast Guard as operating in

On the Circle, you can pick your weather [PHOTO BY ROB MOORE, *LATITUDE 38*]

Guam and the South China Sea, the Red Sea, and beyond. For more about the Coast Guard command, see page 30.

The Brooklyn Basin fixed bridge effectively closes off east-side access to the channel. To go farther, you will first have to go back around Coast Guard Island. From there, a complete trip around Alameda will take you under a lifting railroad bridge and three bascule bridges at Fruitvale Avenue, High Street, and Park Street, respectively. Unless your mast height is 13 feet or less, you'll have to get those bridges open to sail on into the marshy San Leandro Channel and the waters of the great South Bay.

THE SOUTH BAY

The South Bay is shallow, and lack of water limits the cruising, but the South Bay has its attractions, especially for locals who think they've seen it all. Marinas are the only likely destinations except at Redwood

City, which has its own marinas and, nearby, sloughs for the anchoring with egrets on the march.

Sailing into the South Bay from the north, you will find plenty of water initially. These are active waters for cruising and racing. North of the San Mateo Bridge, even a deep-draft boat will find plenty of room to play, but a glance at the chart will reveal how quickly it goes shallow, especially along the eastern reach. The most northerly of the marinas — Brisbane, Oyster Point and Oyster Cove — are located just north of the San Francisco International Airport. They are modern and well equipped, with guest docks, friendly natives, pumpout stations and restaurants. Oyster Point, which has the Oyster Point Yacht Club and a fuel dock pumping gas and diesel, is surrounded by a 33-acre park with trails and promenades and a sandy swimming beach.

San Bruno Mountain is the most prominent geographical feature here. The mountain creates a wind hole out in the bay that can make for ideal drifting, lunching, and basking early in the day. When the seabreeze gets serious, the hole shrinks in a hurry.

South of the airport, Coyote Point Marina can be recognized from afar by the dark clump of trees that top a small hill there. The shoreline farther south will appear on a range to the left of the hill, no matter how close to the western shore you sail, because the shoreline turns steadily to the "left." The forested hill is part of a park that surrounds the marina, the Coyote Point Yacht Club, and a restaurant. The South Bay is in full character enroute to Coyote Point — the long expanse of open water, the golden hills to the east, the industry lining the shore.

The beach just north of Coyote Point is a popular windsurfing site, favored for the seabreeze that funnels in south of San Bruno Mountain, through the San Bruno

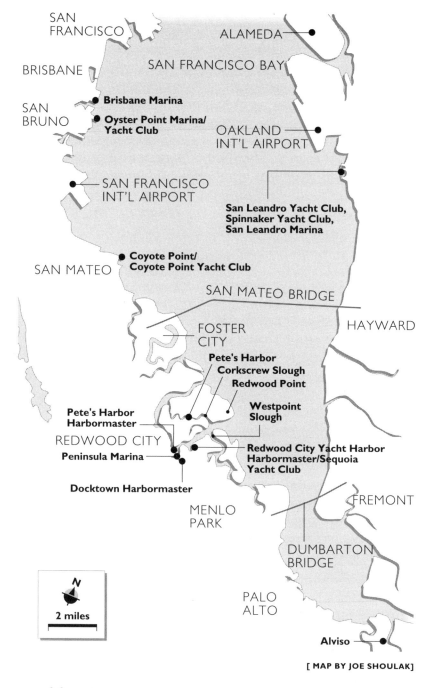

[MAP BY JOE SHOULAK]

Gap. It's a tight reach out and a broad reach back (see page 113).

Across the bay from Coyote Point is San Leandro and the San Leandro Marina. Spinnaker Yacht Club and the San Leandro Yacht Club are here, and guest berthing at the marina is free the first night. If you arrive after hours, tie up below the office. The fuel dock sign says Friday through Sunday, but if the office is occupied you can probably get fuel at other times. Boats do not anchor out. The marina is high quality and aggressively marketed to the local boating community. It is the only east-side port in the South Bay. (South of San Leandro, along the eastern reach, the only cruising destination is Newark Slough — rich in wildlife and part of the San Francisco Bay National Wildlife Refuge, but not a refuge for deep-draft boats).

The San Leandro entrance channel is about two miles long and 200 yards wide. It is marked by stakes and dredged to a depth of six or seven feet. There are four restaurants at the marina, which is surrounded by parkland and a golf course. The nearest grocery stores and laundry facilities are about one mile inland.

Sailing ever deeper into the South Bay, toward the San Mateo Bridge and points south, the sailor will find the seabreeze (feeding through the San Bruno Gap) bending to the south and settling in at about 290 degrees between the bridge and Redwood City. By the time you get to Redwood City, generally, temperatures are up 10 or 15 degrees from West Bay temperatures, and winds are down 5 or 10 miles per hour.

There are radical depth changes too, but they're no secret. Look at the chart, where the channel approaches the San Mateo-Hayward Bridge from the north, and you will see how the western side of the channel drops off in depth — as if you were running into a wall — when all you can see on the surface is the bridge coming closer. But there's no Big Lesson here. Look at the chart and stay in the channel.

If necessary, we could say it again, very slowly …

Early on a summer day, you might find winds from the north or east near Redwood City. It happens whenever a local thermal develops and draws in the surrounding air (see page 113). The local thermal ends whenever the seabreeze takes over. Redwood City is the most popular destination in the South Bay, with boatyards, restaurants, and three marinas. Redwood City was born as a shipping point for redwoods. Now it is an industrial seaport, with ocean going ships to 30,000 dead weight tons calling here, usually for recycled, shredded metal or gypsum (useful in making plaster of Paris and fertilizer). The ship traffic is not heavy, perhaps 25 ships a year, but there are many more barges that come here to load aggregates (gravel) that are trucked in from elsewhere, or the ships load salt taken from evaporation ponds that occupy much of the southern shoreline. At Redwood City you might see white mountains of salt being shoved around by road graders. Most of that salt goes to the Pacific Northwest for use in the paper industry, but some of it is on its way to your table.

Redwood City offers areas to anchor out in the sloughs at a near remove from marinas and industry. Here, in the marshes, the atmosphere is a bit like that of that of the Delta. Egrets pick their way through the tules. There are blue herons on the hunt and seals slipping through the deeper waters.

The Redwood City entrance is authorized to 30 feet and dredged to something close to that. The first turn to the south leads into Westpoint Slough, where local sailors go to raft up, party, and watch the sun set. A mile and a half farther in, Smith Slough turns off to the northwest, feeding into Steinberger Slough, which is navigable at high tide (by dinghies and kayaks) and leads back out to the bay. The sloughs separate Bair Island from the surrounding land and marshes and turn it into a defacto nature preserve. The chart indicates a depth of five feet at the mouth of Smith Slough, and 50 footers sometimes anchor here.

Sequoia Yacht Club is located in the 200-slip Redwood City Yacht Harbor, where there are guest slips, pumpouts, and a restaurant. Farther along are the Peninsula Marina (with 417 slips, guest dock, pumpouts, laundry facilities, and nearby restaurants) and Pete's Harbor, with 280 slips, guest berthing, pumpout and the Harbor House restaurant. There's a movie theatre within walking distance, but not a grocery store. And by the time you get to the head of Redwood Creek, as far as you can go, the scene is thick with industry, boatyards, and anchored boats, some of which seem to have gone there to die and almost succeeded.

South of Redwood City, the waters are seriously shallow. Marshland and salt evaporation ponds line the shores to the right and left. However, a boat with a draft under five feet will be okay, especially if you bring a dinghy and a kedging anchor. The fishing is good, and there are so few visitors that you feel like an adventurer. Palo Alto used to be a destination, but the city chose to let the harbor silt in and return to wildland; there are windsurfers sailing out of Palo Alto, but no keelboats. The only cruising sites south of the Dumbarton Bridge are the quiet anchorages of Newark Slough, just south of the Railroad Swing Bridge, and Alviso, once a busy sailing center but silted in and languishing now — by turns tumbledown or pristine but rich in character. Coyote Creek and Alviso Slough wind for more than four miles, growing shallower as they go, before they reach Alviso. You can anchor along the slough or continue to the South Bay Yacht Club, where shrimpers often occupy the docks but yachties are always welcome. You needn't be afraid of the wintertime. Folks here keep a huge pile of firewood handcut by members. There aren't a lot of visitors, however, and once you arrive, your docking options are zero. So call ahead.

South Bay YC is a turn of the century frame structure, well broken in, homey and friendly with a view across the tules on one side and down into sunken Alviso on the other. Along the slough, the tules are taking over — a recent phenomenon, locals say — and not many of the boats there appear to be navigable. Most are sinking roots into the mud.

Alviso was a major shipping port until a railroad arrived in the 1880s and stole the port's trade in shipping grain and fruit north, mostly to San Francisco. The wells that were dug to make agriculture reliable, meanwhile, caused the subsidence that helps make Alviso a memorable call for people with a certain sense of adventure. Without levees, the town could flood and cease to exist. There are grocery stores and good restaurants just a few blocks from the tules, and over it all lies an atmosphere that is close to surreal. Picture a bright, prim Victorian festooned with petunia pots sitting next to a rumbling semi-trailer truck lot next to a collapsing industrial building that would be a collectible item, if the right artist signed it. I liked Alviso, and it is absolutely as far south as you can take a boat. When you've been here, you've been to the end of San Francisco Bay. ⚓

"When I leap into a pit I leap headlong." Dimitri Karamazov [PHOTO BY DON HILBUN]

OUTSIDE: BEYOND THE GATE

"It's the wilderness experience that brought me into sailing. It's more of an escape route, or dynamic, than anything else I've found." — ALEXIS MONSON

"Forty on the stupid!" — SARAH B.

IMAGINE A CLEAR EVENING, with a westerly breeze to stir the sails and the downtown towers flashing gold astern. There's an ocean off the bow, and that's the goal. Let the gentlest of chop lick the leeward rail. Let a quick tug on the leech cord take the flutter out of the jib. As long as we're dreaming, let's make it good.

The fishing fleet of the day is inbound through the Golden Gate, and passing among those boats, we're not going to assume that every skipper is driving instead of filleting. This is part of our instinct of self preservation. And if it's as cool as we expect, we'll be dragging out the long underwear and extra socks long before the sun hits the horizon. We'll probably be pulling them on even before we pass under the arc of the bridge with its load of growling traffic (homebound to canyons where Mercedes are common as dirt, and cheaper).

The north wall of the strait is made of scarfaced Franciscan sandstone rising to a peak of 938 feet at Wolfback Ridge. Below the surface, the canyon wall plunges 350 feet to a layer of thick silt and beyond that to the carved bedrock that, in the ice ages, was a river bed and a mountain pass.

Off the quarter, the late sun bends into rainbows in the spray.

Off the bow, the front yard stretches all the way to Hilo, Tonga, Sydney, Hong Kong, Vladivostok …

Beyond the wind funnel, the winds ease. The hull lifts and falls on long swells, and the view opens to a line from Point Reyes on the north to Point San Pedro on the south. The lighthouses are already switched on, and the channel buoys are flashing.

The sun grows large, and it sinks all at once, leaving a mercury, twilight glow.

This is the peace of the sea, and the purposefulness in simply being, that lies at the center of Alexis Monson's not-so-accidentally contradictory "escape route, or dynamic." All who love the sea have felt it. When it is good, there is nothing better. Those who love the sea beyond infatuation love it all the more for knowing the other moods of the sea as well: the days of too much weather, of slabsided, bonechilling waves and bumps and bruises and the thought, "Yessir, if Sarah could see me now, she'd bet the whole forty on me."

THE GULF OF THE FARALLONES runs thirty-four miles, northwest to southeast, from Point Reyes to Point San Pedro; it runs twenty-three miles, northeast to southwest, from the Golden Gate to the Farallon Islands. During most of the "sailing season," the windflow is northwesterly, but there's one occasional variant we haven't talked about yet: Point Reyes, jutting into the windstream, can act as a spoiler, with an eddy trailing off to the south and a mild breeze working north inside it. And, if you sail offshore often enough, you will discover that an obstructing land mass — Point Reyes for example — can speed the wind around it and turn a stiff breeze into a gale.

The deepest part of the Gulf of the Farallones is the trench carved by the tidal currents as they rush through the Golden Gate. Surrounding that, just as you would expect to find at the mouth of any river system, there is a silted, sandy region and a shallow bar that sometimes kills boats and people.

The San Francisco Bar arcs in a semicircle around the entrance to the bay, extending halfway to the Sea Buoy. It is prevented from damming the approach by the scouring of the tides and the occasional intervention of dredges, which maintain the shipping channel at a depth of 55 feet. That depth is just barely enough water to accommodate large ship traffic and create a safe route in most, but not all, sea conditions.

The northerly segment of the bar, the Fourfathom Bank, hits depths of less than 23 feet in places — and a lot less than that, in the same places, when big waves suck water out of the troughs. The shallowest and most dangerous portion lies closest to Point Bonita. We call it the Potatopatch Shoal, or simply the Potatopatch.

Small boats can cross the bar in reasonable safety in mild to moderate weather. Fishing boats often work right on the bar. But you have to remember the im-

pact of shallow water on the action of wave and swell. The generalities are simple: Over shallow water, waves grow higher and steeper. The particulars are more complex: Rarely, but definitely, small boats have been destroyed along with the people aboard on golden, calm days. Waves come out of nowhere. Something steep and breaking rolls in cross-pattern, landing on the deck like a hammer as the keel grounds on the sand and then busts through the bottom of the boat. Yes? Maybe? It's hard to be sure.

Small boat traffic is not barred from the bar. But don't go there in rough weather, ever. And don't go there in mild weather without think-

GREMLINS AND BLACK HOLES ON THE SOUTHERN BAR

THIS CORRESPONDENT ONCE BLUNDERED into a stormy night on the southern bar and never even saw the wave that dropped right out from under the boat.

The sensation of tumbling into a black hole ended in a solid "whack" at the trough, and I was marooned for an instant in a pit in the ocean that felt as deep as the pit-fall in my stomach. The helm of our thirty-foot yacht afforded an arresting perspective on the moving breaker that towered above us, briefly, then crashed down hard and cold. Hard enough, and spilling water deep enough, to touch a moment's wonder: Have we been cashed in?

Then — our little champ popped up, on her feet and sailing. I love that boat. Maybe I was needing a good, deep breath when we got to the top of the next wave, but instead, I choked. Up ahead, shining in the loom of the lights of the city, something vastly more vast than a breadbox was breaking from all the way

left to all the way right. And just when I had seen enough to believe, the bottom fell out again. It was three o'clock in the morning. Since the witching hour, after steering some nine hours, I had been seeing little green gremlins dancing on the wavetops. Now I was suffering visions of icy, dark fluids wriggling about my knees.

Some wave.

And on top of that one, the view was unchanged. Granddaddy was still breaking. A little green gremlin perched atop the sheet winch, saluted smartly, and said, "Standing by to alter course, Sir."

It was a tricky turn. If we were caught broadside in the dark and rolled over, we wouldn't come back. And if there was any lesson in helm versus sea — any principle that you could copy on parchment and post on the bulkhead — I would certainly share it. But, all I remember is surviving the turn, thanks to a good hand on the sheets. That gremlin can sail with me anytime.

In recollection, that was one of the great thrill rides of my life, but I never went back for a re-ride. In a southerly the bar is at its worst. Wave patterns mix unpredictably. The resulting nonpattern hints at a treachery undesirable in the medium that supports one's vessel. In English, that means stay away.

ing of the early Greek mariners. They experienced the behavior of the sea as explorers and interpreted the things that happened to them as well as they knew how. Everything that happened, they believed, was the whim of a god, and the gods who followed them over the sea were perverse, unpredictable, spiteful, and scary.

The modern, sensual sailor expects to see water on deck from time to time, but how many of us have every stood ankle-deep in a fast-moving river of potatoes? Coastal schooners laden with spuds from Bodega Bay lost many an escaping deck load on the northern bar, and they cursed this place as the #|!@|! Potatopatch Shoal. Or so the story goes. Several yachties since have had their own inner potatoes whipped and mashed in the Potatopatch.

Northbound, anything smaller than a ship (definition: ships carry boats) can use the Bonita Channel, a narrow way leading between the Marin headland and the Potatopatch. Three red-flashing buoys mark its western border. A green-flashing, green buoy marks the shallow Sears Rock and Centissima Reef to landward. The Bonita Channel is only three-tenths of a mile wide, with currents that run north to south through most of the tide cycle. Bonita Channel currents ebb (south to north) only during the two hours or a bit more before maximum ebb. It's worth remembering … No, let's say it this way: Never forget that, when the bar is breaking, some of the whitest, nastiest water in the whole Potatopatch boils up just west of the channel, and breakers often intrude into the Bonita "Channel."

There is no colorful name attached to the Southern Bar, which shoals to as little as 32 feet, even in the so-called South Channel that parallels Ocean Beach. This one is simply not an option on a foul day.

The Main Ship Channel runs in an almost straight course, bearing slightly to port inbound. Where the channel cuts through the bar, the lane is roughly 900 yards wide and marked by eight buoys, four in line on the north side flashing green, and four in line on the south side flashing red. This holds with the old rule, "Red right returning." Inbound, a vessel in the channel will have the red buoys on its right, or starboard, side.

Inbound ships keep to the south side of the channel. Outbound ships keep to the north, and little boats keep out of the way.

The southern side of the shipping channel is usually smoother than the north side, and there is room for a small boat to sail just outside the red buoys (south of them) while keeping deep water and avoiding the ship channel at the same time. In low visibility, this might be the most comfortable route.

The channel is the safest place to be, but don't assume that it's always an easy ride. In his *Marine Weather Handbook: Northern & Central California*, NOAA commander Kenneth Lilly, Jr. documents a day when a 12-foot ocean wave pattern, while building up 20-foot breakers on the bar (at indicated water depths of 24 feet), produced waves in the outermost part of the channel of 15 to 18 feet. That will get your attention. At the same time waves decreased in height in the deeper waters farther east until they were down to six feet in the Golden Gate.

Commander Lilly includes a reminder that when we hear wave height reported or predicted, we are speaking of significant wave height, which is taken as an average of the highest one-third. Lilly's book is a good one, out of print as we went to press but worth snapping up if you find it on the used market.

Beyond the bar, the sand bottom drops away steadily until it reaches a depth of one hundred feet at the Sea Buoy, or "Lightship," 11.1 nautical miles west of the Golden Gate Bridge.

San Francisco sailors still sail "Lightship" races, even though there hasn't been a ship on that station since 1971. There were several that came and went in the seventy-three years preceding, however, the first of which went into duty in 1898. The last arrived in 1950, a 133-footer painted bright red with a working crew of sixteen, riding to an anchor rode one thousand feet long. The lightship was easy to spot but expensive to maintain. It was replaced with a less personable but more efficient large navigational buoy, or LNB — 40 feet in diameter, with a bank of humming generators and a two-year load of fuel — that was replaced in turn by an even-more efficient solar-powered buoy. The new buoy arrived in 1994. It is nine feet in diameter and equipped with Racon, a high-intensity strobe, and a light flashing the Morse code for Alpha. The Bar Pilots call it the Sea Buoy, which is simple and illustrative, so in this book, Sea Buoy it is.

One mile east of the Sea Buoy is the pilot-boat cruising area, where

San Francisco Bar Pilots board inbound vessels and disembark from outbound vessels. The pilot, by definition, is a specialist trained to know a given body of water as well as it can be known and licensed to guide ships into a harbor, or out. When a pilot is aboard a ship, the pilot makes the decisions, informing the officers of the bridge of the headings and speed to be maintained to hold the ship in narrow channels, avoid obstructions, and pass through traffic zones in safety. Unlike an arriving stranger, the pilot does not have to search for Blossom Rock Buoy against the background of Treasure Island; the knowledge of its position is beaten in so hard and so deep that it can never be erased.

Pilots are at the apex of the business of moving ships. All of them have worked their way up through the ranks. They might be former sea captains or tug captains; always, they hold Coast Guard licenses as captains and pilots, and they have passed a state examination that requires them, in effect, to memorize the charts for 200 miles of waterways from the bar through the bay and into the rivers. That means hundreds of soundings, hazards, buoys, ranges, beacons, and light characteristics.

The role of the pilot goes back at least as far as the Greeks. Pilots have been a legal requirement in British ports since Henry VIII issued a decree in 1541. Here on the bay, pilots have been on the scene since

A ROSE BY ANY NAME

© San Francisco Chronicle, by Kimball Livingston

PAUL AND RUTH TARA SPENT SOME OF THE BEST YEARS OF their lives in a racing dinghy, blasting through the waters off Santa Cruz with spray in the face and the boat leaving a white track through the brine. Then they decided to try something completely different. Paul got a new crew and a new boat. He called it, *Ruthless*.

The naming of any boat is bound up in the diversity and perversity of human emotion. A forthright skipper like Franklin Snyder calls his cabin cruiser the *Floating Loan*. A punster like Frank Baldwin comes up with *A-Tiller-the-Hun*.

Feminine names are big. A quick study of the Yachting Yearbook will turn up *Donna Kay* and *Dorothy Ann*, *Jenny Jo* and *Gracie O*. The *Dinghy Sue* belongs to Tom Curtis, way up in Ignacio.

But romance is one thing. The reality of the sea comes in pungent doses. So along comes Scott Owen, a reliable threat on the race course, and don't mess with *Sweaty Lorna*, or *Uptight Emma*, for that matter.

Some names are born with the boat. Warren Wilbur won the Moore 24 Nationals sailing *Moore Burgers*. Charles Hall and Jesse Hollingsworth took delivery of hull number 30 from the Olson 30 line and named it *Thirty-Thirty*. From the classic Bears come *Teddy Bear*, *Smokey*, *Circus Bear*, and *Goldilocks*. From the Birds, *Falcon*, *Petrel* and *Swallow*.

Fast boats like 505s inspire fast names. One team takes its thrill rides on an *Orangegasm*. *Recreational Pharmacology* won the class Worlds. And *Lord Nelson*, shipped here from Denmark by Jorgen Schonherr, stirs history buffs to marvel that a Danish yacht should be named for an English admiral who forced the surrender of Copenhagen. "When I bought my first boat," Schonherr explained, "it was called *Lord Nelson*. The name came with the boat, and when I changed boats, I kept the name. What's one little invasion?"

Jaren Leet once owned 37 feet worth of fiberglass sloop he called the *Rational Harpoon*. "It was a takeoff on the magazine National Lampoon — we figured we could rationally stick it to'em." When Leet moved to a custom ocean racer, after a searching study of his motives, he named the new beauty *Irrational*. Score one for honesty.

Sue Rowly cruises the Bay and Delta with a husband, kids, and a bright yellow *Awesome Possom*. Score one for whimsy. Score two for whimsy with Leonard and Patti Delmas, who have one big happy family, all daughters, and a crimson sloop that is just *Another Girl*.

Some names are harder to live with than others. Imagine the poor blighter on a cruise with the Aahmes Shrine Yacht Club motor fleet, who has to check in at the office. He asks his host, Walter Snow, for the boat's call numbers. Then he turns on the radiotelephone and calls the marine operator. The operator in turn dials the office and announces, "A ship-to-shore call from the *Pickled-Ding-A-Ling* ..."

One of the most famous trios in American life is composed of Tom, Dick and Harry. In their local incarnation, Tom Bookwilder and the Scottish sea captain William B. Richardson (the Richardson of Richardson's Bay) undertook the role in the Mexican port of the 1830s. The fledgling California State Legislature made bar pilots official in its first session, in 1849, and the job has grown from there.

At all shipping ports of the West Coast, all foreign vessels and American ships under register in the foreign trade are required to carry a pilot entering and leaving. If their masters are licensed pilots for these waters, American boats traveling coastwise may do without. A number of Chevron tankers, for example, have skippers who are also licensed pilots, but the largest ships in their fleet use Bar Pilots for every passage into the Gate or out. Pilot boats cruise on station continually. Fog makes it impractical to use helicopters, as pilots do at some ports, and the volume of traffic is another reason for keeping a pilot boat on station, while other boats shuttle pilots in or out. The bay averages some twenty arrivals or departures a day. A typical day for a pilot is one ship out, and another in.

UNTROPICAL ISLES

In clear weather, it's easy to see your way around the Gulf of the Farallones. There are prominent landmarks ashore and powerful lights at Point Bonita, the Sea Buoy, Point Reyes and the Farallones. In low visibility, the job is tougher, but it's become much easier since the original edition of *Sailing The Bay* was published in 1981, with its concern for the use and misuse of LORAN. Geographical Positioning Systems (GPS) are the wave of the present and the way of the future for their precision and general ease of application. But, whatever the means, no sailor worthy of the name will go out lacking a method of homing in bad weather — or bet all his cookies on electronics.

West of the Sea Buoy, the sandy bottom is mixed with patches of mud and shells, deepening gradually to about 180 feet near the Farallon Islands. The main ship route westbound lies just south of the Farallones, a small, craggy colony of rocks breaking up some seven linear miles of ocean and marking the last vestige of the North American continent. Beyond the islands, the shelf drops rapidly, reaching depths greater than a mile.

The rocks and shoals of the Farallones are dangerous, especially for boats approaching

Dick Aronoff were the owners. *Harry* was the boat, and they made a happy threesome for a while. Now it's just Dick and *Harry*. Tom got married.

In the bay's fleet of International One Designs there are classic names to match the classic lines, names such as *Contessa, Iorana* or *Quickstep II*. Decidedly nonclassic is *Icfigin*, an acronym beginning, I Can Feel It ...

And, while it's not unusual to find wives who love sailing as much as their husbands do, or even more, most purchases continue to be made for the man of the house. Every port has its *Mama's Mink*, and many, many boats are named for the little lady. In that tradition, and twisting it a bit, we find Hugh Jacks, a feisty fellow who declares, "I'm going to name my next boat after my wife: Mrs. Hugh Jacks!"

Some names are born with the boat
[PHOTO BY DON HILBUN]

from the north and closing on hazards that are low or even submerged. The northern extremity, Fanny Shoal, is marked by a lighted buoy with a whistle — a nice touch that surely would have been appreciated by the master of the clipper *Noonday*, which struck a then-uncharted rock and sank on New Year's Day, 1863. The *Noonday*'s crew was saved by a pilot boat, but the ship and cargo sank in some 280 feet of water. The rock it hit, eighteen feet below the surface, is charted now. In the tradition of naming rocks for the boats that hit them, you will find it marked as Noonday Rock.

For most sailors, the granite-faced Southeast Farallon is everything we need to know about the islands. It is the closest to the Golden Gate, the largest, and — at an elevation of 350 feet — the most visible. Except for fishing boats on the hunt, it is the target for almost every excursion to the Farallones. Technically, at present sea levels, the Southeast Farallon is two islands, but the gap between is impassable. Seas build to a massive scale here, even on a mild day, as deep ocean swells meet the continental rise. For sailors rounding the island on the western face, towering breakers are an awe-inspiring reminder of the power of nature, and good reason not to sail too close.

The Southeast Farallon was once a haunt for hunters and trappers who decimated the wildlife. Now the island supports only an automated lighthouse and housing for a handful of naturalists who "come aboard" by crane, lifted in a basket from the heaving deck of a small boat. There is no pocket of water protected enough for docking or safe anchoring. Visitors are not allowed. The Farallones are owned by the Federal Government, with jurisdiction split between the Gulf of the Farallones National Marine Sanctuary (below the high tide line) and the U.S. Fish & Wildlife Service (above the high tide line). The Point Reyes Bird Observatory is under contract to provide stewardship and research regarding wildlife on the islands and in the waters surrounding them. The Observatory's professional biologists and volunteers share a pair of cozy cottages surrounded by some 200,000 birds and 7,000 to 10,000 seals and sea lions. Of 800 bird species in North America, 380 have been spotted on the Farallones. Bird populations have declined over the last two decades; seals have increased. The waters around the islands witness the seasonal processions of some 200 blue whales, 400 humpbacks, and thousands of grays. In fall and winter, when the elephant seals come to haul out and

A RORSCHALK TEST FOR SAILORS

OCEAN SAILING IS POPULAR. People love it. But we have to wave caution flags on the matter of crew companions. Don't take your shipmates for granted. And before you commit, apply the Oreo test.

The trained eye can detect critical potentialities elicited by highly-reinforcing external stimuli — Oreos, for example — in easily-replicated studies of manual dexterity and cognitive adaptation as displayed by test subjects in response to repeated exposure. [See Litrownik, A. and Laszlo, F: Murder, Madness, and Soggy Cookies Offshore. University of Northern South Dakota. 1997 38 (3), 529-533]. In projecting the arc of a crew relationship in either qualitative or quantitative terms, no theory and no laboratory device can replace the simple Oreo placed alluringly on a smudged fiberglass housing. As your subjects take the bait, weigh the evidence closely:

Does a proposed watch captain wrench-and-split? If so, using one hand, or two?

With the cookie in two halves, does our subject then scrape the icing off with the teeth?

Using the upper or the lower teeth?

A little icing at a time, or all of it at once?

Does our specimen perhaps lick the icing slowly, savoring it, appraising it between licks as a sculptor studies stone?

Or is your proposed watchmate a precise aesthete who will deftly wrench-and-split, keeping all the icing in a single, smooth layer on one surface, then turn over the opposite half and press it down to leave a print of ОЗЯО? Does he line all his cookies up, in turn, to see which came out the best?

Or do we uncover a primitive who paws up cookies whole?

Choose well your long distance companions. No one who has been to sea soon forgets how big is the ocean, or how small is a boat.

mate, they bring with them a following of white sharks — big, mature white sharks who know how to make a living.

As islands go, the Farallones aren't much, but they're what we've got. The Southeast Farallon is the turning mark for the Farallones Race, the classic local ocean race dating from 1907, also for the Singlehanded and Doublehanded Farallones Races and more.

In a "standard" northwest wind, a boat leaving the Golden Gate on starboard tack can fetch the Southeast Farallon Island (rarely) or nearly fetch the island (usually) in one tack.

Since they expect to have to tack at some point, most skippers prefer to tack early, through the Bonita Channel or soon after clearing the bar. There might be a wind-direction advantage, a current advantage, a smooth water advantage, or even all three at once.

An obvious case for not using the Bonita Channel would be a Farallones-bound or north-bound passage leaving the Gate at two hours after maximum ebb, when there is a weak flood running past Bonita and a powerful ebb outbound through the Main Ship Channel (see Figure 4, page 43). Otherwise, the Bonita Channel is worth considering. With a bit of northerly distance under it, a boat enroute to the Farallones is positioned to profit, later, as it clears the coastal climate and enters the ocean climate. You take the profit on the approach to the island, where the sea turns to a deeper blue and the swells build. The wind comes more from the north, providing a starboard tack lift in the last few miles. The boat to the north is inside the lift, for maximum gain.

Now you're smelling, and looking at, the true ocean.

CURRENTS OFFSHORE

In the summertime, the prevailing flow off the coast is a wind-driven current moving southeast at an average two-tenths knot — the California Current — driven by the prevailing northwesterlies. Currents inside the Gulf of the Farallones, however, flow northward as an eddy.

The California Current, some five hundred miles wide, duplicates Pacific weather patterns. Given ten to thirteen months, it will carry a raft to Hawaii. In the depths below the California Current runs a compensating countercurrent headed north. During the winter, when the prevailing northwesterly of summer disappears and winds blow often from the south, the California Current shifts farther offshore. A northward-trending current builds inside it — a current that, in the thinking of oceanographers, represents the surfacing of the water that previously flowed six hundred feet below. Along the Northern California coast this northerly set, the Davidson Current, is usually active from November through February.

The California Current and the Davidson Current flow through ocean waters outside the Gulf of the Farallones. In the shallower waters inside the islands (to hammer on a critical point) the currents are more variable, with strong influences from tidal flow through the Golden Gate. Just outside the San Francisco Bar is a slight current to the north and west, averaging one-tenth of a knot. Strong ebb tides can reinforce and increase this Coast Eddy Current, especially in periods of high river runoff. Current speeds then can reach a ripping three knots. A muddy ebb-tide plume will spread nearly to the Farallones.

In average conditions at the Sea Buoy, tide-related currents reach three-tenths knot on the flood and four-tenths knot on the ebb, changing direction about fifteen degrees each hour and covering the entire compass. The flow is described in a knotty diagram in NOAA's Tidal Current Tables: Pacific Coast of North America and Asia. Storm-driven currents running south to north reach seven-tenths of a knot.

Tidal currents are the strongest under-foot forces near the Golden Gate. In the flood cycle, flood currents appear sooner along the shoreline north and south than near the Sea Buoy. As the flood develops, the currents converge on the strait. In the ebb cycle, most of the ebbing current flows straight out the Gate on a west-southwest heading through the Main Ship Channel, the line of least resistance. In the strait, Bonita Cove on the north and Baker Beach on the south are the sites of major eddies during both the flood and ebb tide cycles. Boats bound against the current will duck into these backwaters rather than stem the tide midchannel.

Flood tide currents tend to set straight in, with a slight northward tendency. Ebbs near Fort Point set slightly toward the south. Fogbound shipping captains ignorant or forgetful of this basic fact have piled up on a variety of south-shore rocks and beaches. But this is not the greatest danger on the local ocean.

DISASTER

The worst tragedy of U.S. ocean racing occurred in the Gulf of the Farallones on April 10, 1982. To a human, that sounds like a long time ago, but in geologic time, or in the building and passing of storms in storm-seeding regions of the open ocean, it might as well have been yesterday. Four sailors died in the Doublehanded Farallones Race and two cruising sailors died nearby. Six boats sank, capsized, or were driven onto rocks. Three were deliberately beached. Two were dismasted.

There was a pattern to it.

The fleet that sailed out the Gate that morning had reason to suspect something blustery from the south, but the upgrade from small-craft advisory to gale warning came at 8 a.m., exactly at starting time, when most skippers were preoccupied with the race. Later still, they had other preoccupations.

The warm front drove through in late morning with a moderate southerly wind and sheets of hard rain. It was uncomfortable but not terrifying, and when it passed, the weather appeared to be improving. The biggest, fastest boats made it home in the afternoon. Then the cold front hit with thunderstorms and winds that peaked at the Point Bonita recording station at 67 knots. At that point, many of the people still on the ocean were so busy managing boat and sails and trying to stay on board that they couldn't employ a radio, even if they were among the lucky ones whose radio hadn't been swamped by rain and incoming seas.

The worst of the storm arrived at 5 p.m. and roared through the night. A Coast Guard spokesman said, "Our choppers are capable of fighting winds to ninety knots, but they were having trouble making headway out there."

Survivors agreed that they had been cold and fatigued no matter how much clothing they wore and even though the rain was "warm." The cold and fatigue marked early stages of hypothermia.

The first broadcast distress case turned up in mid-afternoon, when Sam Weeks decided to "attack the shoal" rather than try to sail around it. His catamaran capsized, but Weeks and his crew were picked up by another boat.

By sunset, there was havoc on the ocean and on the beach. Fourteen boats were unaccounted for. Half of those boats were sailed by people who had quit, successfully, and gone home, happily, without letting the race committee know their whereabouts.

Never leave any race without notifying the race committee.

By 10:30 p.m., with committee members calling phone numbers from the sign-up lists, the missing had been reduced to seven boats, but it wasn't only the racers and the helicopter crews who were taking it in the shorts. Commander J.W. Haugen, chief of Search and Rescue for what was then the 12th Coast Guard District, commented, "Our 44-footers roll 'till they make the toughest people sick. If you've been on one for six hours, you're dead tired."

But the crews of those boats stuck it out all night. Helicopter sorties ended at 10:30 p.m., and the last flight brought home two living.

All wrecks took place from Point Bonita north.

The coast eddy current, setting north, and reinforced by powerful winds from the south, swept the fleet off course. Many people were hardpressed to control the boat and just hang on. They sailed pre-planned compass courses that they thought would bring them home, and they did not, or could not, do any position finding. Even survivors who popped out (briefly) into clear visibility in time to find the Gate reported being surprised to find themselves far north of where they thought they should be.

To make a clear, inbound passage through the Main Ship Channel, you need to make good a course between 70 and 80 degrees magnetic. On boats that worked hard for the southing they needed, the crews suffered in high, steep seas that crashed in from dead abeam and threatened to roll them over. Those who were too far north when they recognized the problem had no chance at all of making the channel.

Paul May grounded his Cal 30 on Duxbury Reef. Greg Sawyer, who had led the fleet in the first hour with his 27-foot catamaran, turned back when the storm hit, at about mile 19. The return was, "uneventful," he said, "except the wind and sea were blowing us off course to the north, and we were unaware of it until we could see the shore. And

WHEN YACHTS FLY

FOR WINDSURFERS, THE FIRST GREAT RACING ADVENTURE was the Golden Gate Crossing, all the way from Crissy Field to Sausalito. "An epic," Ken Winner called it, and in the early years — on stock Windsurfer boards with no footstraps — an epic it was. But not for long.

By 1979, as Diane Green recalls, "We had new boards, we had harnesses, and the Golden Gate Crossing was just too easy, so we went looking for the next challenge. That's how the Bay Classic got going. But the Coast Guard was pretty skeptical about letting a bunch of boardheads race from Crissy Field to Berkeley. They wouldn't give us a permit unless we had one crash boat for every seven or eight competitors. That's why we made it an invitational. There were 13 of us in the first one."

A pre-race test of a possible course through Raccoon Strait led Green and Barbara Ockel into the lee of Angel Island, and it was well past dark when they finally made Berkeley. After that, it was clear that the course had to stay in the wind funnel no matter how many times it criss-crossed the bay.

Windsurfer Rockets — with footstraps and improved daggerboards — were the hot ticket in 1979. The way Steve Silvester recalls the race, "It was foggy. A lot of the time you couldn't see other people, and it wasn't super windy, but we had enough wind to make us go."

Robbie Naish won the first one, with Winner second, and they repeated that order for three years (as well as we can piece it together), and meanwhile, the scene was moving fast. "Boards became much more capable in that time," Winner said. "By 1988, people were using slalom boards, and the equipment was pretty much what we see at the Olympics now and expect to see in the near future."

Again, with better boards, the racing became too easy. First a triangle was added to the under-the-bridge leg, then another triangle was added to that, just to keep the challenge in it. "And now," Green said, "there's a race back to Crissy after the race."

A final note: It was 16 years after the first Bay Classic that *Sailing the Bay* turned to the original players to piece together this account. Their guesstimates on the timing of the inaugural covered a nine-year span, and three different names were put forward as the inaugural winner. As far as we know, the Bay Classic is the oldest surviving windsurfing event on the Blue Planet.

Lt. Crissy was a flyer too... [PHOTO BY DON HILBUN]

then we saw Bolinas." At that point, Sawyer's cat was trapped between the shoreline to the north and the bar to the south. With his crewman and close friend Dennis Madigan (killed in the same race one year later), Sawyer tried to work offshore but couldn't make headway. "There were waves halfway up the mast," he said. "We'd take a tack out and back and end up exactly where we started." Closing on the bar on his last pass, Sawyer spotted the overturned hull of Sam Weeks' catamaran (and a rescue underway), and decided to go for the beach instead. With the daggerboards up, he and Madigan landed north of Bolinas unharmed and spent the night with friendly natives, who took them in while rising waters destroyed the boat.

Offshore, the night was miserable but passable. Jocelyn Nash headed out to sea to escape, not the storm, but the worst dangers of the storm. While other boats were breaking up, trying to get home, Nash headed west in her Hawkfarm class sloop *El Gavilan*, and she made enough offing for security. Nash didn't go for home until daylight arrived on the day following, and the wind moderated. Only weeks before, preparing for her fourth Singlehanded Farallones Race and a Singlehanded Transpacific race later in the year, Nash had said, "The Transpac, in the open ocean, is safer in some ways than the Farallones course. On the long race, you can pace yourself for sleep. The Farallones is a sprint that can last all night, and you have extra hazards — big ships, narrow channels, and a lee shore."

One month later, Commander Haugen, who wasn't bucking for promotion, said it simply: "If you're going to sail in the ocean, you're going to continue to lose lives."

But not very often, unless we forget.

THE CALL OF THE SEA

It's important to talk about the dangers of the sea, and once you start, it's hard to stop. Who's been hammered hardest by what-size waves makes a better story (and I like a story) than who's seen the prettiest sunset. The category of Lessons Learned draws heavily on the scary stuff, and Lessons Learned is the heart and soul of this book. If there's no balance here, so be it. There are plenty of people selling the

"Wake me when the weather moderates." R.C. Keefe [PHOTO BY DON HILBUN]

magic and the adventure of offshore sailing. Heck, they sold it to me. I've been there, and I'm going back.

Two of the worst and finest experiences of this sailor's life occurred on the same race boat, just weeks apart. The worst was losing a man overboard in a predawn broach and crash off Point Sur, and getting him back, barely. We were a full racing crew making a pre-Transpac familiarization and delivery trip down the coast. It was a bad crash, and we came out of it one man short, with one crewman injured below deck, a damaged boat that wouldn't sail to weather, and lines in the water when we started the motor and put the prop in gear. But the worst did not turn us into the worst case imaginable. The prop did not foul. And our man was wearing a Type III vest, so when we finally worked our way back through the whitecaps and made contact — on the second pass — he was still on the surface of the Pacific Ocean rather than under it. No, he couldn't help himself. He was hypothermic. He was in shock. But all 220 soaking pounds of him was ours. Skip Stevely almost singlehandedly lifted him aboard the same way that mothers lift schoolbusses off trapped children. Three thousand miles and a few weeks later, we were racing down the Molokai Channel. Honolulu radio was announcing our boat as the Class A winner and inviting people down to the Ala Wai Yacht Harbor to greet us. I could hear the guys on deck stomping and yelling as the boat surfed the big ones, but I was in a wistful mood. I stalked the cabin below, studying the dials in the nav station, the instruments spewing out numbers that no longer required attention. I sorted a few dishes back into the rack where they belonged, noted in my Official Star Wars Fan Club Notebook the previous day's thought that, "there is no sweeter feeling at sea than drifting off to sleep to the sound of someone else doing the dishes," and wandered forward, stepping over sails, wishing it wouldn't end …

We were ten days out of Point Fermin, and I could have kept right on going.

LONG DISTANCE TRAVEL HAS TWO PEAK PERIODS for San Francisco Bay sailors. There's summer, for Southern California or Hawaii, and fall, for Mexico and beyond.

One of the great world cruisers of an earlier generation, Eric Hiscock, commented on a voyage to California that anyone who could manage this coastline could sail anywhere. Those who have followed him agree. Hiscock did not mean that we have the most extreme conditions in the world. He was speaking instead of the long distances between ports, the fog that makes visual piloting difficult, and the elements that nearly always oppose northbound traffic.

Every once in a while someone takes a boat north to Portland or Puget Sound, finds the sea mild along the way, and maybe even lucks into a southerly. More often, it's an uphill battle. Heading south is a different case. That's usually "downhill," and sailing to Southern California can be a lark. You keep California to the left and the northwesterly at your back. At Point Conception, where the coastline turns left into the Santa Barbara Channel, you hook a turn and follow it. Then you're in the protected and generally mild waters of the Catalina Eddy (see figure 8, page 55), extending beyond the Mexican border.

Or, you could get kicked in the pants all the way down the coast, so you'd better be prepared. Midsummer winds at Point Sur and Point Conception can really howl, and even an eighteen-knot breeze, sustained, will build a whitecapped sea with waves to six feet. First timers will find it quite impressive; to a nervous soul, it may look like the devil's own storm.

Between San Francisco and Point Conception, cruisers can stop in places such as Santa Cruz and Monterey for shelter and full services, or in the beautiful, partially-protected anchorage at San Simeon beneath high coastal hills. At San Simeon, you anchor off and use a small boat to tie to the pier. It's a long climb up a vertical ladder to the deck of the pier, and when the swell is in, the boat-to-ladder, ladder-to-boat leap is quite an adventure. (Anyhow, it used to be. If you get there and find wall-to-wall condos, just figure you were a bit too late.)

Not far down the coast from San Simeon is Morro Bay, a well-protected harbor with a population that is justly celebrated for its hospitality to traveling sailors. It is also almost exactly halfway between San Francisco and Los Angeles, with a mound of hard rock nearly 600 feet tall marking the entrance, so Morro Bay shares the advantages of convenience and recognizability. The entrance is hard to approach in a blow, however. To be more precise, it's downright dangerous in a heavy sea whether the wind is blowing or not. Boats have been rolled, pitch-poled, and cashed in. Big boats. The good news is that the natives here take better care of sailing visitors then just about any group of people we've ever heard of.

Otherwise, there are only a few points of refuge on the Central Coast. To learn where they are — and get the finer points about using them — consult any of several good coastal guides and seek advice from veterans. This is not a guide to the coast. This is a selected highlights tour. It's offered because you cannot be a complete sailor on San Francisco Bay unless you understand where you fit in as a sailor on the West Coast of the Americas. So, in that spirit …

… and with apologies, we must note that Point Conception has been referred to as "the Cape Horn of the Pacific." We can't let those other books out-hype *Sailing The Bay*, so there. We're on record. And Point Conception has earned the name. Thirty knots at Conception is not exactly uncommon, and it can get much worse. Then, right around the corner — in the Santa Barbara Channel, in the lee of the Santa Barbara Mountains — the wind can shut off completely. The contrast is dramatic no matter which way you're going, and it poses a great tactical problem for racing fleets bound to ports in Southern California. When do you turn left? (Or, alter course to a more easterly heading, as our nautical friends say.) If the destination is Santa Barbara, the navigator has no choice; he has to cut the corner close. If the destination is a bit farther south, Los Angeles Harbor or Catalina Island, navigators will often bypass the Santa Barbara Channel and hold on in the outer coastal waters until they have cleared the westernmost of the Channel Islands, San Miguel, and the lonely, windswept Richardson's Rock. In another version, they might work the south side of the channel and then duck between two of the islands. Either way, they have a chance of holding more wind longer. Even then, it often happens to racing fleets that the wind dies on the final approach, boats drift with slatting sails in sight of the finish line after 300 miles on the course, and all the odds are reshuffled. It's an old dilemma in California coastal racing. There is no Ideal Destination. The Ideal Finish would be right at the wind line at Point Conception, but the Ideal Race Committee of suicide volunteers has yet to step forward.

Tucked inside the Catalina Eddy, the Channel Islands are rugged and beautiful, yet they're often overlooked by people who forget that something so good could be so close. The anchorages are exotic, with a sense of the wild and faraway. Wandering among them offers all the rewards and challenges of cruising in distant places. It's something like the California of 100 years ago. An abundance of wildlife, semi-wild horses on Santa Cruz Island, a few old ranch buildings, unmarked Indian sites, tall cliffs, protected beaches, clear water — all go together to make this not only an inspiring destination but also an excellent school for the long distance cruiser. And if you come up short on a few items, half a day's sail will get you to the happy shopping grounds of Santa Barbara or Ventura. One version of an ideal Mexican cruise would be to summer in the Channel Islands, then go. Or, just go to the Channel Islands and then come home. You'll have gone somewhere. The rub is climbing uphill to get home, but, you either like wet socks or you don't. You'll need a Channel Islands guidebook to plan your trip, and don't expect to be allowed ashore without a permit from Channel Islands National Park headquarters.

The mainland side of the channel is quiet and almost deserted. Just inside Government Point (on the protected, channel side of Point Conception), you will find Cojo, an anchorage used by generations of sailors steeling themselves for that northward beat, or looking to take a breather after a windy ride south. Cojo has good holding ground, and it feels as far off the beaten track as most of the places a traveling yacht could visit in a year's worth of voyaging. There's terrific surfing nearby, an array of impressive vistas as you cruise the coastline — and the threat of some very big and sudden spurts of wind blasting down the canyons. So, be alert. Why get rolled off the canyons of California when you can save that adventure for the Mistral coming down out of the Rhone Valley on the other side of the world?

If the goal is Hawaii, either cruising or racing, summer is the window and June and July are the popular months. Then you have the best chance of catching a classic tradewind ride to the islands. That would mean two or three days of possibly wet-reaching across a cold north-westerly until the wind fairs, warms, and informs you thus that you have entered the trades. North Pacific winds circulate clockwise around the

Pacific High Pressure Zone, driving surface currents with them all the way. The southern side of the cycle should blow you to Hawaii with the wind over your shoulder. In a textbook year, the High will center roughly west of San Francisco — a region of calms and fitful zephyrs — and the best course will loop around it to the south, sailing on the starboard jibe and finding the strongest breeze on the 1020 millibar line. Racing yachts pressing for the fast track occasionally hold starboard jibe until they are one day out of the islands and then jibe onto a "hot angle" for the final approach. Along the way, the water grows brighter and the skies grow warmer. Flying fish break the wavetops, and puffy little tradewind clouds pass overhead. But watch over your shoulder for the squalls. They pack a wicked punch.

How easy is it to get to Hawaii? Very easy, if you're a good sailor and seaman with a mastery of your boat and its mechanical systems, experienced in navigation, and already comfortable with shorter passages. As ocean crossings go, California-Hawaii is a milk run. But you won't get there by "following the airplanes." You won't see the planes. And yes, given enough time, wind-driven ocean currents will carry a raft to Hawaii. By then, you'll be a year older, almost, and you might miss by forty miles, which is good for another year before your bleached bones wash up on some atoll in the great outback of the Pacific. From Hilo to Hanalei Bay — from the Big Island on the south to Kauai on the north — is a distance of 300 nautical miles. That's a big target, but just the same, people have missed Hawaii and not recognized the problem until days later, when they faced an upwind, upcurrent return against the same forces that made it all seem easy, for a while.

As far as San Francisco Bay sailors can tell, non-textbook years on the Pacific Ocean are just as common as textbook years. I once found myself beating to Honolulu on port tack — instead of reaching on starboard — and Dan Newland, a repeat winner in the Singlehanded Transpac and a veteran of many fully-crewed crossings, summed up his experience this way: "Every year I've ever gone," he said, "it's been weird."

If the High is weak, or out of position, the trades may not exist, or they may be pushed far to the south, with oddments of breeze lying across the usual California-Hawaii track. It's worth knowing too that Hawaii, even though it's a beautiful destination and a rewarding place to sail, is not the easiest cruising ground. The coastlines are steep and rocky, and the gaps between the islands are natural funnels where the wind and the currents really rip.

IN MEXICO, HURRICANE SEASON BEGINS IN JUNE and ends in the fall. Fall is when boats from Vancouver, Seattle and Portland appear in San Francisco Bay, stopping over on their way south. It's a good time, and by odds the best time, for sailing down the California coast. But there are no guarantees. From September on, there is always the threat of a rainstorm from the south or a howler from the north. By November, there's almost sure to be some sort of extra adventure in the offing. November is not too late to go, but it's late.

South of San Diego, the weather moderates with the latitude. November and December are good months for the voyage down the outside of the Baja Peninsula. The wind might even be light or calm, but the usual caveats apply. You could get a blow from the south or the north. I've sat in Cabo baking in the sun on the Gulf side and then hiked up the hill and looked out across the ocean to see whitecaps and a solid 30 knots of wind blowing down from the northwest. From December on, the warmest, finest cruising in Mexico will be found along the mainland, probably as far south as Zihuatañejo. Cruising season in the Gulf of California begins when the weather warms. Boats will be found coming north from the mainland and into the Gulf to catch the good weather of May, June and July.

Mexico is a favorite of Richard Spindler, publisher of *Latitude 38* and founder of the popular Baha Ha Ha that rounds up cruisers in the Gulf of California for what is probably the greatest annual high-kicks, low-key sailing event on the planet. "Putting out the magazine never left me enough time to burn out on sailing," Spindler says. "There was a La Paz trip one year, and I remember the sunset … you can't describe it, but I was just so damned glad to be alive." ◆

"They all have to find their own level of stress." Matt Jones, race manager and final word. **[PHOTO BY JOHN RIISE, *LATITUDE 38*]**

THE DRIVE TO COMPETE

Competitors are born. After that, they find what smokes 'em. Paul Cayard, famous in San Bruno for fouling out of high school basketball games — a victim of testosterone delirium — was on the road at the same time to becoming one of the great figures of yacht racing. On the road, literally, almost every day of his teenage years, rolling up Highway 280 to 19th Avenue and the docks of the San Francisco cityfront. On the way, he remembers, "I used the traffic to sharpen up. It was a question of how to control the fleet, manage a crowd, keep it smooth, make sure I was the first car out of Golden Gate Park. The drive to compete — that was born in me."

— PAUL CAYARD

GET TWO BOATS IN SIGHT OF EACH OTHER, and they'll race. Oh, they might pretend not to. This game can be felinely sur reptitious. Perhaps it's just a nonchalant tweak to the genoa sheet when no one seems to be looking. The hard-core cruiser is not immune, especially if that first, nonchalant tweak produces a hope of winning. The next stage is total concentration, not to look at the other boat.

And, those are the cruisers.

Summertime race committees on San Francisco Bay enjoy a rare luxury. They can count on the wind, most of the time. That's a luxury for competitors, too, but it carries a price. With the wind taken for granted, tidal currents are so important that they dominate strategy and sometimes even tactics. Often, there is one narrow tidal lane where a boat must go to win. Things are different in other parts of the world, and bay-trained sailors who go away to race will face a steep, new learning curve. The exceptions are the ones who grew up with dinghies on the Small Boat Racing Association circuit — mastering not only the bay but the changeable winds of Clear Lake, Folsom Lake. etc. For them it all comes naturally.

Success on most of the waters of the world will depend upon reading the weather signs in the sky, to choose the favored side of the course, and then, from moment to moment, "bouncing" from puff to puff to catch the favorable windshifts enroute to the mark. But San Francisco Bay is a strange bear. We might find our local heroes sailing right through a header and grinning it down for the sake of reaching favorable current. What choice is there? Sail a five-knot boat into a two-knot river running the wrong way, and you've just lost 40 percent of your speed over the bottom. Sail a five-knot boat into a four-knot river, and you'll have time to homestead, build a fence, and paint it.

Which repeats what we already know: The bay is a place where the tides speak with a many-forked and swift tongue, and the wind blows hard. And yet, that's not all there is to it. The image of a bay race as a tide race, swallowed whole, will keep you from winning the big ones. Currents may dictate strategy on the grand scale, but there are twists and turns in the wind that turn the tactical key between the also-ran and the ran-away-and-hid. Sometimes the windshift is the race because everybody in the fleet knows what the tide is doing, and nobody's going to get that part wrong.

Back in Melges country, on Wisconsin's Lake Geneva, windshifts turn on the arrival of a weather front, or the passing of a cumulus cloud as the cloud's thermal action sucks up unstable air. On San Francisco Bay, on a seabreeze day, we don't have unstable air. Instead, the seabreeze flows in beneath the warmer inversion layer above. It's smoothly stratified. You could say that it's roofed in. While the bottom lamination of the seabreeze can flow up and over obstructions — if there's enough force driving it — the breeze would much rather flow around an obstruction. Topography rules. So on the bay we have an accumulation of wind currents turned in predictable ways from the prevailing wind direction. As you enter or leave them, you will experience predictable shifts.

Topographic shifts are as reliable as the seabreeze itself.

In the racing world of the bay, the 400-pound gorilla of topographic wind effects is the Point Blunt Shift, where the seabreeze bends around Angel Island and turns north. This is a phenomenon that sailors really depend on and use. The Point Blunt Shift affects big boats racing "up and down" the bay and many boats racing in the East Bay. It is truly as reliable as the seabreeze, and every racing sailor will get a shot at it eventually, perhaps often. We'll come back to it when we look at the Olympic Circle. For now, let's consider a different set of topographic shifts that are reliable from day to day, even from hour to hour, but fickle as a cheerleader from moment to moment.

Now we're on the cityfront …

And we learn that even San Francisco Bay is not devoid of oscillating shifts. As once explained by Paul Kamen, chief technical consultant to the celebrated columnist Max Ebb, oscillating shifts occur along windward shorelines, "or downwind of large obstructions due to vortex shedding." Lay that on your next blind date. Significant windward shorelines include Tiburon, Yellow Bluff, Coyote Point — and the San Francisco cityfront as you approach Crissy Field, where the wind arrives by way of the Presidio hill.

Short-tacking against a flood tide, the cityfront will always bring windshifts into play. They may not be the thermal-related shifts of a Midwestern lake sailor or even the progressive shift of the Southern California coastal sailor, but they're windshifts, and they're ours. Think about them in terms of vortex shedding, if you wish. You won't read much about them in the how-to-win-races books because they also fit into a limited-application category we might Stuart Walkerize as Geographically-Induced Semi-Random Windshifts. Meaning, stuff gets in the way, so the wind acts funny. Picture elements of the breeze blowing across the interference of the Richmond District, bending and roiling along the edge of the Seacliff, and edging down the Presidio hill — all with the wind slot as adjoining, accelerated flow — until the breeze arrives at Crissy Field with light spots, backfill, and sudden puffs.

Cityfront windshifts are not identical from one beat to the next, but one day's grab bag looks a lot like the next. What's predictable is the tendency for the shifts to come from the beach, shifting left, with light spots off Crissy Field. It happens even on days when the breeze to leeward, off the breakwater, is steady by comparison, and even if the breeze of the day is strong. (When the fog is heavy, look for the core breeze to come more from the south than on a clear day, and that breeze too will have its shifts to the left.) A really sweet port-tack lift will let you sail parallel to the beach or almost parallel, in water that is flood-tide protected to one degree or another, aiming at the mark or even above it. But the lift probably will not hold to the mark. The leaders — the few who have a shot at clear air — are likely to be led, eventually, by the boat that achieves the best balance between tide and wind. Sometimes that boat will be the starboard tacker that finds a ten degree header and tacks, even though it's 400 yards away from the beach at the time and everybody knows the beach is the place to get the most in tidal relief.

Along this stretch, there are periods in the flood cycle when the zone of general protection is broad and the zone of maximum protection is narrow — too narrow to occupy for very long. And yet, the fleet may queue along a narrow lane of slightly-less-adverse current, with each boat spoiling the wind behind, and continually making it worse for the boats in back.

The how-to-race books will tell you that it is always good to be inside the lift (to windward of the competition on the lifted tack). Along Crissy Field Beach, however, you're not working your way up the ladder of a wide-open course. You have a different set of problems, so run this scenario through your list of possibilities: Imagine a fleet that has just cleared the St. Francis Yacht Club and now is working toward Anita Rock and Presidio Shoals. There are two starboard-tack boats that might be considered equal contenders for the lead, though in fact they're separated by 75 yards. One boat is about to tack just short of hitting the beach. The other, roughly straight out from it, has less protection from the current. But to what degree?

A shift arrives, coming "from the beach" as we expect. Both boats tack to port, one to avoid hitting the beach, the other for the sake of catching that tasty port-tack lift. The boat close to the beach is in the better water, but the mark — half a mile upwind — is not on the beach. It's out in the wind, and the outside boat is now sailing on the layline.

Time passes.

The port-tack lift passes through. It's gone. The inside boat hits a hole in the wind and stands up straight. The outside boat, missing the hole but no longer on a layline, treats the shift as a port-tack header and tacks to starboard, aiming back toward improved tide. Then another shift "from the beach" comes through. The boat close to the beach, going slow, gets the breeze now, but it's given up distance, and it may even have to ease sheets to aim at the mark. The outside boat tacks and has a good, fast line to lead to the mark.

Too simple? Too many presumptions? You bet. There would be multiple tacks and plenty of chances for both boats to blow it before one of them rounded the mark in the lead. And eventually, everyone will arrive at the dock muttering truisms on the order of, "It was all about who made the fewest mistakes."

Years ago I sailed an invited-skipper race in the Folkboat fleet, and aside from the unfamiliar feeling of how slowly the boat turned (I was coming from J24s) what I remember vividly is falling into a hole off Crissy Field. When I came out of it, I was contending for last place with the man who towered over competition on the bay, Tom Blackaller. Tom had suffered the same fate.

"Hey, Kiiiimball! Can you write your way out of this one?"

The sound of Blackaller's voice coming over the water is something that an entire generation of sailors will never forget. And both of us sailed comebacks. His comeback was better than mine, though, and it would make a dramatic story if Tom had gone on to win the race. Instead, in one lap, reading the tide and playing the shifts — with the boat's regular crew and sails — he worked his way through 80 percent of the fleet. In this book, that's the same thing as winning. Which is, for example, why the racing mark off Crissy Field is now known as the Blackaller Buoy.

Wherever you race, if you're good, your bets will average out. If you're going to be a winner, you'll still make mistakes, but you'll be quick to sort your mistakes into two categories of response: 1) Wait it out and sweat it out, which takes discipline; 2) Make a quick and painful correction. The latter case was covered by Chris Corlett: "If you have to eat sh— take big bites."

In a forty-footer, you might be lucky to catch two usable windshifts on a two-mile beat against a flood tide. In a twenty-footer the options increase. A twenty-footer can shave the beach closer and accelerate more quickly out of a tack. In a dinghy, the game is wide open. Tacks are instantaneous. So is acceleration. Brains and boathandling will carry the day.

ODDS AND ODD ENDS

The Olympic Circle is a much larger geographic area than its namesake, the circle of eight YRA-maintained racing marks just north of the Berkeley Pier. In the local lingo, any race course from the pier to (almost) Richmond is "on the Circle." All these waters are shallow, clear of the shipping channel, and removed from the fastest current. International regattas are often sailed on the Olympic Circle, "to minimize the effect of local knowledge." It works, judging by the number of outsiders who win national and world titles here at the expense of the locals. Or perhaps local knowledge is overrated.

Olympic Circle currents tend to flow in broad sweeps in and out with the flood and ebb, or north and south during the transitions (see page 42 for a discussion of the tidal interchange between North Bay and South Bay). Olympic Circle race courses are free of the narrow rivers and countercurrents that dramatize West Bay sailing. However, this is not a patch of water that rewards the simple-minded. With an ironic view, you might even think that it's easier to read those narrow rivers and countercurrents of the West Bay, especially when there is brown, whitecapped water running out and blue, smooth water running in.

The Olympic Circle per se (aka the Berkeley Circle) is two nautical miles across, with eight marks on the perimeter and another buoy, X Mark, at the center. Club races and midwinters often start at X Mark. The circular arrangement around X allows a race committee to select another buoy one mile away that is reasonably close to an upwind bearing, and that's the one that becomes the weather mark. The Circle is tremendously useful, for example, to the Berkeley/Metropolitan Yacht Club Midwinters. Those races are sailed in off-season winds that may come from any point on the compass.

Major championships are handled differently, and so are most other "Circle" regattas. A race course may be set well north of the permanent marks, and then it becomes a new course, with new considerations of wind and current. Inflatable marks can be set for the wind of the moment and adjusted for small changes. Starting lines can be laid at the bottom of the course rather than in the middle, to let the fleet sort itself out over a two-mile weather leg.

In the summertime, sailing on the north side of the Circle brings you closer to the lee of Angel Island; you can count on lighter wind. Moving south brings you directly into the breeze from the Gate; you can expect more wind.

You can also expect less wind on the bottom of the course and more wind at the top — from a different direction — wherever the race is sailed. This is most noticeable early in the day, while the breeze is building. The seabreeze on the Circle tends to arrive from the south-southwest and shift to the right as it builds, yielding marked differences in the wind readings at the top and bottom of the course. That is, a stronger breeze at the top mark is more to the right than a lighter breeze at the bottom mark. At those times, you'll be rounding out the sails in a big way at the bottom of the course and perhaps wondering if you could change sails quickly enough (now, for the light stuff at the leeward mark, and again, later, for more wind near the weather mark) to make it pay. Usually, the answer is no, you can't make it pay. When

the wind hits 25 knots, it's a different game. That shallow East Bay water gets choppy in a flood and ugly-choppy in an ebb. Any wind-velocity difference between the weather mark and the leeward mark amounts to a subtle modulation of a screaming emergency.

A classic beat to weather on the Circle works the right hand side of the course, the north side, all the way to the "corner." Winners sometimes sail a one-tack leg. Losers too. When the Circle is working by the book, the broad effect of the Point Blunt Shift is to give the right-hand side of the course a double crank: a lifted angle followed by a header followed by a tack and a lift. The strategic implications of the Point Blunt Shift dominate most of the racing decisions on the Circle — and beating out of the Circle to marks in the West Bay.

If the seabreeze is solid and strong, it will be hard to avoid the temptations of the north side of the Circle. Here are three situations, however, when you ought to consider alternatives. 1) If the course is laid on the southern extremity of the Circle, the influence of the Point Blunt Shift is reduced, so the south side has more chance of being productive. 2) Wherever the course is laid, if the breeze is light, the left side or the middle should have the strongest wind. Going right takes you deeper into the wind shadow of the island. 3) If the tide is just turning to slack before ebb (because the South Bay ebbs first), the left side may offer favorable current on the weather leg.

The 1992 Star class worlds were sailed on the Circle, and there were moderate-air races in which the tide favored the right-hand side and the wind favored the left. The equation, generally, favored the wind. Moreover, "working the middle," as we might call anything short of a one-tack weather leg to the right-hand corner, offers the option of tacking on the shifts. Joe Londrigan, a sailmaker living in San Diego, almost won the '92 worlds. Later, he recalled that, "I had never sailed in San Francisco until the weekend before, but I knew that current would be a factor. I went to the Bay Model, I listened to anybody who would talk to me, and all the information agreed. It was going to be a big fleet, so it was obvious that you had to get a good start, and everybody figured you had to get onto port (which aims you toward the right-hand side) right away. But the committee was favoring the pin end (the left end) of the starting line, so I made my starts down there.

I did that for traffic control, mainly. It was too crowded at the other end. Everyone was jammed up, trying to be the first boat to get free and go right. To do that, they risked putting themselves in bad air, and that's what I was avoiding. I'd make my start and get over onto port like everybody else, but the wind was a lot freer for me, and I could tack on a shift if I wanted to."

Tides and currents, wind currents, topographic shifts — these are matters of strategy that you can plot before the race. When the fleet engages, you're down to tactics. The strategic demands of the Circle don't change much from day to day, but no two tactical races are the same.

Olympic medalist Jeff Madrigali looks at the Circle this way:

"If your course is on the north side of the Circle, you're going to be dealing with the wind that bends around Point Blunt. You go for the shift on the right, but you expect the puffs to come from the left.

"The key is knowing where you want to be on the starting line, because that's going to set you up for how you arrive at the corner, and turning the corner sets you up for approaching the weather mark.

"I like to go from the middle of the line or maybe the left. As soon as we start, sure, I'm going to go off to the right along with everybody else, but I've got my options open. Maybe it's a day when you want to go all

THE CHECKUP

INTERIOR. DAY.
THE DOCTOR'S EXAMINING ROOM
Thin light penetrates blinds drawn shut for privacy. We see the doctor removing his gloves, signaling the end of an examination. He moves as if to exit, then turns to speak. The voice is somber, solicitous — and chilling.
Doctor:
When you get dressed, I'd like to speak to you in my office.
Female Patient:
(Whispering to herself)
Oh my god …

INTERIOR. DAY.
THE DOCTOR'S PRIVATE OFFICE
The Female Patient sits in an upholstered chair in front of the doctor's desk. Her legs are crossed, arms pulled close in body language expressing deep anxiety. What's it going to be? Cancer? She studies the doctor's face. Yes, of course, it has to be cancer! The wait is killing her. At last, he speaks:

Doctor
(Slowly, carefully)
Is there … anything you'd like to talk about?
Silence.
Doctor
You can talk to me.
Female Patient
(A quizzical look. She was ready for anything but this.)
Doctor
Sometimes, a woman just needs someone she can talk to.
Female Patient
(Beginning to wonder about the doctor)
I'm sorry … I'm … I … really … I don't think I understand.
Doctor
You can trust me. That's what I'm here for.
Female Patient
(More fearful and confused by the minute)
But I just don't know what you're asking.
Doctor
(Penetrating, ironic)
So I suppose you got those bruises on your legs and hips from walking into a doorknob?
Female Patient
(Seeing the light, laughing hysterically)
Oh, Doctor! It's all right. Nobody's beating me up. I'M A SAILOR!

the way to the corner. Fine, but sometimes, the way to get there is to go from the left end of the line. If you start from the right-hand end, you might get to the corner first, but maybe your end of the starting line wasn't favored, and then you're hosed — you're not the fleet leader, you're blocked, you can't tack, and you're forced to overstand the layline.

"Where you tack back is critical. In the corner, the wind goes right some more — you get headed — and late in the day, that right swing is even more pronounced. Then, when you come back for the mark, you get lifted on starboard tack. And the tide's never neutral. You're going to get pushed one way or the other. A strong ebb is going to make the layline hard to call, but the early flood is the time when it's hardest to get around the mark. Another thing you see with laylines on the Circle — lots of times people go to the corner, and they come back on what looks like the layline, but then the wind goes back to the left a bit, and they lose what they paid for over in the corner.

"And it doesn't go the same from one beat to the next. On the second or third beat, if you're forced to take a clearing tack coming off the bottom mark, there's a tendency to get caved in (on your next port tack), right back onto the track of the boats that rounded ahead of you.

"How you play the first beat also depends on how far up you're going. We sailed a Soling Worlds on the Circle, with a starting line that was close to Brooks Island and the weather mark very far up. It was also farther left than usual, and we had early starts, about noon, and an ebb tide. There was a lot of ebb coming out of the South Bay, then sweeping out toward the Gate. That South Bay ebb was really working for the left side. We'd go off that way, and it would help us, but then we'd look at the guys who had gone even farther left, and they were looking better than we were."

Thanks, Madro. Here are three principles to believe in: 1) The more international champions there are on the course, the more like-

SHORT-TACKING THE CITY FRONT

UNDER THE RACING RULES, a boat that is "pinned" by another as they approach the shore has the right to request room to tack, but only if it is impossible to tack without hitting the other boat. If the pinned boat can tack and duck, it's not really pinned and there is no right to hail.

Coming off the San Francisco cityfront on port tack, a boat that has hailed for searoom loses its privilege, becoming just another burdened vessel, as soon as there is enough water around it to tack again and not immediately go aground. Even if a right-of-way boat forces it to maneuver with the speed low and the sails stalled. Even if, instead of tacking, it has to aim toward Berkeley and duck five transoms. Multitiered overlaps and reasonable warning time come into play, all on the instant, in the midst of noise, distractions, and a potential for violence. The real competitor will employ his right-of-way tacks with diabolical timing, to catch an opponent at the worst possible moment. That is how the game is played: sailshape, hullform, water, wind and chess. And noise, those cries of

STARBOARD! Searoom! STARBOARD! Searoom! that cut through the rattling of the sails. The experts play it close, and it's not strange to see a starboard-tack, right-of-way skipper wave a port-tack opponent across his bow. The rules require everyone to avoid a collision if possible. There might be tactical concerns, too. Maybe the starboard-tacker would rather have his opponent cross his bow and go away than tack into a lee-bow position where, very soon, he'll be hailing for searoom. Perhaps it's a question of mutual survival, and the starboard-tacker knows full well he'll be a port-tacker momentarily, and there are minor fouls going on all over the place, and we bought these boats for fun …

Those who carry a foul to a protest hearing should keep one fact in mind. Their protest may well be heard by well-versed, well-intentioned people who did not witness the incident and, after listening to different versions well-presented by the crews of both well-sailed boats, will wind up with no earthly idea what really happened. Then they will turn to each other and say, "We'll have to rule according to the burden of proof." The racing rules specify which boat must prove its case in a right-of-way dispute. Where doubt remains, that's the boat that gets chucked.

A spectator sport [PHOTO BY JOHN RIISE, *LATITUDE 38*]

ly that someone will work the left, or the middle, with success. 2) If it's blowing 25 out of 225, don't even think about it. 3) It always pays to go right, except when it pays to go left.

Go right? Go right? That's the rule of thumb for most of the racing on the whole West Coast. Up and down the coast and in Southern California, too, these "one-way race courses" are built on a summer seabreeze that shifts to the right as it increases, much as a building breeze shifts on the Olympic Circle. A typical Southern California gradient seabreeze comes in at 8-12 knots from 230-240 degrees. Significant currents then are wind-driven, down-coast currents, lighter near the beach. That's the same as to say, upwind is also up-current. The least current is found to the right as you leave the starting line, and the current-favored side is also the wind-favored side. In a growing seabreeze, shifting with the increase, the boat that works upwind on the right-hand (up-coast) side of the course is sailing toward the increase and sailing toward a port-tack header that equals a profitable, progressive starboard-tack lift toward the mark.

Around Marina Del Rey and down to Redondo Beach/King Harbor, a 12-knot peak is typical for a summer day. Just to the south of Redondo Beach, the Palos Verdes cliffs break up the wind flow, creating a venturi on the southern side of the hill that makes San Pedro/Long Beach/Alamitos Bay the windiest spot in greater L.A. Afternoon winds might peak at 16-18. Then, moving south again, the breeze drops off again. Newport Beach falls into the "lucky to see 14" category, and in San Diego, which has some truly great sailing, there also are plenty of days of an eight-knot breeze in a sea condition known as "the San Diego slop."

Which is enough information, and true enough, to be dangerous. Here's how complicated it can get:

For a long time, Newport Beach sailors worked their patch of water according to the go-right formula, but Dave Ullman (sailmaker, world champion, Yachtsman of the Year, and home town boy) calls that approach "obsolete." Newport Beach lies downwind of Catalina Island. The island's influence on the breeze redefines everything, Ullman says, and current is a major consideration.

Off Newport Beach, a gradient breeze — coming around the upper end of Catalina — will build a down-coast current. Meanwhile, the way race courses are laid out here, you cross from shallow water to deep water on the way to the weather mark, about halfway up. A 10-knot breeze only three days in a row can build a down-coast current that runs twice as fast on the deep side of the shelf. (I've never measured those currents, but even if it's only a half-knot, consider what you would give for a reliable, predictable quarter knot of speed-in-the-bank.

Or, if a summertime low pressure system is moving off the coast (we're not speaking of a winter storm), the wind will come from the south, eddying off the lower side of Catalina, and the current then will turn from down-coast to up-coast, shifting first on the shallow, inner side of the shelf. In the transition, Ullman says, it is "not uncommon" to have an up-coast current on the shelf and a down-coast current in the deep waters off the shelf, with a clear color change between them.

In the eddying, southerly winds associated with low atmospheric pressure, the left side tends to be favored. You get the puffs first on the left, and on average, you get more breeze. When high pressure returns to the region, and the gradient breeze builds again, the tactician returns his attention to the go-right formula. In 12 knots from 240 degrees, the right side produces more wind and a shift. (However, if the wind doesn't build, if it sticks at 6-10, the right side gets the shift but no increase. Boats on the left, outside, get more breeze. Usually, but not always, more breeze wins.)

Santa Cruz is another go-right race course, but it's a little more complicated, what with being tucked into the northern side of the Monterey Bay bight.

First, there's the predictable clockwise shift on a building breeze as the fog burns off on a "classic" day. Or, if the fog doesn't burn off, the wind won't blow as hard, and it will stay "more to the south." Among the experts on Santa Cruz sailing, Morgan Larson likes to emphasize the effect of geography upon the wind; Dave Wahle likes to emphasize the effect of geography upon the current.

"It's definitely a right-hand favored course," Larson said. " The wind bends along the shore, so you have a good angle coming in on port, and you get lifted going out on starboard. There are times when you have less wind close to the beach, but if it's already blowing eighteen knots, you can afford to go for the angle."

Wahle agreed that it's a right-sided race course: "It has a lot to do with the current. The coastal current back-eddies at Monterey, then it hooks up into Santa Cruz. I've sat on the committee boat at the starting line and seen it streaming dead upwind against the current.

"If the breeze is steady at 240, you have to go right," Wahle said. "You slowly get lifted on port tack going into the corner, and then, as you come out, you get into the seabreeze, and that lifts you on starboard tack. It's a good feeling both ways. There are just two more things to say about it. For some regattas — a world championship, say — we move the course offshore far enough to get out of the up-coast current. And we have an ocean swell down here, so, unlike the bay, there's always a chance for some serious surfing. Try it. You'll like it."

One quirk worth knowing about is the windflow eddy that sometimes occurs — near the beach you get a southwesterly instead of a northwesterly. And when you go to Santa Cruz, remember, spirit counts. One pair of sailors from Kenya earned legendary status for the way they overcame all obstacles to race at a 505 World Championship. A dock strike intimidated many foreign entries, and kept them at home, but not the Kenyans. They shipped their boat to Mexico and unloaded there, bought a rusted Cadillac from the first guy they met on the beach, and headed north with the radiator steaming and the springs creaking. They wrung every ounce of life out of the old behemoth, which hemorrhaged and died as it rolled into the parking lot below the Santa Cruz Yacht Club. There the Caddy ended its days, abandoned, as a spot for teenage trysts. So the story goes, if you believe the ex-teenagers.

The edge of the fog. Almost anywhere, but especially in the West Bay, you should expect the wind to be gusty at the edge of the fog. You can get some very big blasts. It happens, probably, when two layers of incoming air are mixing vertically, and the higher wind aloft gets sucked down to mast level.

Should you "play the cone" at Alcatraz? Here's a tactical question that comes up sooner or later for most racing keelboats, and cruisers can profit if they know the tricks.

From the sky, Alcatraz looks like a motorboat going through the water. It leaves a huge wake. Fighting a flood, you can make big gains if you stay in that wake, where the current is blocked. The Alcatraz Cone is especially attractive on flood-tide racing legs between Treasure Island and Crissy Field.

Early in the flood, the cone is the fast way to go. Late in the flood, it's a disaster.

Where's the cutoff? We're looking at a westbound leg against a countercurrent. We want to avoid the channel, or minimize our time in the channel, so we have to choose between protected water behind the island and protected water close to the San Francisco cityfront. At some time during the flood tide cycle, the advantage shifts from boats in the cone to boats on the beach, and several generations of tacticians have settled on this rule of thumb: You use the cone up to one hour after Maximum Flood; later than that, you go to the beach.

It pays out this way. Early in the flood, with the current running strongest close to the cityfront, there's no rush to be there. Later, when the flood is fully formed and running strongest in the channel, there's still no rush to get to the cityfront, because Alcatraz is such a good tide blocker. However, at one hour after Maximum Flood, the current slows dramatically along the beach. Eddies and backcurrents form. From then on, if you're trying to get to this good stuff by crossing the channel from Alcatraz, you will lose big to the boats that are already there.

"Playing the face" of the island is a secondary option, and it pays off until about Maximum Flood. Suppose you have tacked up behind the island, keeping your boat inside the cone. Now, instead of ramming the island, and instead of taking off on starboard tack for the cityfront, you poke out into the channel, on the city side, just far enough to get around the rocks — the heroes play it spitting close — and then you go back to sail in the protected "bubble" on the western face. You might even discover a bonus countercurrent waiting for you there.

Eventually, whether you work the face or not, you have to cross the channel, hit the cityfront, and short-tack from wherever you make contact. If you can set yourself up to clear the last of the Fort Mason piers and sail directly into the protected water at Gas House Cove, you won't be sorry. With the flood working the entire bay, the best protection and any available countercurrents will be found in the shallows close to the beach.

THE NORTH CHANNEL, between Alcatraz and Angel Island, has the strongest currents inside the Golden Gate. It also sees some heavy traffic, with races passing through between West Bay and East Bay marks — and it's worth remembering that the heaviest ships use the North Channel going both directions.

Upwind legs through the North Channel often begin in the East Bay, with a rounding of YRA 24, east of Angel Island. Turning upwind at 24 and strapping in the sails makes for a tactical moment that is all but unique on the local scene — we make the same move whether the tide is ebbing or flooding. Since we're "behind" Angel Island, where we expect the wind to be affected by the Point Blunt Shift, we sail toward the island on port tack. If the tide is ebbing, the ebb is pushing us sideways in a good direction. If it's flooding, we're aimed at less flood.

So, here we are leaving YRA 24, on port tack behind Angel Island, aimed at the island. With an ebb current running, we're not tempted to sail too close, where the wind might go light. Instead, we tack to starboard while the breeze is solid, keeping ourselves in good current flow. The challenge is to choose our tacking point, because we also want to set ourselves up against the competition. Preferably, we're closer to the island than they are without being too close, and here's why. After we tack to starboard, and we approach Point Blunt and sail into the wind that's blowing off the West Bay, we'll be entering a starboard-tack lift. We want to be "inside" that lift (just as we'd like to be the inside boat on every lift for the rest of our lives).

Time passes, and here we are on starboard, clearing Point Blunt and sailing into the breeze from the main part of the bay. Next, we're clear of the buoy, and we tack — immediately, for a Point Knox finish

> *"San Francisco Bay sailors need to spend a lot more time in light air. There's a whole world of light-air sailing, and there's a whole world of technique that surrounds it. People here forget there's such a thing as finesse, and as soon as their boat slows down they flip out, they tack, and they go down the tubes. When the wind goes light, everything slows down. You have to slow down too, and you don't tack unless there's a reason."*
>
> — DAWN RILEY
> America's Cup challenger, *America True*

line, or a little later (for maximum wind and current) if we're going to Harding Rock or Yellow Bluff. Look back to the Current Diagrams on page 43 for an overview. The big ebb is out in the channel. What you won't see pictured are the current swirls that form on the backside of Point Blunt in ebb or flood.

Leaving YRA 24 in a flood tide race is a bit more complicated. Clearing the mark and beating toward the island on port, we'll have to balance the advantages of going close, for tide protection, with the risk of light spots in the lee of the hill. It's yet another version of the conundrum, out for the wind or in for the tide. We've heard that winners bet with the wind, but we also need to be inside that lift, don't we? Hmmmm. And on the way, close in, there's that one rock that you'll never find on the chart, but deep draft boats can't clear it, and only those who have found it, know it. (Believe it.)

Rounding Blunt against a flood, it's common to tack immediately and sail a course close to the island. "Working the face of Angel," they call it. However, there's a bubble of light air that forms on the windward side of the island, and you can hurt yourself by sailing too close. Two boats side by side but fifty yards apart can be sailing in different wind velocities with little difference in current. The later you go in the flood cycle, the less the tide-advantage of being in close.

Elsewhere, the shifting surface of our local playing field is rich in details that you have to learn sooner or later. Here are a few.

♦ At Harding Rock, relative to the mid-bay breeze, the wind tends to be a little bit lighter, and it comes more from the south. Approaching from a cityfront mark, you will experience the change as a lifting, fairing breeze. Probably, this has to do with a northerly split in the breeze from the Golden Gate, drawn off by Raccoon Strait and light spots in the lee of the Marin Headlands.

♦ At Yellow Bluff, the wind blowing over the headlands is full of holes and puffs from odd directions. On most days, the lifts come from the left, favoring the boat inside on port tack — at the same time that the tide often favors boats sailing in from the right.

♦ Off downtown Sausalito, the seabreeze that rolls in over Wolfback Ridge will sometimes bounce back up, leaving a hole that is filled by an easterly backflow. It won't happen unless the main body of the seabreeze is strong, and it won't last if the seabreeze builds to a scream.

♦ Around Richmond, you can make some pretty good guesses about wind strength in different, adjoining patches of water depending on whether or not you can look through Raccoon Strait and see the Golden Gate. If you can see the bridge, the wind can see you. Sail out of Keller's Cove and turn north toward the Richmond Long Wharf, and you will soon come to an area where you can look through the strait to the Golden Gate. Expect an increase in wind. Sail north beyond that (or north-ish), and you will enter the lee of Tiburon. The wind will drop. And here's a different wrinkle on the same theme: "If I'm running down from Raccoon Strait to Richmond," says Jim DeWitt, "I make better time if I stay to the north of a straight line. It adds a little distance, but it keeps me in the breeze."

Another DeWitt tip has to do with the way the seabreeze fans out from the central part of the bay, blowing across the Olympic Circle and bending north toward San Pablo. Thinking back to one race in particular and a leeward mark close to the Richmond breakwater, DeWitt points out that boats in those waters, sailing on a reach from south to north, are caught up in that changing breeze. Usually, it will go lighter on them, so it just might pay to sail below the rhumb line. That way, when the breeze does go light, the boats to leeward can reach up to a hotter angle for more apparent wind and a chance of sailing right around the rhumb-line bound competition.

♦ Patrick Andreasen, a dinghy sailor who grew up stomping around Coyote Point and environs, likes to say, "That's pretty much it," after he fills you in on the one great, tactical, weather-leg move for racing upwind out of Coyote Point: "Go to the beach."

In a summer seabreeze, a boat working to weather on port tack (port tack being the long board enroute to the usual weather mark, the birdcage north of the airport) will experience a port-tack lift. Boats closer to the beach will be inside the lift, and they'll make out.

Andreasen also notes that Coyote Point is a good place for windsurfing almost all the time, but especially when the currents are no good at Crissy Field. At Coyote Point, port tack takes you out on a tight reach; starboard brings you in on a wide reach, "and the wind doesn't shut down all of a sudden; it gives you some warning. It won't just leave

Keep a stiff lower lip [PHOTO BY ROB MOORE, *LATITUDE 38*]

you out there with a great view of the sunset."

♦ One of the peculiarities of Redwood City sailing is the occasional summertime northerly or easterly sucked in by a local thermal. The peninsula is wide enough here to build up a heat pocket with enough thermal action to accomplish exactly that — until the seabreeze fills and backs the whole shebang around 50 to 90 degrees.

When the westerly is late, perhaps with a high pressure cell incubating on top of the region and drooling out oddments of wind, the race committee's job becomes a matter of philosophy. Any site chosen for a weather mark may lie to leeward in ten minutes. Worse yet, a windward-leeward course could turn into a set of reaches.

To wait for the westerly or not to wait, that is the question. If there seems a reasonable chance that it will come, most committees will wait, "to provide the fairest race possible." Considering the realities of bay sailing (the strong tides and the poor chance that any odd sliver of wind will support a whole race), that's not a decision to quarrel with. But it might leave bay sailors shortchanged on the total experience of yacht racing.

Which brings us back short circle to Jim DeWitt, full time artist, sometime sailmaker, and the first bay sailor ever to win the men's na-

---

ENSENADA BOUND
© San Francisco Chronicle, by Kimball Livingston

I HADN'T SAILED THE ENSENADA RACE since the Federales tear-gassed me in front of Hussong's Cantina. Maybe that was a sign.

Picture a fleet of boats big and small, new and old and six hundred strong, reaching down the coast in such a grand, hungry hoarde they could be taking orders from Cecil B. DeMille himself. Picture flags flying and Heineken flowing.

It's billed as a boat race, but this overnight Bull Run from Newport Beach to Ensenada is also renowned for exploits ashore. Any veteran will have stories about Rosarita, tequila, and the crewmates he bailed out of the Ensenada jail (or in my case, the Newport jail — a clean, well-lighted place, and we hadn't even started yet).

The proposition that twelve equal-cost partners ought to charter an old, unsuccessful America's Cup boat and race it on the ocean just has to grow horsefeathers someplace. But it's hard to resist the allure of these rare, quirky thoroughbreds. They are fascinating as sin. I told my friends, "This is what yachting is all about."

Valiant was built for the 1970 defense of the America's Cup. She is 63 feet long and weighs 69,000 pounds. In her moment of glory, Twelve Meter U.S. 16 marked a turning point, but it wasn't a good turn for *Valiant*. This was the design where Olin Stephens discovered that he had gone one step too far making each new hull a little longer than the last one, and giving up sail area to accomplish it. *Valiant* was heavy and underpowered. The boat did not make it to the America's Cup finals. Many years and indignities later, and fallen into strange hands, she called to mind the passage in *Black Beauty* where the poor beast, aging and weak, staggers uphill under the cruel traces of a coal wagon.

That was something to think about when I found myself flat on the deck in the flak-attack position, with the boat yawing wildly out of control under full sail and a calm voice announcing, "Yep, there goes the rudder." But I'm getting ahead of my story.

The moment I saw her, Valiant gave me a lift. My eye and my heart together took in the tall mast, the sexy transom and the familiar snub nose of the America's Cup breed. Admittedly, Dennis Conner wouldn't have touched it, and the howls of laughter from Chris Dickson or New Zealand's winning Cup skipper Russell Coutts would have curdled the bilgewater that continually leaked in.

But Valiant was the real thing, a boat with a past, and she was all ours for two weeks. Fresh paint hid the worst of the recent crimes, and our charter shares included the "opportunity" to revamp everything: winches, electricals, sails. Having been charged with running the foredeck, I scurried about and tried to look intelligent.

I felt minimally intelligent being hauled up the mast in the bosun's chair, higher and higher off the deck, to inspect the many points at which critical wires disappeared into pools of rust. The halyard I was hanging on, for example.

The start of the Ensenada Race is one of

tional championship, the Mallory Cup. DeWitt won the Mallory at Annapolis, on the Chesapeake, an experience that reinforced his faith in the meaningfulness of racing in eccentric, light winds. DeWitt believes in the competitive values that lie beyond the textbook race. "Sailing in junk," he calls it. "It's good for you. There's character in it. Maybe it's just because I grew up sailing on Lake Merritt, and I feel at home in that kind of stuff, but when you go traveling and you get outside San Francisco Bay, there's a lot of it to contend with. It's a trial, and it's honest. It's less physical and more mental than twenty-five knots."

OAK, ASH, AND CARBON FIBER

When Hemingway wanted to give us a picture of his romantic heroine Brett Ashley, he said she was "built with curves like the hull of a racing yacht," and he let our minds fill in the rest. But *The Sun Also Rises* was written in the 1920s, when boats were built with curves to rival the alluring Lady Brett. Nowadays, with Hemingway soon to become a writer from the early-to-mid portions of a previous century, you have to figure that noodle-thin spars and anodized winches do not spell the romance of mahogany and brass, even if they make for deucedly effective machines.

Whatever your taste, the Bay delivers. The springtime Master Mariners Regatta, a revival of the working boat races of the 1800s, now draws the likes of little *Freda*, built in Tiburon in 1885 and still, wherever she goes, a special place to be, a magical helm just to touch.

Bird boats were born in the 1920s as a syndicate boat for match racing, and they've since competed in thirteen matches for the San Francisco Perpetual Challenge Trophy. In the process, they have grown into an active class of twenty-two surviving boats out of twenty-six built. (When the first edition of *Sailing the Bay* was published, the survivors were twenty-three; then *Falcon*, hull number five, opened up and swallowed the bay on the second leg of a Master Mariners Race. The fleet now lists *Falcon* as deceased, one mile southeast of Angel Island.)

One of the great bay classics, the

---

the world's great traffic jams. With the helmsman half blind, part of my job was to keep skipper Ted Ritter up to speed on the zigs and the zags. Our space-age communication-headsets flopped, so we returned to the grand traditions of yachting. We hollered our heads off.

The rest, the race, was a routine familiar to all who have sailed offshore in moderate winds and a mild sea. Sails were adjusted and re-adjusted. Sandwiches appeared and disappeared. We soon left the herd behind.

Our class rival, another old Cup boat called *Newsboy*, was safely tucked away astern. *Valiant* quickly, quietly made strides. Dolphin rocketed through the quarter-wave, and the long afternoon deepened into night with the moonlight bright on the water. I paced the deck and worried, "How do I get a story out of this?"

Then, at midnight, the wind came.

Cup boats are highly-stressed machines. To keep a mast upright, bearing a perfect airfoil in sails strong enough to pull a 69,000-pound boat at flank speed, powerful forces have to be guided and controlled. Parts, when they break, blow with explosive force, and they're likely to take

out the next thing in line. Lose control and you can lose the mast, which is why I hit the deck, flak-attack flat, when I felt the helm go.

The wind was twenty-six knots apparent. We were headstay reaching with our biggest spinnaker up and the lights of Ensenada ahead.

Then we weren't.

The next hour had all the romance of wading through a swamp of snakes — getting the sails down and the boat under control. It was exhausting. It was dangerous. And it was only ten miles from Ensenada.

We spent the rest of that night and the next day limping slowly back the way we had come to an arrival in San Diego, the closest reasonable port of repairs and far more attractive on that scale than Ensenada. Less attractive on other scales, but meanwhile the rudder was cocked off 60 degrees from where it belonged. We had one big question: Would it stay there, requiring only a new rudder stock, or would it drop away entirely, requiring a new rudder and many, many dollars? Would my one-twelfth share of a new rudder wipe out my plans for that new windsurfer?

I sighed, "This is what yachting is all about."

El Toro pram, was developed from a wooden design of the 1930s. Eight feet long and still commanding devotion from skippers eight to eighty, El Toros have a senior division that begins at age 19 and includes people such as Pete Blasberg, who qualified for the division more than half a century ago. Pete won't quit till he gets it right. El Toros race in the lakes, in sheltered arms of the main bay, and once a year across the Gate from Sausalito to the cityfront in the aptly named Bullship Regatta. John Kostecki, world champion, Olympic medalist, and America's Cup tactician, grew up racing two boats — his father's Cal 20 and his own El Toro. When he looks back now, Kostecki says, "I liked crewing on the Cal 20, but most of all I liked the El Toro. On that boat, I was the skipper. I was in control."

The Bullship finishes off the St. Francis Yacht Club, right where international ocean racers finish in the Big Boat Series, the bay's signature annual event. The Big Boat Series is known offically as the club's Perpetual Trophy Regatta and unofficially as the West Coast Convention of Yacht Racing. Boats come down from Seattle and up from Los Angeles. It's a hard-traveling bunch, but the crews like to come here. As one 70-footer owner put it, with only a slight exaggeration, "We like it because everyplace else we race is kind of ho-hum."

From the Richmond Yacht Club's Big Daddy Regatta to the Singlehanded Sailing Society's Three Bridge Fiasco, the bay is rich in special events and special opportunities for racing. Organized competition on the bay goes back to 1869. That was the year the San Francisco Yacht Club, as an early order of business, staged the club's first regatta. The winner was the sloop *Emerald*, a dark-hulled beauty with a graceful sheer and a cutter bow. The newly-formed club started its race from the station of the time, at Mission Rock, just south of China Basin. From there, the course reached south to a stakeboat at Hunters Point and across the South Bay to a stakeboat near Oakland, where the fleet turned upwind for a beat to a stakeboat near the Golden Gate. The second half of the race was a return to the starting line, rerounding all marks.

A course like that is unthinkable today, but those were simpler times. In place of the complicated time allowance systems we have now, the San Francisco Yacht Club's handicapping fit on a single sheet of pa-

per. By 1877, the system had developed so far as to recognize two classifications, schooners and sloops. Yawls were lumped with the schooners. The club gave allowances of three-fourths of a minute per foot of waterline length. In the 1880s, the allowance was increased to a minute per foot, and somebody was always griping about an unfair rating. The more things change, the more they stay the same.

Compared to Europe and the East Coast, an unusually large number of San Francisco Bay sailors skippered their own boats. There were names such as Charlie Chittenden and Isidor Gutte. The famous yachts of the 19th Century — the likes of the *Sappho*, *Chispa*, *Casco* or *Lurline* — were big things by present thinking. But it wasn't just the fat cats that wanted to race. Little boats were out there too, and "mosquito regattas" sprang up to accommodate them. Sailing canoes were popular in many corners of the bay, including the south shore of Alameda, where the skippers included more than one commodore of the Encinal Yacht Club. Small boat racing was successful enough to persuade its enthusiasts that they needed a forum of their own, which had a lot to do with the launching of the Corinthian Yacht Club in Belvedere in 1886. To make sure that it remained a small-boat club, Corinthian's bylaws stated flatly that no boat over forty-five feet would be admitted. Perceptions of size have changed, since then, and so has the Corinthian Yacht Club.

Our oldest sailing prize is the San Francisco Perpetual Challenge Trophy, a big bite of silver first contested in 1895 under the auspices of the two senior clubs, San Francisco and Corinthian, and endowed by members of those clubs along with others from Encinal, Pacific (RIP), and California (RIP). By the luck of the draw, Encinal became the first defender of the new trophy, and San Francisco became the first challenger. Encinal commodore Joseph Leonard told his friends, "When I drew the slip of paper which made the Encinal Yacht Club the first custodian of the cup, I could see a smile go around the company, which was as much as to say, `Well, it is lucky you drew the cup, for that is your Club's only chance in the world of ever getting it.' "

Leonard, however, had his own ideas. He was the proud owner of a new and very racy sloop, the *El Sueño*, 36.5 feet on the waterline and 52 feet overall. Leonard had designed it himself, with a rounded

The launching of *El Sueño* at South Beach, Alameda, on April 6, 1905. A photographer's note reads: "Realizing they are stuck fast."
[COURTESY OF EVELYN CRANE AND WOODRUFF C. MINOR. PHOTO BY FREDERICK ZIEL]

"whaleback" cabin and decks to shed water and lower wind resistance. The boat also had an eight-horse, triple-cylinder gasoline engine with a retractable propeller that made it the first auxiliary yacht on San Francisco Bay, according to our authority here, Woodruff C. Minor's history of Encinal YC, *On the Bay*. *El Sueño* was the natural choice to defend even though Leonard had to alter a brand new boat to meet the challenger's terms. Some 300 square feet of sail area was trimmed from the boat's designed 1900 square feet — to bring it within ten percent of the challenger's sail area — and the boat's auxiliary engine was removed. It was then the first former auxiliary yacht on San Francisco Bay, but not the last hopeful to soak up money and attention going into a match for the Perpetual Challenge Trophy.

Race day dawned August 31, 1895. Both boats had ringers on the helm. The San Francisco Yacht Club's challenger was the *Queen*, a Stone Boat Yard-built sloop owned by Frank Bartlett and skippered by Capt. Edward Howard. *El Sueño* raced under Capt. James Hanley, who had quit Maine and the maritime trade for a real estate career in Alameda. EYC, as defender, set a 15-mile course (a modified version of its club course), with a starting line off the Alameda Ferry Pier (RIP). The opening leg lay upwind to Blossom Rock Buoy, and Howard and Hanley split tacks early. Howard short-tacked close to Goat (Yerba Buena) Island. Hanley worked longer boards in deeper water and nursed El Sueño to Blossom Rock with a three-minute lead. From there, rounding subsequent marks at Hunters Point and Mission Rock, he stretched his lead and ran for home with a finish-line difference of eleven minutes. In Alameda, as they say, the crowd went wild.

Joseph Leonard served five terms as EYC commodore. He was the towering figure of East Bay yachting in the 1890s. At the same time, his construction company built a sizable chunk of everything that went up in Alameda, including a shingled mansion for himself on the "Gold Coast." In 1898, with the economy in recession and his business on the rocks, he left for the Klondike.

If you're looking at the old days, the history of yachting makes a pretty good history of the Bay Area, period.

The San Francisco Perpetual Challenge Trophy deed of gift invites challenges from distant clubs, and the trophy spent fourteen of its first 100 years at the Los Angeles, San Diego, or Balboa Yacht Clubs, with no end of bother. Whenever a Southern California boat skips off with this one, it's a matter of honor to get it back. And it's never cheap. Locally, the Corinthian, Aeolian, Sausalito and Sequoia yacht clubs have all held the prize.

The St. Francis Yacht Club took the Perpetual away from Balboa in 1987 and held it — the club's fourth possession — until 1994, when the San Francisco Yacht Club won it away and set the stage for a centennial rematch. In 1995, 100 years to the month after the original contest, the Encinal Yacht Club was the challenger and the San Francisco Yacht

STEVE TAFT HAS SAILED umpteen jillion laps of San Francisco Bay as helmsman, tactician, or both at the same time. When he talks about, "using the cone up to an hour after Maximum Flood," he's talking about a course that will sail up the cone, cross the channel, and arrive at the cityfront at about that bell-ringer hour of Maximum Flood plus one. And he doesn't take the tide book for granted. "The trick is to determine when max flood is really going to happen," Taft says. "Over the course of a year, the book averages out very nicely, but there are times when it just doesn't match up. If the book happens to be an hour off on the day of The Race, and you don't know it, you could look pretty bad. I make it a practice to check a bunch of different marks on the way to the race; that helps me to figure where we are relative to the book-tide. And when I'm down at T.I., I look up toward Pier 39, and I can learn a lot about what the tide's doing close to the beach by watching the boats up there. You have all kinds of considerations. If you're down at T.I. and there's a lot of south in the wind, maybe the cutoff point comes a little earlier in the flood tide cycle. Instead of going to the cone you get yourself to the beach and you sail a long, port-tack board instead of making tacks up the cone. You really have to think through this business of cone or the beach, beach or the cone, because once you've made a commitment, you're going to live with it."

Club was the defender. Both had ringers to drive: Christopher Corlett for EYC; Jeff Madrigali for SFYC. The two clubs settled on one-design J-105s for the match, as Madrigali said, "because in the old days, a lot of the boats that raced were so different from each other, the race was over before anybody put up the sails."

Skies were clear on the morning of August 26, 1995. A wispy fog topped the headlands north of the Golden Gate, and a solid, heavy line of fog lurked offshore, gray and distant. Berkeley YC's Montara fleet worked outbound, heeled to the breeze, with Albert Holt's Olson 30 *Run Wild* chasing the big guys and fated to return seven hours later with a corrected time win. Richmond YC's Tri-Island racers were off for roundings of Red Rock, Angel and Alcatraz, either way (north-around proving the fast route by four minutes for Ralph Rhoda's Etchells 30, *Sabik*). Handicap Divisions were beating toward Yellow Bluff from the Sausalito YC's starting line at Point Knox, One Design Classes were beating up the cityfront, and Golden Gate YC had the Woodies — the Knarrs, Folkboats, and IODs. In short, it was a normal day on San Francisco Bay, and that accounted for only the action in view from the West Bay. The Treasure Island YC was meanwhile running 505s and International Canoes, and at Redwood City, twenty-some miles to the south, Sequoia YC was racing fleets of Sunfish, Lasers, JY15s and El Toros.

Back in the West Bay, in the Alcatraz Channel, the SFYC committee-boat *Victory* laid a line that ranged straight up Laguna Street to the crest of Pacific Heights. Then *Victory* called *Blackhawk* (belonging to Art Ball) and *Chimo* (belonging to Chuck Winton) to answer the guns. The prestart was a lively bit of aim-at'em-duck'em-dodge'em-scare'em, and Madrigali got the best of that. He locked out Corlett on the left end and took a clear-ahead start across the flood, aimed on starboard tack at the tide relief on the beach. "Corlett didn't have any options at that point," Madrigali said. "He had to follow us to the beach to get out of the tide, and he had to eat our gas to do it."

When Madrigali tacked on a header, well short of the beach, Corlett kept going, and Madrigali let him go. From that point EYC was in better current and aimed at better yet. SFYC had more wind, also more current opposing, but an angle, as Madrigali said, "that had us laying the mark."

And then it didn't.

When *Chimo* sailed into a light spot and a header both at the same time, the day suddenly looked glowing for *Blackhawk* and Alameda, ashen for *Chimo* and Belvedere.

And then it didn't.

The wind came back for *Chimo*, and that reversed the reverse, and that was that. It was yet another example of the old "out for the wind or in for the tide" non-equatable equation, with the boat behind trying to force the issue and this time failing. The SFYC defenders rounded 31 seconds up at the first mark, with speed to stretch the lead on every leg.

Both teams looked flawless. *Chimo* set the tone of things at the first leeward mark; Madrigali, Winton, Chris Perkins, John Sweeney and bowman Hogan Beatie had the gennaker down, the decks cleared, and the weight on the rail one fat half-second before they wound the boat up around the mark. EYC — Corlett, Carl Schumacher, Glenn Hansen, Sean Svendsen and Bill Columbo — were just as good if quite a big busier going around Mark 1. They couldn't afford the luxury of an early sail change.

SFYC stretched on every leg, helped by a gennaker that pulled them lower and faster. EYC took a flyer out to the middle of the bay on the last upwind leg — there was nothing else to do, and maybe the laws of hydraulics had been canceled for the day — but the net effect was a finish line difference of five minutes, 52 seconds.

Glenn Isaacson, out from Belvedere to view the proceedings, observed that, "In a flood tide race, the rich get richer."

Corlett announced that, "I finished second, and those poor guys in the other boat — they were next to last."

Then they all went home, and that was the beginning of the next hundred years.

Racing to Hawaii, bay sailors have their choice of two races that start right here at home: the West Marine Pacific Cup, and the Single-handed Sailing Society's Singlehanded Transpac.

The Pacific Cup was developed by the Ballena Bay Yacht Club as an alternative to the Transpacific Yacht Race, which runs from San Pedro to Honolulu in July of odd-numbered years. The Transpac history is

Zounds, little *Suds*. Thou must not port-tack the mighty *Brigadoon*! [PHOTO BY DON HILBUN]

packed with great names and great boats; it's a who's who of 20th century California yachting. In the 1980s, however, the Transpac followed the international trend to hotrod boats and crews that were often semi-pro or pro. That meant goodbye to loading up the boat with your friends and nephews and hello to piling on the ringers who might or might not respect you in the morning. The Pacific Cup was created so that "family" crews would have a race to Hawaii where they wouldn't feel like bumpkins driving a station wagon at the Indy 500. Later, a recession rang the bell on the highrolling Eighties. Then the glamour fleet shrank, and the formerly-oversubscribed Transpac, suddenly short of entries, began to court a broader constituency, somewhat like the Pacific Cup. The Pacific Cup — now the West Marine Pacific Cup — was meanwhile going great guns. It's a West Coast success story. It runs in even-numbered years, and the fleet draws a spectrum of talent that ranges from top pros to mom-and-pop operations that have done their homework.

The Singlehanded Transpac is a rare and indigenous flower. While sponsored Europeans race across the Atlantic at breakneck speeds in giant multihulls, unsponsored Californians can be found soloing across the Pacific, sometimes at breakneck speed, in anything from fast multihulls to ultralight monohulls to antique schooners. Bob Counts was a time allowance winner once in *Sanderling*, Golden Gate class sloop Number 16 — a 1957 hull built to a 1931 design. Sanderling's elapsed time of 18 days, 4 hours was a few days over "average" but not off the scale. Other, racier boats have been built or chartered especially for the race, but for most entrants, it's all about sailing what-you-got. From time to time, members of the SSS fret about how to turn their event into a transAtlantic-big-bucks equivalent. But if they ever succeed, the heart will go out of it. After two decades now, the Singlehanded Transpac is something special. It's a grass roots race, with real people sailing their own boats without techno-promotional wizardry. The skills of the people at the top — Dan Newland and Mark Rudiger come to mind — don't yield an inch to the heroes of the Atlantic route. But the Singlehanded Transpac remains a forum for people who want to reach inside themselves. "I've seen the people who went out there to prove something to somebody else," said Dan Newland.

"They're the ones who don't make it."

The City by the Bay missed out on hosting the original Transpac through a fault entirely our own, the San Andreas. It was in the dawning years of this century that a gentleman from Honolulu, one Clarence MacFarland, got it in his head that a race across the Pacific would be good for the sport of sailing and good for the economy of the islands. To that end, he came yachting over in the spring of 1906 in his schooner *La Paloma*, expecting to stir up a race home from the lusty descendants of the Forty-Niners. Instead, he arrived right behind the San Andreas earthquake to find a tent city still smoldering, still in shock, and needing shelter and commerce more than a 2,500-mile lark. *La Paloma* sailed on to Los Angeles, where MacFarland found his race, and finished last.

Citizens of the quake-ravaged city faced more than a few challenges in 1906. At the Stone Boat Yard, located then where the St. Francis Yacht Club stands now, the immediate problem was to hoist the sloop *Yankee* back onto the ways so they could finish building it. Ribbed and timbered fifty-two foot hulls do not pick up handily after they've been dumped on the floor, but the Stone crew managed, and the *Yankee* grew to be a happy boat. The very next year, under the colors of the Corinthian Yacht Club, she won the first ocean race sailed out of San Francisco Bay.

Probably, that first ocean race grew from a seed planted by Clarence MacFarland. Or perhaps it was simply time for it to happen. The course began in the Golden Gate strait, led around the Middle Farallon, and returned — more than sixty miles, figuring in the tacking angles. San Francisco Yacht Club commodore Francis Phillips put up the cup the *Yankee* won. In those years, the San Francisco Yacht Club was still located on pilings off Bridgeway in Sausalito (now occupied by restaurants). The club's seniority and deep water anchorage (and the demise in 1905 of the Pacific Yacht Club) meant that nearly all the larger yachts of the bay were on its rolls. SFYC still hosts the Farallones Race, but with changes. The turning mark is the well-lighted, beaconed, nearer Southeast Farallon, the race is part of the annual ocean series, and it is only one of many races that turn at the Farallones.

The *Yankee* has had many more adventures. It has since been rerigged as a schooner, and though it hasn't won an ocean race in quite a while, the *Yankee* sails on, a piece of our history, cutting a clean wake in Master Mariners events and resting in her quiet hours on the cityfront, close by her birthplace, downwind from the beach where those whippersnapper windsurfers rig up. You can hear the volleyballs bomp in the afternoon air.

ASSOCIATIONS, ASSOCIATIONS, ASSOCIATIONS, ASSOCIATIONS, ASSOCIATIONS, ASSOCIATIONS …

As work expands to fill the space allotted, associations expand to fill the universe. There's always room for one more group devoted to shorter seasons in longer boats, or longer seasons in shorter boats, or a new, improved time allowance system guaranteed to cultivate a wholesome, fast racing boat with a comfy interior and a proud future as a cruiser.

The Yacht Racing Association of San Francisco Bay was formed in 1928 and allied with the then North American Yacht Racing Union (later, with Canada subtracted, known as the U.S. Yacht Racing Union and now, for marketing purposes, renamed U.S. Sailing). The YRA umbrella takes care of many time-allowance and one design classes, and the YRA office at Fort Mason (415-771-9500) is a source of information for anyone who wants to get into the game.

Most YRA races run long circuits of the bay, turning around any of a number of marks and finishing back where they started, all under the eye of the race committee of the sponsoring club. The YRA spring opener is a different case. The spring opener is a stampede to Vallejo, rooted in traditions going back to the turn of the century. With half a thousand boats entered and a course that crosses microregions and microclimates — and with a history of armies of boats sometimes failing to finish — most fleets gave up long ago on counting the Vallejo Race toward season points. But this is a race you have to do.

The modern Vallejo Race starts in the East Bay, with a short weather leg to sort out the fleet. Then comes a long reach to the corner, at the Richmond-San Rafael Bridge. On this leg, you will probably find the wind shifting around behind you as you leave the weather mark, YRA 8, and head for the bridge or perhaps a close rounding at Point San Pablo. In some years, sailing low pays off on this leg, so let's say that again with numbers — between YRA 8 and the Richmond-San Rafael Bridge, the wind direction difference can be as much as 90 degrees. Later, the seabreeze turns again as it follows the path of least resistance into San Pablo Bay (first it took a left; now it takes a right). In San Pablo Bay, light spots are common, and deep holes are not unknown, but usually the seabreeze fills in to carry the fleet on to the Vallejo Yacht Club, at the mouth of the Napa River.

The overnight raftup and Saturday night party contribute nothing eye-opening to Sunday morning navigators looking for the fast track home. On Sunday, they say, you can hear the windshifts. Peter English, now the owner/skipper of a lovely, wooden sloop named *Chorus*, made his first Vallejo Race as a boy in 1953. "When we got to the finish," English recalls, "we found that the Vallejo Yacht Club had set up supper in a big, red barn. It was a spaghetti feed, and they had these long tables all lined up, and spirits were running high. I remember toward the end of the evening the mayor of Sausalito jumped up on our table, grabbed a banner that was hanging overhead, and ran with it the length of the table, spaghetti and plates and all. I was thirteen at the time. It made quite an impression on me."

The Small Boat Racing Association was formed in 1937 to handle the needs of three centerboard classes, of which only the Snipe remains. Lasers, Lightnings, Finns, OKs, FJs and others have been added to the roster since. SBRA regattas are held at many places around the bay, preferably in sheltered water. Richmond is a favorite, and there is a lake circuit through Clear Lake, Lake Yosemite, Oroville, Folsom and on. SBRA organizers usually schedule a one-hour break between races. You can't wait any longer, they say, or you have to re-train the crews.

Many more organizations exist in the tradition of, "If you don't like it, start your own." The Small Yacht Racing Association was formed in 1957 to cover the needs of small keelboats. There is a South Bay YRA, a Northern California Youth Sailing Association, a KIF (Knarr-IC-Folkboat), a Singlehanded Sailing Society, a Bay Area Multihull Association, a San Francisco Boardsailors Association, an Offshore Yacht

Racing Association, a Midget Ocean Racing Association, a One Design Classes Association, a Handicap Divisions Association and on and on. Many of these are also members of the YRA. They work together to create an annual schedule with the fewest possible traffic jams. It may seem confusing, but, with practice, those OYRA's and BAMA's, HDA's, ODCA's, IMS's and PHRF's will roll off your tongue like butter. If you have a better way to impress your mother-in-law, let's hear it.

BANANA SPLITS

Certain maneuvers are basic to the sport: the tack, the jibe, the trimming or easing of sails to different points of the wind. On San Francisco Bay we might add, among the basics, one maneuver that is considered rather exotic elsewhere. That would be the laid flat, prostrate, pancaked, stub-toed, gravel-up-your-nose *broach*.

Some boats are born to sail straight. Others are not. There was a whole generation of IOR boats shaped like watermelon seeds that couldn't sail straight to save themselves. Most of those old war horses are emeritus now. New designs go faster and straighter. The 1990s crop of fashionable boats placed the emphasis on high performance with a minimum number of crew. "Too many sandwiches to bring along" was an old complaint, and, "The boats are too hard to sail." The new fleets address both problems, but this is San Francisco Bay. Even a boat that doesn't have a hard mouth can be a handful under spinnaker in a summer breeze against an ebb tide. And if the 1970s-80s boats are also on the water, you can have a day with more spinouts than a Hollywood stock-car race.

A boat under spinnaker develops its power aloft. The sail pulls forward and up, but the sheet and the afterguy carry that load to the rear of the boat. That force tends to lift the transom and drive the bow down. It takes rapidfire coordination between the trimmers and the driver to keep the boat on its feet, and if the boat is overpowered — if the helmsman is losing — only a quick ease on the spinnaker sheet will save the moment. Also a quick ease on the mainsail traveler. Forget the mainsheet. That's too slow.

Easing the spinnaker sheet depowers the sail. Do it before you lose

control of the boat, and, probably, you won't lose control. As the rudder digs in, re-trim pronto and you can keep the kite from popping the rig. Otherwise, it re-fills with a bang that's hard on the gear and even harder on the owner's nerves.

When the going gets tough and the tough get going, one trick the tough use to keep going is to choke the spinnaker down before things get out of hand. They ease the spinnaker pole forward and down and cinch the foreguy tight. They might also take the spinnaker sheet to a new lead farther forward on the deck. That way, the spinnaker is depowered, and the driver has a better shot at performing his job description — to keep the boat under the sails.

And yet, spray flies in the face of the just and the unjust. Sooner or later, for richer or for poorer, you will go down. The trick is to go down but not out. Top racing crews take it for granted that the spinnaker will stay up in any wind until the best helmsman aboard crashes more than once. To take that attitude, they have to be confident of their ability to handle a knockdown. As Han Solo put it, "Don't ever tell me the odds."

So there you are, dragging sideways toward the South Forty with the deck vertical and the sails flogging and the competition waving at you and chortling, echoing the late Bob "Big Daddy" Klein, "Byeee, Sweetie!" On the way down, the spinnaker trimmer dumped the spinnaker sheet and the mainsail trimmer dumped the traveler and maybe some sheet, but it didn't work. So what next? If you had Warwick "Commodore" Tompkins along to freeze-frame the emergency and talk you through it, you would be hearing the words of a man whose boat-handling credentials are second to none. His words are for the helmsman: "The boat wants to go, so let it go — straighten that rudder."

The very form of the hull makes it want to go forward. Meanwhile, the rudder is stalled. If the rudder were not stalled, we wouldn't even be in this position, right? We've got to get the rudder working again. Given its own head, a thirty-six footer will not turn into the wind much farther than the beam, and it will make three or four knots in full broach. That speed is the key. Oh, to be sure, it's speed in the wrong direction, and the sails are rattling the boat right down to the keel. But the mast (probably) will not break. The sail (probably) will not rip. Life (probably) will not end.

Big game hunting [PHOTO BY KEITH NORDAHL]

So the helmsman straightens the rudder, and the boat gains speed. As it gains speed, waterflow across the rudder makes the rudder effective. Now the driver can really do something. There will be a moment when it's time to set the bit and turn the beast to course, being careful as hey-ho, and up she rises, not to trip right into an overcorrection in the opposite direction, wrong twice.

If the broach is so complete that the boat is truly being dragged sideways, and isn't going forward, the helmsman might ask for a little mainsheet trim, to give the boat some momentum. Meanwhile, as the helmsman searches for the perfect instant to turn the boat, crew weight belongs on the high side and aft, the leverage point for kicking the bow around to a civilized course. (If the vang or a preventer strap is holding the boom up in the air, consider easing it, very carefully. It will be loaded, and it will try to run away and kill somebody, so be sure of your moves. Stay low, and stand ready to re-trim a preventer at the instant of recovery). And don't leave any fingernail marks in the deck.

A boat broached "to leeward" has spun out with its lee rail in the water. A boat broached "to weather" has spun out with its weather rail down, with the boom sticking up in the air and the spinnaker pole aimed at the water. This is far more serious than a broach to leeward, and if the spinnaker pole threatens to hit the water, the foreguy should be eased instantly to keep the pole high and dry. Otherwise, you can break the mast. If the pole is already in the water, the foreguy should be cast off. Then maybe, just maybe, the pole will lift out and clear. Otherwise, in the water, the pole loads up and transfers that load to the mast at a point where most masts are unsupported. The mast-breakage curve steepens sharply. You cannot stem christie a racing yacht.

Also among the blunders available to the hardworking crew is one that is worse than most and very easy to make: releasing the afterguy along with the spinnaker sheet. Aboard a boat that is raced hard, sails are constantly being trimmed. The afterguy will not be cleated at the moment of the knockdown. As the driver starts piping a jittery, "Ease the sheet! Ease it!" the person holding the tail of the afterguy will have a powerful impulse to ease the thing in hand. As a basic mistake in one of the bay's basic maneuvers, easing the afterguy in a broach invokes an arresting array of consequences. The sail flies farther from the boat. It wants to fill no matter how far the sheet is eased. Being so far from the boat, it makes for very effective sideways drag, and it's going to be bodacious hard to get it back under control when the boat stands up, if ever. Useful procedures for anyone caught holding the afterguy in a knockdown are: (1) cleat that sucker, and (2) repeat the silent mantra: "I am controlling the afterguy. It must not be eased. I am controlling the afterguy. I am …"

Now, isn't that just like San Francisco Bay? It'll send you off talking to yourself, every time. ◈

BIBLIOGRAPHY

Clancy, Edward. P. *The Tides: Pulse of the Earth.* Garden City, N.J.: Doubleday & Co., 1968.

Conomos, T.J., ed. *San Francisco Bay: The Urbanized Estuary.* Lawrence, Kansas: Allen Press. For the California Academy of Sciences, San Francisco, 1979.

Gilliam, Harold. *Weather of the San Francisco Bay Region.* Berkeley and Los Angeles: University of California Press, 1962.

Jorgensen, Victor. *The First One Hundred Years of the San Francisco Yacht Club.* Belvedere, California: The San Francisco Yacht Club: 1977.

Kotsch, William J., Rear Admiral, Ret. *Weather for the Mariner.* Annapolis: Naval Institute Press, 1977.

Lilly, Commander Kenneth E., Jr., Ret. *Marine Weather Handbook: Northern & Central California.* Sausalito, California: Paradise Cay Yacht Sales, 1985.

Minor, Woodruff. C. *On The Bay: A Centennial History of the Encinal Yacht Club.* Alameda, California: The Encinal Yacht Club, 1994.

Neumann, Gerhard, and Pierson, Willard J. Jr. *Principles of Physical Oceanography.* Englewood Cliffs, N.J.: Prentice-Hall, Inc., 1966.

Newton, Sir Isaac. *Mathematical Principles of Natural Philosophy.* Translated by Andrew Motte. Berkeley and Los Angeles: University of California Press, 1934. Reprint. Chicago, London, Toronto, Geneva: Encyclopaedia Britannica, Inc., 1952.

Rousmaniere, John. *The Annapolis Book of Seamanship.* New York, N.Y.: Simon and Schuster, 1989.

Smock, Jack. *Transpac: A History of the Great Race to Honolulu.* San Diego: The Maritime Museum Association of San Diego, 1980.

U.S. Department of Commerce, National Oceanic and Atmospheric Administration. *Tidal Current Tables: Pacific Coast of North America and Asia.* Rockville, Maryland: National Ocean Survey.

U.S. Department of Commerce, National Oceanic and Atmospheric Administration. *United States Coast Pilot, Pacific Coast: California, Oregon, Washington, and Hawaii.* Rockville, Maryland: National Ocean Survey, 1980.

And the documents file at the J. Porter Shaw Library of the National Maritime Museum.

INDEX

*Page references in italics
refer to illustrations*

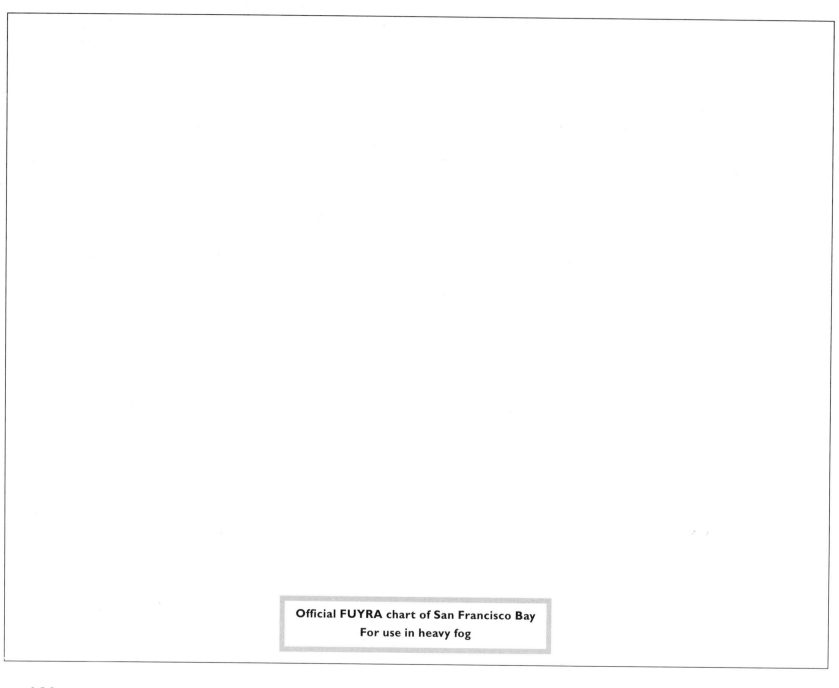

Official **FUYRA** chart of San Francisco Bay

For use in heavy fog